RESPONSIBLE MAN
The Atmaan Beja of North-eastern Sudan

RESPONSIBLE MAN

the Atmaan Beja of North-eastern Sudan

Anders Hjort af Ornäs
Gudrun Dahl

Published by
Stockholm Studies in Social Anthropology, SSSA
in cooperation with
Nordiska Afrikainstitutet, Uppsala
1991

Cover: The top of a wooden Beja comb, used by men to embellish their Afro-style hair. The figure in the upper section is a man's head. The middle section shows a number of utensils used in the coffee ceremony: fan, stove and set of *jabana* pot and cups. To the right of the rifle in the bottom section is a pack-sack for a camel.

Drawings by Gudrun Dahl

Typesetting: Kerstin Edlund, Uppsala University, Uppsala

ISBN 91-7146-905-2

Printed in Sweden by
Reklam & Katalogtryck, Uppsala universitet, 1991

Contents

Preface   viii

Some terms used in the text   ix

1 . The Atmaan Amar'ar and their country   1

    The area and its inhabitants   1
    An outline of the study   8

2 . From the Red Sea to the Nile Valley: An historical
    background to the Beja's resource situation   13
    The origins of Beja economy   15
    Desert routes, harbours and early trade   20
    The Beja and the Hadariba   22
    Beja groups in the 19th century   29
    Egyptian rule   31
    Harbours and routes during the Turko-Egyptian era   33
    Osman Digna and the Beja: slave trade religion and wars 35
    The British impact on the Atmaan and other Beja   38
    Conclusion   41

3 . Territory, resource control and solidarity among the Atmaan   45

    The lineage system, a folk model of historical links 49
    Diwab ideology and livestock property   55
    Physical and social territory   57
    Urban resources and diwab structure   62
    Territoriality, kinship and neighbourhood   64

4 . The responsible man   69

    Key male virtues   70
    Honour as a collective resource   75
    Leadership and arbitration   82
    Management of honour in a mixed cultural environment 84
    Reflections on hospitality, alliance and hierarchy   88

5 . Gender roles, marriage and brother-sister relations   91

    Inside and outside   91
    Brotherhood and marriage   92
    Gender and work   98
    Womanhood and marriage   102
    The limited significance of marriage   107

6 . Getting grain   109

    Farm land and the question of ownership   112
    The cultivation process   117
    The local grain trade versus the world market   122

7 . Family herds   127

    The camel in local life   128
    The camel population   132
    Three patterns of camel pastoralism   134
        Aririit camel pastoralism in Aulib   134
        Matiaat camel pastoralism in the khors   136
        Shallageea camel pastoralism on the coast   137
    Small stock herding   139
    Shepherding: production and vulnerability   142
    Change and constraints   146

8 . The dwindling resource base   151

    The modern history of drought in Beja lands   152
        The Sanasita period 1888-89   154
        Environmental hazards during the post-Sanasita period   156
    A summary of general trends in land control by the Beja   162
    The scope of local observation   164
    Trees and poverty   168
    Talking about disaster   172
    God and the Beja's new neighbours   173
    Unification and division   175

Appendix: Early Beja history   177

    Beja country and Nubia in ancient times   177
    The Beja in Early Arab times   180

Bibliography   185

Maps

1. North-eastern Sudan   6
2. The Beja and other Cushitic groups   16
3. The Red Sea in classical times, and some places mentioned in the text   19
4. Caravan routes of significance for the Beja   24
5. The core area of Atmaan traditional rights and settlements   47
6. Catchment areas in Red Sea Province   113
7. Natural vegetation in north-eastern Sudan   114

Figures

1. Amar'ar groups and subdivisions   48
2. Genealogies of the Atmaan recorded in 1935 and 1980   51

Preface

This study is based on fieldwork carried out during different periods. The authors spent five months each in Red Sea Province in 1980. Hjort af Ornäs returned for a two-month period later that year. Dahl spent two months there in 1986/87. In view of the methodological problems involved in studying the Beja, we would have preferred to have spent more time in the field than has for personal reasons been possible for us. As a consequence, the present volume is as much built on reviewing the available written sources on the Beja as on field data, and it is more exploratory in nature than conclusive. Nevertheless, we hope that the present volume will contribute to identifying interesting fields for further research among the Beja.

Our fieldwork was carried out mainly among the Atmaan, who constitute the major part of the Atmaan-Amar'ar, with families centered on Waheda (outside Port Sudan), Musmar and Ariaab. Our own field data apply to them but, particularly in the chapters on history and on recent changes in the resource basis, we have had an eye to the broader region of the northern Beja in general. It is difficult for us to judge the extent to which the people we have been dealing with are more Arabicized than the Beja living at greater distances from the main routes, but our impression is that various groups of Hadendowa, Atmaan-Amar'ar and Bishariin have enough in common to be treated as one single culture.

The work has been financed by SAREC (the Swedish Agency for Research Cooperation with Developing Countries) and by the Swedish Academy of Science. Their contribution is gratefully appreciated, as is also the assistance of many Beja friends. This has to be a collective acknowledgement. Among individuals we wish to thank are Waffa Osman and Ali Salah of Sudan Central Records Archives, Safia of the Anthropology and Sociology Department, Peter Walker, Nicholas Meadows, Penny Nestle and Suzanne Quinney. Thanks also to M A Mohamed Salih for his comments on the early draft of this book. The language editing was done by Tim Caudery and the maps were drawn by Peter van Gylswyck. Typesetting, finally, was executed by Kerstin Edlund.

Anders Hjort af Ornäs and Gudrun Dahl

Some Beja terms used in the text

Please note that this list is primarily prepared to help the reader with terms used in the text. This means not least that many tuBedawiet words are listed here with the masculine or feminine prefix.

Ababda the most northern of the Beja groups
adarharob red durra
'adlib Suaeda fruticosa Forsk., a bush
amab Tamarix aphylla for making wooden poles
angareb rope bed
aririit type of camel: fair milk producers. Main advantage is endurance
asl customary title to land
Atmaan a Beja group
ayb taboo
balat'harob durra which is identical with *himeisi*, Stapf variety
balbal weeds
Bedawiet Beja
Beni Amer (Khasa) ethnic group with links to the Beja and the Tigre, but ethnically distinct from both
billtub dukhn (Ar.); finger millet
Bishariin a Beja group
dameini to cover
dayb ground pits for durra
dekab a shelter of timber for giving hospitality and holding councils
diwab major clan group
dukhn (Ar.) finger millet
durareit honour (n)
feddan measure of land area. 1 feddan = 1.038 acres
gangar durra cob
gefareeb Salsola baryosma a bush, camel fodder
gudamantib development
gwadabb symbolic recognition of land ownership; front leg of animal
hadara civilization
hadarenini to be hospitable
Hadendowa a Beja group
halagen bride-wealth

harob durra (Ar.); sorghum
hedareb hospitable people
i'damar the permanent home place
i'mara rights; the rights obtained in exchange for the *gwadabb*
jabana Turkish coffee
jawal 90 kg sack of durra
kantar 1 small kantar is 44.928 kg. For cotton, a big kantar is
    141.523 kg.
kirrab a water catchment
kurai the grazing territory to which a Beja claims customary rights
matiaat the fastest and most slender of the Atmaan camels
mish'ariib camel herder
mugud a durra type
mushuk date residue from wine production
nandab shade tree
o'di smoke-bath
o'mkir the act of consulting an elder of one of the property-holding
    diwab
o'slif customary law
o'tam durra porridge
omda lower level "headmen"
qalla work gang in port
qole the distance a land-owner can throw his walking stick
rafig (Ar.), a sponsor to vouch for one's good faith
rattel 1 rattel is approximately 0.45 kg (various sources indicate
    7.25 rattel = 3.5 kg; 100 rattel = 44.928 kg, and 1 kg = 2.25 rattel)
safiia 1 safiia = 15.14 litres
Sanasita 1888-89 drought disaster
shallageea type of camel: the sturdiest and the best milk producers
sheikh leader in the kinship system but also a Quranic teacher
shetariit (Ar. fetarita); see *harob*
shuush Panicum turgidum perennial grass; excellent camel fodder
silsila a lineal chain of religious succession
suganneit insult, provocation against collective honour
sulh property rights to land
sumatu individual reputation
t'angash (Ar. *saluka*) a digging stick
t'anna sheep
tajjer compensation in gold or money

ti' hibqualda see matiaat
ti' sagane Acacia spirocarpa
ti' smaya namegiving
Tu'Durarey or synonymously *o'rya*: honour
tubahala the (dry) period lasting from November to March
TuBedawiye the Beja language
tuhoobi rainy period
wahalas the afterbirth
yategaab shepherd
yomiia a day's work in port

1

The Atmaan Amar'ar and their country

The area and its inhabitants

In the Red Sea Hill region of north-eastern Sudan live a people referred to as the Beja, but who in their own language call themselves *Bedawiet*. The ancestors of the present Beja have been exploiting the semi-deserts of Egypt, Eastern Sudan and possibly Eritrea for thousands of years. They were probably among the first African peoples to breed camels, around the time of Christ. Controlling the desert route from Red Sea ports to the upper Nile Valley, the Beja have since that time made good use of this beast, both for nourishment and as a riding or transport animal when acting as caravan traders or guides. Sheep and goats are also very important for their subsistence, as is *durra* (sorghum) cultivated by flush irrigation in the dry river beds that criss-cross the area.

As the vegetation is sparse in the typical Beja landscape, the home-steads of the Beja shepherds used to be widely scattered in the valleys. They consisted of two or three low tents made of palm-leaf matting, and each dwelling was situated at some kilometres' distance from the nearest neighbour. Today many Beja live in more permanent houses of sundried mud or concrete bricks in desert villages or on the outskirts of Port Sudan, Atbara and Kassala towns, combining urban employ-ment with small-scale animal husbandry for the urban market.

The Beja language, *TuBedawiye*, is Cushitic, and thus related to some languages spoken in Ethiopia and on the Horn of Africa. After close interaction with Arabs for more than one thousand years, the Beja culture represents an intermarriage between Arabic and Cushitic influences. An even longer relationship with the Nubian people of the Nile valley has also given the Beja very much in common with the Nubians. Although the Beja stand out as ethnically distinct from the rest of the population in northern Sudan, there is probably more to connect them with than to distinguish them from other Sudanese.

Descriptions of foreign cultures have often been coloured by a wish to measure "us" and "them" on a scale which exists in two versions. In the first, the two extremes of the scale represent the blissful original natural state and the decay of human life qualities in modern society. In the second, the polarities are the misery of primitivity and the glory of modern utopia. Some cultures would appear to be particularly easily fitted into such descriptive frameworks, and their available ethno-graphy is accordingly either heavily romanticized or highly deni-grating.

The Beja culture is one which appears to invite biased description. One reason is that the visual impression of the Beja at first sight con-jures up images of antiquity in the head of the European observer. With his curls and carefully arranged "Afro" hair, his long wrapping of dusty white cotton, his crusader-like sword and round shield, the handsome Beja camelman reminds one of ancient Egyptian frescos as well as of Medieval knights: yet the Beja are not living in the past any more than the observer. They are very much contemporary people with contemporary problems.

2

Still, many observers have, like Clark (1938:4, 20), commented on the conservatism inherent in Beja culture. There are good reasons why a society such as that of the Beja is conservative in the sense that they strive to maintain traditional values. One is a dominance of domestic production forms which are subject to great climatic risk. Such conditions tend to discourage openness to social or economic innovations. But there are also structural reasons why innovations are likely to be confined rather than spread in the Beja population.

As we shall see in following chapters, Beja social structure is extremely familistic. Social life is oriented towards one's own small family confederation (*diwab*), and within that towards yet tighter units. In contrast to other pastoral societies where stock-friendships or exogamous affinal alliances are important, such as is the case is among East African cattle nomads,[1] Beja custom restricts rather than encourages a wide network of contacts. Cultural convention places no primacy on fixed or continued alliances on a group level, and marriages are used to consolidate the extended family group rather than to reach out and establish wider contacts. Relations between family confederations are characterized by distrust, as — for good historical reasons — is the attitude toward representatives of foreign cultures. The social structure does not provide many cross-cutting links between extended families and kinship groups that could encourage a quick spread of cultural innovations.

The Western writer often uses the picture of "the other" in order to throw light on her or his own culture and society, and this by necessity implies a certain distancing from the object. If the foreign observer has a tendency to project ideas of a spatial and temporal distance on to the description, this may in the Beja case be aggravated by their attitude toward strangers. For the distinctions between "our trusted people" and "others", between "hosts" and "guests" and between "well-known friends" and "potential enimies" are the most pervasive themes in Beja culture, and of central concern in this book. They are not just relevant to the boundaries between the Beja and non-Beja. Relations between the Beja themselves are equally marked by these dualities. Within the narrow confines of the Beja lineage or closest family, expressions of warmth

---

[1]Pastoral societies differ widely in the extent to which individual alliances are used to enhance secure access to productive resources. For illustrations of this see Hjort af Ornäs (1989).

and constant concern contrast with the suspicion directed towards the outside.

Reading texts on the Beja, the researcher continuously runs into the problem of filtering facts from prejudice. But if the values of those who wrote the literary sources are a major stumbling-block, the anthropologist doing fieldwork among the Beja also encounters problems in coping with Beja values about how information should be handled, and with their emphasis on the ideals of a honourable life. There are many fields of information which the Beja regard as being delicate. These include those which touch directly upon the virtues of one's own clan members, such as those pertaining to gender relations. Sexual issues and female chastity are tricky topics but so are questions of male success as providers of food and physical protection. It is also risky to talk about these matters in relation to members of other clans, as that can be seen as a challenge to their honour. Other delicate issues relate directly to resources necessary for survival, to property claims to livestock or land, and to challenges against such claims. Much of the practice relating to ideals of honour concerns keeping up a facade.

This problem is both ethical and practical. The Beja can be hospitable to the stranger to the limit of physical self-denial; yet at the same time, they have learnt to be wary of the alien, and even among themselves their society is turned inwards, towards the closest family. Anthropological "networking" is virtually impossible, and formal interviewing about socially loaded information has to be abandoned in favour of pure "hanging-around". Nevertheless, we hope that we have succeeded in writing a text that will convey our respect for the Beja as a people of cheerful, patient, honest and hospitable citizens without either offending them or unnecessarily idealizing them.

The Beja were very hard hit by the drought of 1984-86. 95% of their herds died. It is not our intention in the present volume to either account for the details of this emergency, its progress over time or its consequences, or to give any comprehensive picture of the responses of the Beja. Indeed, our choice of the Red Sea Hills as an area for study was made after doing work with Boran and Somali pastoralists in the late 1970s, in order to establish a comparative perspective for that work by looking at other Cushitic herdspeople in an even more arid area. We met a culture whose deep historic roots can be traced in outline, a culture which has evolved more or less in defence against strangers and around the management of extremely limited resources.

When we met it, this culture appeared to us to have more in common with Mediterranean honour-and-shame cultures than with the Cushitic cultures we knew about. Such topics are given prime attention in the present volume.

Far from being politically united, the Beja nation is made up of several rival confederations of land-controlling family groups, ideally patrilineally recruited but in practice with many abberations of bilateral consanguinity. The most prominent of these groups are the Bishariin, the Hadendowa, the Amar'ar and the bilingual (Arab-Beja) Ababda.[2] The Tigre-speaking Beni Amer, or Khasa, who contain large Bedawiet-speaking sections, live on both sides of the Eritrean border. They are frequently included in the category "Beja" by people who are neither Khasa nor Beja themselves. Apart from the fact that this categorisation does not agree with local perceptions, there appear to be such large cultural differences between the ideologically egalitarian Beja proper ("the northern Beja") and the more hierarchical Beni Amer that the latter would merit separate treatment. This book is thus not about them.

The Atmaan of the Amar'ar, who are the central concern of this book, exploit the ranges between Port Sudan and the coast and Atbara on the Nile, but have their tribal headquarters at Khor Ariaab, north of Musmar (Map 1).

To the western observer, the territories loved and used by the Beja appear harsh. Living conditions are constrained by the failure or success of mono-seasonal rains. Aulib, the inland plateau, experiences in most years one annual rainfall period from July to September, with only scanty rains. The weather on the coastal strip, Gunob, and in the mountains along the coast is influenced by monsoon winds. Gunob and the Red Sea Hills have their rainy season in November to December. Only a small area between Aulib and Gunob, in the hills and in the foothills to the west of them, may experience two rainy seasons. Frequently, there is grass on the mountain summits even under conditions of general drought, and Beja then, at the cost of considerable effort, collect grass there for their animals. The rains are however unreliable, both at the coast and in the interior, and can, as was the case around 1984, sometimes totally fail.

---

[2] Murray (1935:355) mentions a group of Ababda living as far north as Suez and suggests that they may at one time have controlled most of the Eastern Desert of Egypt but that their general northern boundary was pushed southwards in the 16th century.

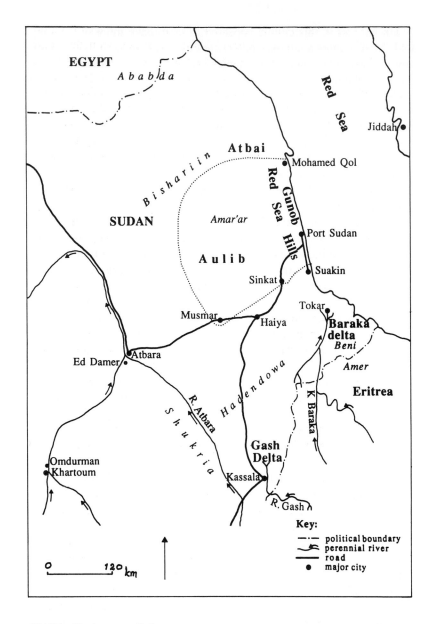

MAP 1: North-eastern Sudan

6

The average annual rainfall is below 110 mm, and the area is classified as arid. Erratic rains fall in November-December on the coast, and in June-July inland. Floods occur approximately every 3-8 years. Only three good years have occurred during the last 22-year period (1968, 1977 and 1986). Ground water is, although not available everywhere, reliable in fracture zones of the granite bedrock. This is so because rainwater seeps into the ground through silt deposits and rock fissures. Water quality is good for livestock except along the coast (salt) and to the north (other minerals). The area of contaminated wells seems to expand southwards during drought periods, due to low groundwater levels. The catchment areas in Red Sea Province are shown on Map 6.

Soils include silt, sand and loam on the slopes of the hills and in river beds. These allow a high degree of percolation, thus adding to groundwater reserves. This means that plants can grow with a minimum of water flow, but also that the soils are susceptible to water and wind erosion. The Red Sea Hills are bare rock, while inland areas are mostly made up of sand sheets, as is the coastal strip along the mountains.

Most of the Beja area outside the territory of the Atmaan is also exceedingly dry, although areas south of the Port Sudan-Khartoum railway allow the herd-owners to keep cattle and sheep, not just camels and goats as is the case in the Atmaan area and further north. Most of the Red Sea Province is made up of sparsely wooded semi-deserts which in the west merge into the Nubian Desert. Some denser tree and grass cover can be found in the drainage lines and wadi beds. The only substantial fertile regions are the Tokar delta on the coast in the southeast and the inland delta of the river Gash immediately north of the Ethiopian highlands, both of which areas are intensively cultivated.

A large range of spatio-temporal constraints shape the particular pattern of mobility dominant in any Beja group. There is the incidence of summer rains in the inland areas, and of coastal winter rains. There is the flushing and flooding of the rivers Nile, Gash, Atbara and Baraka, in response to more faraway rains at their sources. There is the necessity to avoid rainstorms and cold as well as heat which is too extreme. There is the need to travel to markets which are only open at certain times in order to obtain necessary supplies. There is the need for some households or groups to avail themselves of the opportunities to seek work in Port Sudan, Atbara, Gash or Tokar.

For the Amar'ar, the dominant traditional transhumance is between the feeder khors and the permanent wells in the dry season. This is a time of year when maximal adaptation to conditions is obtained by splitting as much as possible into smaller units, in order to make use of very scarce pastures on the mountain tops.

The degree of rainfall regulates the amount of sorghum that can be grown, as well as the goat kidding seasons and the conception of camels. The Atmaan once used to be wealthy in camels, and together with the neighbouring Bishariin they are famed for being excellent camel breeders. The camel has for almost two thousand years been the backbone of Beja society. It created the preconditions for Beja control of the trade routes between the Nile Valley and the Red Sea. Without this asset the Beja would not have had the capacity to remain in the lands they inhabit, classified as being among the driest and hottest in Africa.

Since an extreme three year drought in the early 1940s, however, many Atmaan have been squeezed out of their traditional niche of camel rearing. In 1980, camels were no longer the main basis of the economy of the region. The relative importance of sheep and goats had increased, and many households had been forced to take up wage labour in Port Sudan. The famine during the early 1980s further aggravated the situation. The area now also has a major refugee problem, receiving large numbers of people from Eritrea and Ethiopia.

An outline of the study

The second chapter provides an overview of the historical background. Its aim is to demonstrate how in the past the resource base of the Beja has been determined not only by local technology and ecological circumstances, but also by more comprehensive economic and political contexts. We make an attempt to relieve the image of the Beja of the timelessness associated with traditional stereotypes of them. The vehicle for the penetration of external influences into the local community was long-distance trade. The passage of such trade through the region probably produced an economic contribution to Beja subsistence, but it also brought problems of maintaining cultural and social identity, creating a need to safeguard settlements, herds and water resources from external intrusion. The Beja attitude towards strangers is not an effect of isolation, but rather an adaptation to a constant flow of foreigners through their area.

8

This historical chapter consists of a text-based reconstruction of external influences rather than a recounting of oral ethnohistory. Though it draws mainly on secondary sources, the chapter aims at building up a fairly comprehensive historical picture of the periods during which caravan trade through the area has been significant. The chapter also draws attention to the role of urban middlemen in the history of the Beja.

In spite of the fact that the Beja are among those groups in Africa that are mentioned in the earliest sources of conventional history, their own interest in history is limited. Their historical memory is selectively geared towards an ideology of honour, giving emphasis to heroic behaviour but playing down problems such as starvation periods.

The strong emphasis the Beja place on honour is a key element for understanding not only the Beja historical perspective, but also the current situation. This emphasis has to be appreciated in order to comprehend how Beja kinship, through the lineage (diwab) system, relates to resources, land and livestock. To comply with social norms, the individual Beja man is expected to be "a Responsible Man". By achieving this goal he becomes an honourable person.

The context in which he can act out this role is that of diwab solidarity. The diwab is a kinship group which makes up the basic unit of tribal confederations. It is central to Beja social organization, and is the most important point of reference for Beja identity concepts. The principle of recruitment to the diwab has two components: sharing descent and sharing territorial affiliation. Diwab ideology gives the framework for administering both material and symbolic resources in a collective manner.

Chapter 3 deals essentially with the interaction of kinship solidarity with solidarity of territoriality, acquaintance and neighbourhood. Chapter 4 addresses questions related to honour in relation to the corporate group; these matters are discussed in respect of their importance both to the general male role and to the role of Beja leaders.

Beja society does not of course consist solely of honourable men, but also of women, who act within roles largely defined by the honour of men. It is a society where the division between male and female spheres appears extremely sharp. Chapter 5 demonstrates the implications of this fact for the dynamics of society. It seeks to bring out the main axes of male-female alliance, i.e. marriage and brother/sister-hood. Apart from exceptional cases related to elite strategy, Beja marriage would appear to have very little to do with alliances formed on a collective level, for example between diwabs. In essence, marriage is looked upon as being based on a sexual relationship and thus being in itself a vulnerable institution. In order to last, it must be reinforced with brotherly solidarity. This view leads to endogamous marriages with cousins on both sides, and further emphasizes the tightness of the family as against a world seen as potentially hostile.

In the remaining chapters, the focus is on the traditional system of subsistence, and on the changes in that. Chapter 6 concerns the important production of grain and the way in which the problem of general access to grain has been aggravated. Grain is an essential supplement to pastoral produce, and eating porridge is an important part of "being Beja". Apart from being the archetypal food, durra is important as fodder for domestic animals. Durra (Beja *harob*), or in certain places its substitute, finger millet (Ar. *dukhn*, TuBedawiye *billtub*), is cultivated by almost all Beja groups. The Amar'ar are restricted to dry river beds for growing grain and have to supplement what they produce with substantial imports.

In the rare case of a surplus of durra being produced, storage creates little problem and the harvests of earlier years are used as fodder, primarily for camels. One can safely assume many centuries of barter trade, exchanging pastoral produce for grain. During recent decades much of the durra consumed has come from the Gezira, particularly from Gedaref. This trade is controlled by a few individuals only. It is easy to imagine how the flow will cease in times of scarcity when rural consumption has to compete with the big urban markets such as those in Khartoum and Port Sudan. The substantial illegal trade to Ethiopia and Saudi Arabia has made the situation even more serious.

Access to grain grew more difficult for the Beja during the seventies and the first years of the eighties, the situation becoming seriously aggravated just before the drought and in the period before famine relief arrived. In Chapter 7 we discuss the general trend of a decline in camel rearing that has been going on over the last century. Regrettably, it is likely that the destruction of this system is now irreversible. The herding system for camels required a high degree of competence in order to make quick and correct decisions. With a delay in camel herd recuperation, even this competence may be a dwindling resource. The loss of a family herd of camels is final. For the family that suffers that loss, the only available option in order to remain with animal husbandry is to manage small stock. Here growth rates, at least in terms of numbers of animals, are positive, but vulnerability is greater.

The present book touches upon how the Atmaan have survived over the last hundred years on their scarce resources by using mixed strategies: of herding and cultivation, of moving between urban and rural settings in order to supplement these activities with wage-labouring, and also of involving themselves in commercial enterprises. Such diversifying approaches to subsistence are frequent among pastoralists. It is characteristic of the Beja and other people in the arid regions of Africa that their subsistence requires continuous involvement in several mutually supplementing activities. When they are not able to invest the needed amount of labour, or if the time schedule for the different activities is put out of sequence, the consequences can be devastating. There is always a delicate balance between the amount of food available and the labour requirements for the maintenance of basic resources — primarily the living capital of livestock. When food is not sufficient, the economy easily gets into a vicious circle of lowered productivity. After the blow dealt by the last famine, the question is what remains.

The process whereby "traditional" Atmaan life has become gradually more difficult to live, culminating in the 1984-86 disaster, is linked to changes in their position in relation to the Sudanese economy as a whole, and to Sudan's place in international trade. But it is also linked to the general desiccation of the African Sahel. In the last chapter we take a closer look at the processes of environmental change, as they may appear from the grassroot perspective, and the relationships between poverty, Beja nationalism and new forms of division within Beja society.

We return to the issue of drought, and to the more recent history of the Beja in terms of such experience. We try to place the Beja in their climatic setting, and discuss some of the long-term effects of drought and how the experience of drought relates to the dwindling of resources brought about through non-climatic factors. Emphasis is placed on how the Beja themselves understand their worsening situation and its causes. We hope that some of the more subjective aspects of these problems as seen from the point of view of Beja values will also become apparent to the reader.

2

From the Red Sea to the Nile Valley: An historical background to the Beja's resource situation

The Beja areas were traversed for thousands of years by strangers of many kinds — Egyptians, Greeks, Romans, Persians, Arabs, Turks, Portuguese, British. Yet the Beja themselves seem to have maintained their language and identity fairly intact, and there appears to have been a high degree of cultural continuity during the last two thousand years.

Many of those people who during this long period surrounded and traversed the Beja area left quite tangible traces behind them. Not only did the foreign visitors leave ruins scattered all over Beja lands, but there is also written evidence of their presence there, left in the acient Egyptian, Latin, Arabic and Turkish sources. Beja, or the people who can be identified as proto-Beja, such as the Medjayu and the Blemmyes, are mentioned in these sources. However, the sources have little to say about the living conditions, culture and social organisation of the Beja.

It is extremely hard to build up a coherent historical picture of local society. A sketch of the macro-political and -economic setting in which Beja society has been enmeshed over time may suggest the framework within which cultural influences have taken place. In many parts of Africa, especially further to the south, there is a fiction that international political and economic structures above the level of "intertribal contacts" had little local impact in pre-colonial days. Such a fiction is difficult to maintain in the case of the Beja. Yet, unfortunately, the scarce references to social conditions in Beja country offered by Arab scholars and travellers do not make it possible to reconstruct the social structure and organization of the Beja during this long time span. What we can do is rather to try and identify the basic elements of Beja sustenance and economy, and the extent to which these are likely to have changed over time in pre-colonial days. Prominent in the configuration of such elements today are the combination of small stock husbandry with camel rearing, and irregular flush irrigation of durra and dukhn. With a historical perspective, it is necessary to add the involvement of Beja in long distance trade as guides, middlemen and desert brigands.

Beja country, in particular the desert of the northern Beja groups, was never under tight centralized control. The region was for long periods peripherally related to a series of kingdoms and empires, with a significant economic impact on the local community. First and foremost, one has to consider the effect of the important trade routes that have linked such kingdoms to each other and to the Red Sea, the Ethiopian Highlands, the Nile Valley and Egypt.

In spite of the apparent conservatism of the Beja, it is obvious that their contacts with foreign cultures over such an extended time period have left their mark on their own culture, in terms of both borrowed words and the integration of practices and values. To make an historical reconstruction that defines the limit for speculation about the nature of such influences could be an important goal in itself. However, the historical perspective can also add another dimension to the under-

14

standing of the characteristic traits of Beja culture. We would like here to emphasize the continuity of the existence over a very lengthy period of a situation in which the Beja have had to face the presence of potentially predatory, yet useful, strangers in their area. This presence has to be considered an equally important element of the Beja's regional ecology as the rugged mountains and scorched deserts. Beja culture has been directly influenced by the cultures of these strangers, but Beja hospitality and xenophobia have developed in defensive reaction and adaptation to the strangers' presence.

The origins of Beja economy

On a superficial level Beja culture seems to have much in common with that of other camel rearing Cushites such as the Afar and the Somali.[1] Especially when not looking beyond language and the cultural forms evident in material artefacts, or in social institutions such as a patrilineal emphasis in the pastoral societies, one might be tempted to see an affinity. However, when penetrating the issue a little further, differences rather than similarities become apparent. Linguistic evidence (Ehret 1976:89) suggests that even if the ancestors of the Beja ever were closely related to other Cushites, they broke away from them at least 6000 years ago, i e long before their particular adaptation of combining caravan service, durra cultivation and pastoralism was developed. There are also some striking contrasts in the cultural and technical elaboration of camel rearing. The basic words for camels — o'kam in TuBedawiye (TuB) and gal in Somali — appear to represent two very different linguistic developments from the Arabian gamal. Among eastern Cushitic camel rearers, camels are not ridden but used for loading and milking, while camel riding is a very prominent feature of camel use among the Beja.

Both camel rearing and durra cultivation seem to have been introduced to the area about 2000 years ago (Bulliet 1975:116, Zeuner 1963:353), antedating perhaps by some centuries the time when the Beja are first mentioned by that name, emerging as the descendants of, or perhaps just the successors to, the classical Blemmyes in the Eastern Desert of Egypt and Nubia.

---

[1] The Beja are generally regarded as the most northern of the Cushitic speaking peoples, a subsection within the great Afro-Asiatic language family.

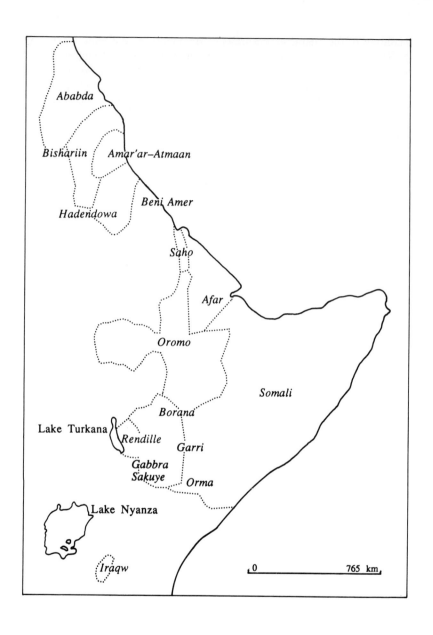

MAP 2: The Beja and other Cushitic groups

16

Around the time of Christ, the inhabitants of the desert were presumably transhumant shepherds of small stock and cattle, utilizing the best pockets of pasture in the hills, and supplementing pastoral production with hunting and gathering. Even today, Beja country contains several wild species of grains and fruits that can be utilized as food.[1] At one stage there might have been denser vegetation and more abundant wildlife to support hunters (Mawson and Williams 1984). Even during the 20th century ariel, ibex, wild sheep, Dorcas and Isabella gazelles, hares and dikdik have been recorded or are to be seen in the mountains and open country, and various large animals such as oryx and wild boars have abounded in the khors.[2] Elephants used to be found in Khor Baraka, and oral history speaks about giraffe hunting.

As to the culture of the early desert dwellers, archaeologists associate the Beja with such groups as "the pan-grave people" (Török 1986) and the "Medjayu" of some Egyptian sources (Bietak 1986:17f), and with the "Blemmyes" of Roman documents.[3]

Durra is thought to have been brought to Africa at around the beginning of our time reckoning, coming, according to Greek and Roman writers, from India. Before its introduction, other grains were available. There is ample evidence of the Beja collecting *shush* (Panicum turgidum) and *hedak* (Aizoon canariense) (Murray 1935:87, Winkler 1936:276, Keimer 1953:376, Hartmann 1865:176). Such wild grains are still used by some desert dwellers on the edge of Sahara (Tubiana and Tubiana 1977:14; Holy 1988:145). In the Nile Valley, certain grains were cultivated from about 4000 BC. Cultivation was, however, hardly a reliable source of food in the Beja area at the time when durra was introduced. Its appearance was therefore less significant in the economic life of Beja than the introduction of the camel.

Camels, thanks to their extended period of lactation, enable their keepers to rely on pastoralism for the full year. Their introduction accordingly created important food and transport resources to use in long distance trade. Camels are, because of their slow rate of biological

---

[1] Among these species are, in addition to shush and hedak (see below), the fruits from Capparis decidua (*sarob*), Balanites egyptiaca (*lalob*), Hyphaene thebaica and Glossonema boreanum (*hambokti*).

[2] For ariel and ibex hunting techniques see Owen (1937b:163) and Parker (1901 SGA 112/11/77, Letter of Inspector of Kassala to Mudir).

[3] Those who are further interested in the ancient history of the Beja are referred to the Appendix and to Adams (1977), Arkell (1955:78), Behrens and Beckhaus-Gerst (1986), Carlsson and van Gerven (1979), Kirwan (1937) and Säve Söderberg (1979). Reinisch (1895:47) derives "Blemmye" from "balami"—desert dweller.

reproduction, an only modestly growing form of capital. They are an asset which can be monopolized. If properly trained the animals provide their owners with combat or raiding superiority; this advantage can in turn be used for subduing small scale farmers or shepherds of small stock.

The records of pillaging raids by the "pre-Beja" Blemmyes against Roman and Nubian settlements in the third and fourth centuries AD (see especially Török 1986) most forcefully raise the possibility of a major political and military change brought about by access to camels. Yet, even if camel breeding was introduced on a large scale at the period mentioned, we cannot postulate that it introduced a resource which was equally accessible to all the Beja — there might have been a division between camel-owning "warriors" and small-stock people. The innovation, however, certainly brought a potential both for internal structural changes within Beja society and for shifts in relations between this society and its agricultural neighbours to the west and south.

Occasional notes exist of transport camels arriving in Africa through Sinai in the context of Assyrian and Persian invasions of Egypt. Yet Bulliet (1975:111ff), along with Zeuner (1963:353) and Trigger (1965:131), conclude that it is only around the time of Christ and with reference to camel-borne trade along the desert routes between the Nile and the Red Sea that one can show camel breeding tribes to be present in the Eastern Desert of Egypt.[1] Specialized camel breeding would be the only way in which an adequate supply of transport animals could be secured at reasonable prices.

Camels made it possible for Sudanese traders to abandon the Elephantine route along the Nile Valley to which they had before been narrowly confined by their dependence on donkeys and human carriers (Amin 1968:36) and also to cross Beja areas more easily. As to the possible introducers of camel breeding technology, Bulliet (loc.cit) points to the presence of early Arabic inscriptions in the Eastern Desert dating from this time, and particularly to the existence of a trade route from the harbour of Leuce Come connected with the Nabataean capital

---

[1] Zarins (1978:45) states that "No firm evidence for camel domestication in the Arabian peninsula prior to 1000BC is forthcoming or convincing". Bulliet (1975:111ff), however, suggests that the camel has been independently introduced to Africa twice. The camel economies further south on the Horn of Africa thus may have an older or separate origin from the camel rearing patterns found in the Sahara, to which the Beja are linked.

Petra on the opposite side of the Red Sea. Thus it would seem likely that the practice of camel breeding for commercial and military purposes in Africa began in the desert areas east of modern Luxor and then spread southwards to the corresponding areas of eastern Sudan. Perhaps the traders encouraged the indigenous desert dwellers to produce such beasts. In any case, the introduction of the camel brought trade right into the Beja desert areas and created a demand for guides and syces which came to be of vital importance for the economy and external contacts of the Beja.

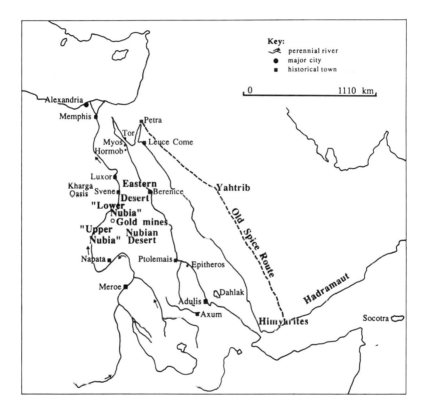

MAP 3: The Red Sea in classical times, and some places mentioned in the text.
Note: Names are not necessarily contemporary with each other.

The question of how durra and camels were introduced to the Beja areas cannot be considered in further detail here. However, it draws our attention to the fact that local conditions can only partially account for the Beja's total access to resources. Innovation has in this case clearly come from the outside. Beja society has never been isolated from the outside world. On the contrary, the outside world has penetrated the local community, so that what we see today is a combination of past technological transfers and a strong cultural heritage, developed partly in defence against such penetration.

Desert routes, harbours and early trade

As the Beja became dependent upon involvement in the caravan business of the hinterland of Red Sea ports, their fortunes also became closely tied to macro-political conditions on the world scene. Almost since time immemorial, the Red Sea route had been one of Europe's three major access routes to the riches of the Orient. The other two were the Silk Route through Inner Asia and the Spice Route via Baghdad to the Persian Gulf and hence to India and South East Asia. The Red Sea route had its own distinct advantages through its vicinity to the East African coast, and to Yemen, but it had to compete with the Spice Route for control of the more easterly trade from India. Depending upon the conditions that prevailed in Mesopotamia and the Gulf, the regions bordering the Red Sea were able to take advantage of the Eastern trade, or suffered from the loss of its profits.

Because trade depended upon shifting macro-political conditions in the region, different parts of the Beja country became involved in the traffic at different times. Four general routes developed. The exact delineation of these varied over the centuries, and the presentation on the map just outlines the dominant routes for different periods. These routes were (1) the Ababda-Bishariin route from Abu Hamad on the Nile via Murat wells and Korosko towards Aswan; (2) the Suakin-Ariaab-Berber route; (3) the Tokar-Baraka-Kassala route (alternatively Agig-Khor Langeb-Baraka); and (4) the southern Egyptian route from Aydhab to Qus.

The Beja coast is characterized by the presence of several alternative small harbours and islands that sea traffic can use. As Crowfoot noted in 1911, they do not differ much in terms of naval safeness or defensive security, but have advantages or drawbacks in terms of the

20

length of the sea journeys implied by their use, and in terms of the accessibility of their hinterlands. A striking feature in the history of the coast is the frequent locational shifts of trading centres and the lack of continuity in the history of ancient harbours. At the same time there is a relative concentration of ancient sites around some strategic khor mouths providing easy ascents to the higher inland regions (Crowfoot 1911:547).

The spice trade dated back far into classical times. In addition to spices proper it concerned itself with incense, various medical substances, pigments and dyes, mordants, and so on (McEvedy 1980:28). When the first Greek descriptions of the Red Sea littoral and harbours were written, Egyptian, Himyaritic and Sabaean traders had already for many generations used them for the monsoon-based trade that linked Egypt with the Indian Ocean and its myrrh-producing countries.

Yet the Red Sea is a difficult route to sail, because of strong northerly winds, dangerous reefs and islands. During the period 900-300 BC, external influences on the Beja coast are not likely to have been very important, for it was better to transport goods by camel through the Arabian desert than by ship on the Red Sea (Doe 1971:13). In contrast to their Arab competitors, it took Greek and Roman merchants until about the year 0 before they understood the monsoon winds, and at the same period the larger *sambuk* type of ship, more suited to the Indian Ocean, became established. These improvements in knowledge and technology made it possible to give greater importance to the Red Sea link from north to south, whereas earlier sea traffic had either crossed the sea or been confined to local traffic along the western shore (Doe 1971:54f).

In the period between 300 and 200 BC, the Ptolemies maintained a series of hunting stations and export harbours along the Southern Beja coast just below the Baraka delta, in order to procure African elephants to be tamed for war purposes and also for ascending to Gezira and the Kassala for some inland products such as ivory, slaves and tortoise shells.

A boom in Roman trade with the Orient through the Red Sea took place during the first centuries AD, but did not last long. This trade became important because of insecure conditions further to the east; the Parthians had blocked the Spice Route through Mesopotamia. Some small harbours on the Beja coast were used as stop-over stations. Trade routes were established in Upper Egypt between the Nile and the Red

21

Sea, passing through what is now the northern end of Beja territory, the present-day habitat of the Mahmedab and Ashabab Ababda. In inland Sudan, the Meroeitic kingdom was an important partner for Red Sea traders. The sources tell us nothing about the role of the Beja in this trade, but it is conceivable that then, as later, many traders travelling through the inland areas would have been dependent upon their assistance.

With the restoration of peaceful conditions on the Spice Route, the Sudanese harbours declined, and so did the Meroe kingdom on the Nile. The Roman sources on "the Blemmyes" and their raids dried up. After Byzantine and Persian interference in Egypt in the 6th and 7th centuries, the Arabs occupied the latter country in 638. From this time on, our sources for the Eastern Desert are mainly Arabic. They refer to the population of the Eastern Desert as "Beja", using the concept in a more inclusive way than we do, however.

The Beja and the Hadariba

The accounts given by the Arab invaders about their relations with the Beja are among the best sources for Beja history. We will in this section try to establish what can be said about Beja society on the basis of such sources. On its way home, an expedition that the Arabs sent to Nubia in 641 came across a group of Beja at the Nile. They did not take the trouble to engage in battle against them (Vantini 1975:59). Later, however, they subdued and nominally converted some Beja at Aswan.[1] A Beja "kingdom" is mentioned (Vantini 1975:48 quoting Al-Waqidi 790 AD), but its status is unclear both in terms of actual political character and of its religion. Christian kingdoms existed in Nubia: Nobatia, Makuria and Alodia. They remained Christian for six hundred years, but came under Arabian dominance politically. They had to pay "baqt", providing Arab Egypt with black slaves. Neighbouring Beja groups were, according to similar agreements, supposed to pay in camels.[2]

The contacts between the Beja and the Arabs intensified when the latter discovered the gold mines in Wadi Allaqi in 946. These were ancient works, and had been exploited by the Egyptians in Pharaonic and Ptolemaic times. A veritable gold-rush ensued (Hassan 1967:40-1,

---

[1]Hassan 1967:31 quoting Ibn Al-Hakam 1920:189 and Ibn Hawqal 1938:51.2, Vantini 1975:59.
[2]Hassan, loc.cit., Vantini op.cit. 625-7, 1981:92, after Macrizi 1922.

22

50ff, Holt and Daly 1979:16-17). Beja and Arab families intermingled, and many Sudanese Arabs possess written family trees which begin with Beja names (Kheir 1982:375). The names given by old Arab sources for the groups they met in the present Beja areas leave no room for doubts about the Bedawiet identity of the inhabitants of the Eastern Desert at that time (see especially Zaborski 1965).

From the early Arab sources it is evident that the Beja were not just desert brigands — though they continued to be so when political control was lax — but that they also acted as desert guides for travellers and caravans. The volume of caravaneering through their area depended upon factors affecting the sea traffic through the Red Sea and the political conditions in the successive Muslim empires on whose periphery they were situated.

In the 10th century, under the Fatimid dynasty, Aydhab, the northernmost port on the Beja coast, was developed into an important link between the Red Sea and prosperous Christian Nubia (Paul 1936). Aydhab profited particularly from the blocking of Sinai during the crusades, which forced all Muslim pilgrims from north Africa to pass through Beja areas on their way to Mecca. The Beja sold honey, clarified butter, milk and water to the town (Maqrizi 1922:272). Idrisi (1864:27) recounts information that presents the Beja as being already commercially oriented at this time. He tells of the Beja village of Bukht, which had a large camel market and a surrounding population of camel nomads. The Hadariba Beja also controlled the difficult crossing to Jiddah by jallab crafts.

In the 13th century another port, Suakin, became prominent under the protection of the Mamluk Turks, who had taken power in Egypt in 1260. It flourished in the 15th century due to wars in Persia and inner Asia, which barred the traditional Silk Route from Europe to the Orient. The town continued to be important after the establishment of the Funj dynasty on the Nile in about 1504. Slaves and ivory from the interior of Africa, as well as camels, ghee and durra from eastern Sudan to Mecca, were typical export goods (O'Fahey and Spaulding 1974:21-22).

In both Aydhab and Suakin, local power and the organization of desert transport were in the hands of people referred to as "Hadareb" or "Hadariba". This name first occurs when Arab sources in the 9th

23

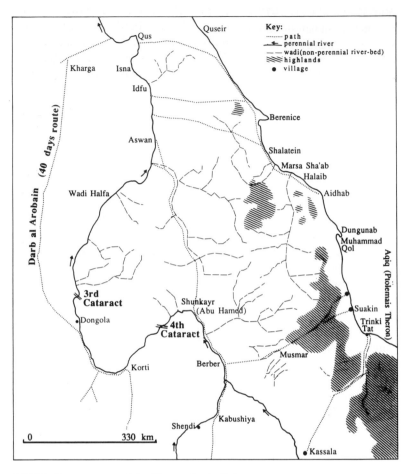

MAP 4: Caravan routes of significance for the Beja

century describe the various inhabitants of the Beja areas. The Hadariba then appear to have been pastoral nomads.

In the most intensive periods of trade through Aydhab and Suakin, the Hadariba seem to have been an urban elite, with continued strong links to the Beja. The Turkish overlords of Suakin were dependent on the Hadariba for obtaining provisions, and the Hadariba were very important to trade links to the Nile Valley (Crawford 1951:123). They

24

were closely connected with the Abdallab, the rulers of Alwa (Alodia), who had been turned into viceroys for the Funj.[1] A similar intermediary group, the Balaw, who were Tigre rather than Beja, were established around Arkiko further to the south (Crawford 1951:131). They competed with the Hadariba and the Abdallab, particularly during the 17th century. In the 18th century, however, Hadariba merchants controlled the caravan trade between Suakin and the gold and slave markets on the Nile, Arbaji, Shendi and Berber. They helped to weaken the influence of the Funj sultan during the last part of the 18th century (O'Fahey and Spaulding 1974:78-82, 96f).

If we look at the earliest documents, those of the Arab chroniclers, it appears that people called the Hadareb were widespread over the northern Beja territory. The Hadareb are mentioned in Yacubi's list (dating from around 872). In the 10th century Ibn Hawqal (1938:56) mentions them as intermarrying with the Rabia leaders of the mine region, and notes that they, particularly the 'Abdak, were overlords over the Rigbat and H.n.d.yba in the Suakin area. Ibn Hawqal, in fact, describes the "Hadariba" living conditions rather extensively:

"They are all cattle-breeders and nomads. Their territory, including that part which is watered by rainfall and sown, and that which serves as grazing land equals in length a two months' journey, while its width is bounded by the Nile and the sea. Their winter camps are on the sea coast and their summer camps are in the valleys in the interior of the country where water is found for their subsistence. In autumn they move westwards near the Nile, where the land has few trees, but provides rich pastures, undergrowth and water pools. They live mainly on meat and milk: the poor eat wild game, gazelles, ostriches and wild asses. They are Muslims only nominally...They speak a language common to all the Beja: they are all illiterate: some of them have a language of their own..." (Vantini 1975:160 2, 1981:100).

A contemporary to Ibn Hawqal, Masudi (d. 956 or 957), not only mentions "30,000 camel men of the Hadariba" (1861:lll:33-34), but notes that the Hadariba are the only Muslims among the Beja. Aswami, however, adds to Masudi's comment that the Hadariba still retain some

---

[1]O'Fahey and Spaulding 1974:26, quoting Barradas 1633 in Beccari 1905-17, IV, 108

pagan customs (Vantini 1975:630-1). He further describes them as the overlords of the Zanafi(g).[1] The Zanafi, he says, are more numerous and once dominated their present lords, but now each Hadariba chief has attached to him a group of inheritable Zanafi serfs who protect the Hadarab and tend their cattle (Hassan 1967:11, n.58, Vantini 1975:624-5, 1981:98). Aswami's description, in Maqrizi's version, is the only one mentioning this relationship between the two categories. It is very reminiscent of the 20th century relationship between the Nabtab and the Tigre/Hedareb as described by Nadel (1954).[2]

The Hadariba category was interpreted by Arabic observers as constituting a tribal sub-unit, and most modern authors seem to take them to be a kind of family or lineage grouping. The term, in fact, crops up continuously in Beja history over a period of one thousand years, and most of the time it seems to refer to a trading elite. Ibn Hawqal's mention of six "butun" belonging to the Hadareb, and his general way of describing them as nomads, suggests in contrast that "Hadareb" was an inclusive category that accounted for large parts of the population.

A word of caution is certainly necessary here. Although it is difficult to ascertain exactly how important traders were in the organization of rural Beja society, the Arab observers are all likely to have moved along trading routes and in places where a merchant elite was particularly likely to be prominent. In fact, despite Ibn Hawqal's description, we do not know whether all the Beja nomads in the northern deserts

---

[1]The Zanafi as such, however, occur in several of the sources. The fact that cattle are mentioned in connection with them suggests that they were living in the area presently inhabited by the Hadendowa or south thereof. North of the present route Atbara-Musmar-Port Sudan there are today no cattle. Murray (1926), however, describes ancient cattle groves from the Bishariin area. Hawqal (1936 1:55) talks about Zanafi staying in the Dukhn area, suggested by Crawford to be the Gash delta (1951:107), and according to Maqrizi, Al-Aswami found them as pastoralists at Shunqayr at the eastern Nile bend, subject to the king of Muqurra but not mixing with the Nubians (Maqrizi, 1922:3:257-8). Furthermore, Zaborski (1965) suggests that Al-Zanafi might be a misreading for as-Zanafi, as "as" is a common element in some southern Beja and Tigre names. There are some other hints that the Zanafi might have been speakers of Tigre. Ibn Hawqal does not mention them at all but names other subordinate groups who were in all likelihood Tigre-speakers. In one of the contradictory versions presented by [Ya'qubi] Yacubi (Kitab al-Buldan 1892:336-7), he claims that the centre of the Zanafi was B.q.l.y.n. In his *Tarih* (1883 vol 1:2l7) he locates them in N.q.y.s. Admittedly, the support for the theory that Zanafi were not Beja proper is weak, but it remains a fact that the word itself has a non-Beja ring. We asked our informants to play with the word to see if they could detect any similarity to any TuBedawiye word, but with little success (the closest they could get was *ti'anamfiq*).

[2]Oddly enough the term *hedareb* in present-day Beni Amer society is used by those who speak TuBedawiye to denote serfs in contrast to Nabtab aristocrats. Tigre-speakers instead use the expression *Tigre*. These two terms also denote the languages (Nadel 1954). Amar'ar and Hadendowa say that the Beja-speaking Beni Amer are hedareb because they, like the rest of the Beja, are hospitable, while the remainder of the Beni Amer are regarded as the opposite.

26

regarded themselves as Hadareb, nor what the significance of slavery and serfhood was for the daily life and subsistence of the majority. One guess would be that the "silent majority" living off the trade routes used to distinguish themselves as *"bedawiet"*, just as the Beja do today, thereby differentiating between themselves and the *"hadarab"* in much the same way as the pair of Arabic concepts *"badawa"* and *"hadara"* was understood by Ibn Khaldoun to denote the binary opposition of civilized and sedentary versus bedouins. Reinisch (1895:112) offers the translation "angesiedelt, sesshaftig" for *"hedare, hadare"*, and Rossini (1928:271) suggests "inhabitant".

Today, the term *Hedareb* essentially connotes a generous and hospitable person, that is a person who fulfils the most basic Beja values. This connotation of "host" is in a Beja context not completely alien to the concept of a town-based, sedentary merchant, for within a Beja tribal section, the town-based member is supposed to provide storage facilities and hospitality for his rural relatives when they come to town, mediating their relations with the non-Beja world (cf. Fawzy 1978:20).

There is also a popular etymology linking the Hadarab to the Hadarmo, people from Hadramawt, which has been taken at face value by several authors writing on the Beja, such as Paul (1954:54; 1959:75-78) and Talhami (1974:109). Zaborski (1965:291) succinctly notes that the folk etymology here contributes to the creation of a prestige-maintaining myth, to the favour of a Muslim elite. However, the alternative translation of "hospitable people" confers at least as much prestige in Beja terms. Today, in Suakin, "Hadarmo" refers to a particular Arabic-speaking, mercantile ethnic group, sharing ancestry from the legendary hadramautian Ba Saffar with the closely associated Arteiga — one of Ibn Hawqal's Hadarab tribes. The "Hadariba" are seen as a largely extinct Arabic-speaking group, once in power.

Probably, all the various etymological explanations of the concept have co-existed for a long time — "civilized", "hospitable" and "coming from Hadramaut". The fact that the latter translation enhances prestige does not of course make it altogether unlikely that some percentage of the original Hadareb were actually from Hadramaut.

The term "bedawiet" at first seems like an obvious Arabic loanword for "bedouin", but it also contains an ambiguity similar to that of "Hadareb". If pronounced "badawiet" it would refer to people living in houses constructed with palm matting (*bad*). "Bedouin", translated *ti'bed*, is used by the Beja to refer not to themselves but to the Rashaida, a group of bedouins coming from the Arabian peninsula during last century and now roaming particularly the Southern and Eastern Beja lands with their camels.

Presently, the main term used in contrast to "Bedawiet" is "Balawiet", rather than "Hadareb". While "Hadareb" is sometimes used to describe speakers of TuBedawiye, who at times talked Arabic, "Balawiet" always refers to Arabic-speaking, urbanized non-Beja.[1]

Returning to the question of medieval patron-serf relationships, the scattered nature of subsistence resources in the northern desert makes it difficult to work out what kind of control any overlords could possibly have had over the bedouins except in times of ecological crisis, when there was scarcity of milk, wild grain or durra. As suggested above, one possibility would be that camel ownership was at that time much less widespread in the Beja community than it was some decades ago. Perhaps large numbers of the ordinary Beja were simple shepherds, camels being a monopoly on which Hadareb trading control was based. That could create a situation akin to the "predatory" camel pastoralism found among some contemporary Saharan pastoralists. This is sheer speculation, which we will probably never be able to substantiate with historical evidence. Neither material remains nor written documents are likely to throw light on this issue.

Another hint of a non-egalitarian structure is contained in Ibn Hawqal's Hadariba description, which sounds familiar to those acquainted with East African pastoral cultures: "The richest among them make it their duty to abstain from wild game and from intercourse with those who eat wild game. They also abhor using the vessels of those who consider game a permitted food. They make no use of them either for drinking or milking." Such "caste" distinctions as Ibn Hawqal here describes are typical of Cushitic herdsmen further south, such as the Borana and the Somali. But the distinctions have been completely forgotten in Beja culture, where no present stigma attaches to wild game hunting as such, although some food is considered less honourable.

Thus, our knowledge of the history of early Arab times indicates that the Beja were a stratified local community, possibly based on patron-serf relationships and low-status caste-like groupings, but

---

[1] Desert pastoralists, whether Beja or not, are referred to as Arab.

especially on class distinction. Class differences also distort the use of tribal names, which at times turn into ambiguous categories. The juxtaposition of "Hadareb" and "Bedawiet" as essentially constituting concepts of class distinction may make the development of the Bedawiet concept easier to understand than if it is regarded primarily as a notion of ethnicity or nationality. Politically significant groupings among the Beja are formed at a much lower level than that of the linguistic group. The type of culturally distinct stranger that most Beja during the ages would be likely to have been in contact with would have been the trader-townsman rather than the pastoralist from another culture.

We know that the Hadariba were very prominent as traders around the time of the Medieval and Funj eras, but we still do not know the extent to which their activities had an impact on ordinary herdspeople.

Apart from the probable extensive involvement of certain Beja groups along the main caravan routes and in Suakin with the trade of the Funj and the Abdallab, the general impact of the Funj rule on Beja life was perhaps small. It has been questioned by Newbold (1935), among others. He observes that "the Abdullab viceroys held Kassala and Goz Regeb and raiding parties probably penetrated the hills, but central and northern Beja...probably resisted all infiltration into their main strongholds...". Perhaps the situation was then as it has also been in more recent times: the Beja allowed themselves to be represented by merchant middlemen in order to skim the cream off whatever trade went through their areas, but they did not let strangers interfere with or even come into direct contact with their own family and subsistence life in the desert and hills. Yet their subsistence living did have room for a certain degree of market production. Apart from the pastoral production of milk and butter that we have mentioned, forest products were sold. For example we know that in about 1800 the Bishariin and Ababda on the northern route gathered and sold wild senna (Walz, *loc.cit*).

Beja groups in the 19th century

With the end of the 18th century we move into the era of oral traditions recorded by European travellers and colonial officers, and more detailed information about identifiable Beja groups, such as the Ababda, Bishariin and Hadendowa. From Sandars (1933) we learn that the Arteiga/Hadariba were during that time in strong opposition to the

29

Bishariin. In connection with wars between the Morghumab and the Batahin, and between the Kamalab and the Messelemia Arabs, the Bishariin, led by Hamad Omran Isa, had moved into the Atbara area from north and west of Ariaab[1] about 1760-70 (Newbold 1935:153). At this time there was no major strife between Ababda and Bishariin. These groups would later contest each other's rights to the Murrat wells on the northward caravan route. Burckhardt (1819) found them grazing peacefully together on each side of the Egyptian border (Sandars 1933:133).

Both groups had long since been established along the northern route, engaging in individual trade and acting as caravan escorts during peaceful periods. In bad periods, they turned to brigandage and the trade switched to the "forty days route" further to the west.[2]

Fawzy (1978:26) describes how the Ababda in the 16th and 17th centuries had been living at Wadi Hodein, their area of habitation extending to Shalatin at the coast. In the early 19th century they migrated northwards. When resources became scarce to the north in the latter half of the century, they started to reclaim their old areas, leading to feuds with the Bishariin in the 1880s.

Within the Atbara Bishariin the most important group were the Hamedab, who cultivated land along the banks of the river up to its junction, and who were rich in livestock. These Bishariin had many conflicts with the Hadendowa. Another strong Bishariin group were the Beni Kurb (Kurbab). It was also during the earlier half of last century that the Hadendowa moved into the Gash, which had up to then been controlled by the Halenga, Segolab, Melitkinab etc. (Newbold 1935:154). These small tribes, according to travellers such as Bruce (1790) and Junker (1890), quoted by Newbold (*loc. cit.*), were under some kind of "shadowy allegiance" to the Funj king between 1770 and 1820. About the remainder of the Bishariin during the 19th century we know little except what can be gained from Linant de Bellefonds (1884), who visited them in 1833. They were anti-Turkish and difficult to control. The Turkish administration consisted only of raids for tribute. The richest groups were the Hamedorab and the Shantirab at Elba, who exported ibex and livestock to Jiddah traders visiting their anchorages.

---

[1]For connections with the Arteiga, see Macmichael 1922:II:169
[2]Burckhardt 1819:153ff, 195, Bruce 1894:294-5, Walz 1978:10,64, Girard 1818:83, 633, 637.

They did not cultivate the land much, and they bought provisions in upper Egypt (Sandars 1933:137).

Sandars (1935), by conjecture but in some detail, summarizes some Amar'ar traditions that can be traced to this period. These concern how various ancestors in the generations succeeding the tribe-founder Atmaan expanded west from their former stronghold at Jebel Akereiribai until they, led by Hamad Hassai ("angry Hamid", ca. 1790-1839), secured their foothold in the khors of the western hill-slopes north of Ariaab. Sandars suggests that this expansion took place into areas already partly abandoned by the Bishariin, but preceeding Hamad Omran's legendary move to Atbara. He is however not able to offer any conclusive answer as to the reasons behind the Bishariin's decline or movement out of these areas.[1] Through intermarriage with the Bishariin and Hadendowa, the Atmaan and Amar'ar are said to have established claims to the plains between Khor Arab and Atbara. These claims drove a wedge into the areas which used to be controlled solely by the Bishariin.

Egyptian rule

Turkey had ruled Egypt since 1260. At the beginning of the 19th century they no longer controlled the country efficiently, although a Turkish-speaking Ottoman elite was still influential. After the defeat of Napoleon, Mehmet Ali was appointed "vice-roy". Under this title he was to rule a relatively independent Egypt. In 1820, Mehmet sent his son Ismail Pasha to recover upper Nubia, where some survivors of the Mamluk army had taken refuge (Holt and Daly 1979:47). It may be of some interest to note that the Ababda provided the caravan transport and guidance for Ismail's expedition (*ibid*). Having been successful, Ismail proceeded to attack Sennar, the capital of the Funj kingdom, which was at this stage plagued by political chaos. Apart from the political motive behind this campaign, the conquest was also motivated by the very same prospects that had aroused pharaonic interest and brought the Arabs to the Sudan: the hope for gold and for secure access to supplies of African slaves for the Egyptian army (Mohamed 1980:15; Schultze 1963:279). It appears, however, that the quest for gold was less rewarding than was the slave trade, which prospered up

[1] Voll (1969:214) hints at a religious background, as many of the Atbara Bishariin were Majdubiyyas. The latter had supported the Funj against the Egyptians. See also Baker (1867:20).

31

till the time of British involvement. In Egypt, Mehmet Ali tried to launch cotton as a profitable alternative to grain cultivation about 1820. This venture later became another important focus for the Egyptian plans for Sudan.

Three aspects of the Egyptian rule are important to consider here, as they were of significance for the Beja economy. The first is the degree of efficiency in the administrative and fiscal systems as relating to the Beja, the second the introduction of alternative models for land use other than those pursued by the Beja, and the third the conditions prevalent for the caravan trade and the harbours during the Egyptian era.

The conquest of Sennar in itself naturally had immediate though limited effects on the Beja. Whereas the riverine peoples were subject to very harsh taxation, particularly in the form of confiscation of slaves, the nomads were at first left in peace by the Turks. However, in 1831-2 a major expedition was organized against the Hadendowa. It ended with the Turko-Egyptian force being wiped out by a Hadendowa contingent led by Mohamed Din (Holt and Daly 1979:63). The next attempt to obtain tribute from the Hadendowa and the Halenga was made in 1840, and was more successful in so far as the Hadendowa and Halenga leaders formally submitted themselves. On the suggestion of the Halenga leader, the Turko-Egyptian governor-general had the Gash river dammed, in order to force the unwilling Hadendowa to pay their tribute. The dam broke, and the scheme failed; the Hadendowa were able to take refuge in the dense bush around the lower Gash (*op. cit*: 66). In 1844 an attempted Hadendowa revolt was brutally crushed (*op. cit*: 69, Born 1964:47). It was during these years that Kassala town was founded, about six km south of the place where the river forks out into the delta. Through its potential for cultivation and its strategic importance at the crossing between caravan routes, the original military camp soon grew into a centre of some importance. In the 1860s there were between 10,000 and 20,000 people living in the town and its suburbs (Born 1964:48).[1]

For those who were living close to garrisons such as Kassala and Berber, tribute-paying may certainly have been a substantial problem. For other groups the information is scanty. Jackson (1926:35) was of the opinion that the Beja generally had less of a grudge against the

---

[1]The successive occupation of the town by Mahdist, Italian and later Anglo-Egyptian troops led to a temporary decline in its growth until the upturn in cotton cultivation in the delta. (Born 1964:48).

Turko-Egyptian Government than other Sudanese people, because no government had been able to tax them efficiently. Sandars (1935:206) notes that the Amar'ar were charged with far smaller taxes than the Hadendowa, but that the burden of having to provide the government troops with camels was felt to be decidedly heavy.

Until the time of the Turkish occupation, farming in the Beja lands had been limited to subsistence durra cultivation on a small scale. Foreign rule did not substantially threaten the land-use system of the Beja. Gash and Tokar were drought refuges for Beja herds looking for pasture, and some small-scale cultivation of durra could take place there as well. Now, however, the Turkish governor of Suakin, Mumtaz Pasha, introduced cotton to Kassala and Tokar in 1870. His ambition, according to Schultze (1963:39), was to put 16 million feddan (6.7 million hectares) under cotton. In contrast to such astonishing figures, Schultze quotes 50 acres[1] as the area put under cotton in Tokar the year 1871, and 2,500 acres as the corresponding figure for Gash (op.cit:44). Internal Sudanese problems with transport and the Mahdist insurrection of the mid-1880s, however, put an obstacle to the further development of this scheme at the same time as the end of the American war quenched the international interest in Sudanese cotton (Shami 1961:148, Holt and Daly 1979:81).

Harbours and routes during the Turko-Egyptian era

The Turko-Egyptian occupation meant an expansion and regularization of the route from Abu Hamad to Aswan. Earlier, the absence of political control either from the Ottomans or from Sinnar had led to brigandage and demands for exorbitant fees from the Ababda, scaring much of the north-bound trade westwards towards the 40 days route. During the Turko-Egyptian period, however, the Ababda became engaged in trade on a more regular basis. The Ababda were permitted to receive 10 % of the value of custom on all exports from the Sudan. They were responsible for policing the route, protecting caravans and providing camels (Hill 1959:128-9, Walz 1978:246 quoting the Hekekyan Papers II:477). The authorities confirmed the Ababda's control over the Murrat wells, over which the Bishariin and the Ababda had earlier maintained conflicting claims (Sandars 1933:138).

---

[1]One feddan is 1.038 acres.

33

The expansion of trade, and presumably the increased security on the route, also led to other groups such as Halfawis and Arabs from Egyptian Nubia being drawn into this traffic (Walz 1978:246, quoting Hekekyan papers II:477). Ivory, gum arabicum, camels and slaves continued to be the important export goods along this route, which was always favoured by the Egyptian authorities. The Turks also negotiated with Beja groups over the control of the Berber-Suakin route. For example, Sandars (1935:205) quotes traditions that they agreed for the Atmaan's Hamed Hassai to protect the route between Ariaab and Obak in return for permission to take tolls.

In 1811, a decade before sending his son to the Sudan, Mehmed Ali had on behalf of the Ottoman Turks re-conquered the Hijaz from the Wahhabis. Control of Arabia meant enhanced security in the Red Sea and revitalization of its traffic. It made it possible for Europe to trade in the Red Sea through Egypt after centuries of obstacles. The coffee trade with Yemen blossomed and the stream of pilgrims to Mecca swelled, particularly in the 1870s and thereafter (Abir 1980:4). The harbours on the western shore also profited from this boom. Although they were nominally under Turkish control, the Sudanese harbours were at first not controlled by the Turko-Egyptian sub-rulers of Sudan. Only after extending their influence from the Nile Valley towards Kassala in 1840 could these rulers aspire to control of Suakin and Massawa. The two towns were instead governed by the authorities of the Hijaz. Mehmet Ali had early in his rule tried to establish full control over Massawa, but had failed to do so. In 1846-9 he was given the two towns on lease for three years. After the lease lapsed they did not come under the sovereignty of Khartoum until 1865 (Holt and Daly 1979:67).

Soon after, in 1869, the Suez canal was opened. It had been constructed as part of the strategies of modernizing Egypt pursued by Mehmet Ali and his successors. But the costs as well as the consequences of the project came to be to the disadvantage of Egypt. Ruined, the country became subject to British dominance, and the ruler had to part with his shares in the company.

The canal drastically changed the conditions for the ancient Red Sea trade. It lessened the importance of Jiddah as a stopover and entrepot for transit goods — and it opened the way for steam traffic and made textiles imported from India and Britain cheaper than Egyptian wares (Ahmed 1974:18). Jiddah remained important for local Red Sea trade.

Since the port facilities at Suakin were bad, import goods such as textiles, perfume, cutlery, tobacco, liquor, timbers and wood had to be brought to Sudan by smaller, local, Egyptian or Jiddan vessels. Then the goods were transported by camel through the Beja areas. During the Mahdiya war, contraband goods such as lead and saltpetre were added to the list (Hill 1959:47, Talhami 1975:84). The exports consisted of traditional goods such as gum, ivory, ostrich feathers, senna, hides and wax coming largely from Ethiopia (Talhami 1975:86; Eisa 1978:53). The dominant exchange medium for transactions in Suakin's market continued to be durra (Talhami 1975:84 quoting Burckhardt 1819:398-400).

Immediately after the installation of Turko-Egyptian authority in Suakin, competition had broken out between the Amar'ar and the Bishariin over who would be the guardians and camel suppliers along the 435 km. long route from Suakin to Berber. The conflicts at times stopped all the trade while the authorities pondered over the various offers, with the Beja impatiently refusing to rent out any camels (Talhami 1975:162). The Atmaan Amar'ar finally won the battle (Jackson 1926:28). There were also strains within the Amar'ar themselves, particularly between the Fadlab and the Hamdab. The Hamdab were finally supported by the Turkish forces stationed at Sinkat (Sandars 1935:27).[1]

Talhami describes some of the ways in which this trade provided a commercial outlet for pastoral produce (*op.cit.*:83). From Kassala the Suakin traders obtained liquid butter and durra, as well as waterskins and other leather products for which there was a demand in the Arabian market. The hill tribes prepared and sold palm-leaf mats, and the Bishariin had for a long time specialized in riding-camels (Burckhardt 1819:396-8).

Osman Digna and the Beja. Slave trade, religion and war

The trade in slaves had been one of the strong factors in Sudan's relations with the external world since times immemorial. In the mid-19th century, European, Syrian and Egyptian merchants were penetrating down into the traditional slave source areas in the Southern Sudan, searching for ivory and providing an increased supply of slaves

---

[1] Sandars suggests that the "present" (i.e. 1935) split between Atmaan and Fadlab dated back to this time.

35

to the northern markets. International pressure forced the Turko-Egyptian authorities to officially ban the slave trade. It continued nevertheless, but in less visible forms. This was no wonder, given the strong economic interests involved, not least among the administrative staff of the Egyptian state (Schultze 1963:35f, 45): by exploiting the formal state monopoly on trade, they could extract a good share. During the last years of the reign of Ismail Pasha (1863-1879), under the governorship of Gordon, renewed attempts were made to put a definite stop to the trade. At that time Egypt itself was no longer a market for slaves; in fact, slave markets all over the world had collapsed. Arabia was an exception, and all trade with slaves was redirected towards the Arabian peninsula, though it was forced to be conducted under disguised forms. One can speculate that this was advantageous to the Beja who controlled the small coastal harbours, just as they today profit from smuggling other goods. Anyhow, it is clear that opposition between slave trading interests and British policy became decisive for development in Beja areas during the Mahdiya.

The most renowned Mahdist leader in Eastern Sudan was Osman Digna, born about 1840. He came from a merchant family engaged in the slave trade, operating between Jiddah and Suakin. The family, as typical Suakinese, apparently had an ethnically mixed descent, claiming to be Kurds from Diyarbekr who had intermarried with the Arteiga and the Hadendowa. About 1877 the family business suffered from British reprisals against slave trading. Osman returned impoverished to Suakin from Jiddah and became a contractor for senna and water to a cotton ginnery. In 1881, when resistance against both the Turks and the British was growing, he tried an abortive uprising in Suakin and was expelled from the town (Jackson 1926:24ff). He then engaged in the trade between Suakin and Berber. After the victory of the Mahdi at El Obeid, Osman was appointed emir, with the task of preventing Anglo-Egyptian reinforcements from arriving by the Suakin-Berber route.

As the Amar'ar were in control of the route and had acted as transport carriers to the government for ten years, they were naturally averse to Osman's attempts to start a war;[1] their leader Hamad Mahmoud kept a low profile when Osman approached him for assistance

---

[1] A Fadlab leader, Mahmud Ali, had a salary of 25 dollars per month for providing protection on the route.

and did not declare open support, only sending an emissary along to represent him (Sandars 1935:207).

Neither was Osman initially attractive as a leader to the Ibrahimab, who held power among the Bishariin, nor to the Beni Amer or to the Ashraf or generally to the Arteiga in Suakin. Among the Beja sections that supported him were the Nafidab Bishariin, the Sharaab, Garaib, BishAriaab, Tankwirab and Maraghei, the Shagalei Arteiga and some of the Abdel Rahmanab and Minniab (op.cit.:29). Much of his support came from the adherents of the Majdubhiya religious fraternity, which was competing with the Khatmiya Mirghaniya for the loyalty of local Muslims.

The final decision on joining or rejecting Osman frequently had a historical basis connected with events during the early decades of the 19th century. Voll (1968) has in his thesis on the Khatmiya summarized the available information on the relationship between tribal affiliation and support for Turko-Egyptian rule. He places emphasis on the importance of relations between the Khatmiya and their opponents, and discusses resistance against the government as being coupled with Majdhubiyya affiliation. The Khatmiya had a role as informal mediators between the Turko-Egyptian government and the people, and had at an early stage won the sympathies of the leaders of the Beni Amer, the Halenga and the Shukriya Arabs. The Majdhubiyya, on the other hand, appealed to groups who rejected the Turks or leaders loyal to them. Thus, the "Beja" were by no means united on this issue; on the contrary, the support for tariqas was linked to internal strife within the tribal groups, as well as to old intertribal conflicts such as the rivalries between the Hadendowa and the Halenga over the Gash (Voll 1969:214 ff using Sandars in Dakhlia 112/11/75).

The Atmaan leaders, to begin with, stood outside this main rivalry. They supported the Qadiriya, who had been established in the area during Funj times (Voll 1969:216). The Fadlab (Voll, ibid. qu. SGA 8-002) leaders, however, supported the Khatmiya, even at this early stage (Sandars SNR 1935 part II:207).

In the long run, the allegiance of many of the various Beja groups shifted with Osman's successes. Jackson, the main authority, fails to offer any comprehensive picture, but it is clear that the Amar'ar were pro-British for most of the period, and that only some of them temporarily associated themselves with Osman, when he was most successful. In 1886, when Osman sent an emissary and 700 men to ask

37

the Amar'ar for tribute, many of his men deserted due to lack of food, and the rest were attacked by the Amar'ar. Osman retaliated by capturing a large number of Amar'ar, leaving at least 150 to die a disgraceful death from starvation or smallpox (Jackson 1926:116). The leaders of the Amar'ar, the Musayab elder Hamad Mahmud and Nurab's Hasab Abdalla, were killed.

Jackson notes the difficulties met by Osman in uniting the fragmented Beja people: "Here the general hostility of one tribe against another or one section towards the other was complicated by minor feuds and dissensions between families or even individuals. However alluring the bait that Osman Digna dangled before the eyes of the tribesmen there was no knowing when some unexpected dispute over a grazing area or a blood-feud about a woman would not upset all his carefully concocted schemes. There was so much intrigue that the people were unwilling to commit themselves and openly declare for one side or the other owing to their uncertainty as to the attitude not only of other sections of their tribe but even of their intimate friends..." (Jackson 1926:122).

During the 1880s and 1890s the human and animal populations in Sudan were reduced to fractions of what they had been before (cf. Schultze 1963:51; Balamoan 1976). Mc Loughlin (1966:111) quotes an estimate that Kassala Province around 1870 had 500,000 people, of which 300,000 died of disease and 120,000 through warfare, leaving a 1903 population of 80,000. All over Sudan, a virtual stop was put to food production by the Mahdist war in combination with the serious drought which hit large parts of Africa. The disaster was aggravated by locust attacks and epizootics of rinderpest striking the herds, and of smallpox and cholera affecting humans.

For Osman Digna the disasters that befell the population meant a loss of much of his material and moral support. After ceding Tokar to the British in 1891 and Kassala to the Italians in 1894, Osman withdrew to Adarama on the Atbara until his final defeat. After some unsuccessful attempts at a come-back, he was betrayed by his adversaries, the Gemilab Beja (Newbold 1935:158, Jackson 1926:160).

The British impact on the Atmaan and other Beja

Apart from the direct effects of war and human and animal disease, one of the problems of the period 1884-1896 for the Beja economy was the virtual stopping of export trade, and thus of the opportunities it brought for profiting from caravan and transport services. The Khalifa, the successor to the Mahdi, was opposed both to slave exports, which might benefit Egypt's neighbours, and to pilgrimage to Mecca; both were abolished. Only a limited export of gum was allowed (Schultze 1963:50). Ismail Pasha had tried to limit Sudan's trade to the Nile routes "due perhaps to his unhappy relations to the Suez canal company" (Ahmed 1974:26). The British on their side put a blockade on Suakin to financially isolate the Mahdists (*loc.cit*) The return of peaceful conditions in the American cotton areas, the constraints on slave-trading, and the general lowering of Sudan's agricultural production shrank the volume of goods to be exported.

After the subjugation of the Mahdist regime, Egypt and Britain ruled Sudan jointly for the periods 1899-1924 and 1936-55. The British colonial administration's prime interest in the Amar'ar Beja was for labour recruitment to the Gash and Tokar irrigation schemes. For the Beja, British administration involved the appointment of "omdas" and "sheikhs" to gather and deliver tribute and to secure order on the trade-routes. In 1901, AC Parker reported that several minor Beja sheikhs had appealed to be made sheikhs independently and not to be placed under the sheikh of any larger "Bedana" (tribal section), on the basis that they had been paying tribute separately earlier (SGA 112/11/77). The sheikhs were expected to deliver taxes in durra, and were to be given 5% of the amount delivered. It was also in order to consolidate their control of the Beja that the British later re-confirmed or re-instituted the Nazir-hoods, by giving the Nazirs comprehensive legal, administrative and tax-collecting rights.[1] For the Amar'ar the British chose to give seniority to the Musayab Atmaan. One reason was the numerical superiority of the Atmaan within the Amar'ar, another Musayab's link to "angry Hamid". When the British selected their Nazir from Hamid's descendants, they gave legitimacy to an idea of "royal blood" which is still very prominent in Musayab discourse. In each case, the tribal Nazirs were selected from what the British deemed to be "the ruling family" (Newbold 1935:160).

The Amar'ar Nazir was encouraged to settle at Musmar by the Government, but to the Atmaan the true centre for the Nazir continued to be at the wells of Ariaab. The prospects of Ariaab and other caravan

---

[1]This was done in 1914 for the Hadendowa, 1915 for the Beni Amer, 1927 for the Amar'ar and 1929 for the Bishariin.

centres, and for the camel-born trade as such, had however darkened. When the general conditions favouring Sudan's export trade improved after the turn of the century, important changes had also been introduced into the infrastructure of this trade by the new British general governor. These were to radically change the conditions for the Beja's involvement in services for the long distance trade. In 1922 the old port of Suakin, which had gradually declined due to its technical inadequacy, was superseded by a new port at Sheikh Marghub, later Port Sudan, which could take larger ships than the small Arabian dhows (Eisa 1978:62). Suakin continued to function mainly on a seasonal basis to cater for pilgrims, until air service took over this role. A railway opened in 1906 between Port Sudan and Atbara, roughly parallel to the old caravan route. The connection to Kassala, substituting for other old routes, was inaugurated in 1924. Another railway link had already been opened between Wadi Halfa and Abu Hamed in 1905, west of the old caravan route of the Ababda and Bishariin; the Ababda's experience was put to good use during its construction (Amin 1968:174).

The reason for these investments was that new commercial opportunities had become apparent to the British. The idea of irrigating the Gezira was first launched as a way of turning this area, situated between the two arms of the Nile, into a granary for all of Sudan (Schultze 1963:64). Soon, however, it became obvious that high quality cotton could be produced here, at the same time as the British Cotton-growing Association, formed in 1902, was looking for suitable areas for development. It also became important to further the development of the Gash and Tokar deltas for the same purpose.

The first large scale cotton crop from Gezira was exported via Port Sudan in 1925. However, any substantial growth of the town came about only in the forties with the growing demand on the world market for Sudanese cotton, and in response to the strategic importance of the town during the war (Oliver 1966:55). As we shall see in later chapters, and as has been demonstrated by, among others, Salih (1976), the commercialization of delta cultivation led to losses of important drought resorts for the Beja, and so has negatively influenced their pastoral resource base. Most directly, the Hadendowa were affected. The territories of the Atmaan and Amar'ar (apart from the Tokar Nurab) did not contain areas of immediate commercial value, and they seem to have been regarded mainly as reserves for producing labour

40

for cotton-picking and harbour work. Colonial records were constantly preoccupied with the problem of motivating the Beja to take employment when milk and durra production was successful, and only barely managed to mask the administrators' satisfaction when bad conditions forced the nomads to work for a wage.[1]

At the end of the forties, the Atmaan lost large parts of their herds due to drought, and many looked for jobs in the expanding harbour. In response to conflicts between stevedores and contractors and between non-Beja workers and nomads who had lost their herds, a system of registered dock worker gangs benefitting the Beja was organized around 1950. Loading and unloading trade unions were established in 1951 (Hejazi 1975:305, al-Deen 1975:106). From 1967 to 1975 the harbour suffered a slack period due to the closure of the Suez Canal, but stevedoring has up to the present remained a very important part of Atmaan economy (see Lewis 1962, James 1969, Milne 1974, Gutbi 1989).

The port traffic of Port Sudan has since the construction of the harbour always been very vulnerable to disturbances on the international level. The depression of the 1930s and the Suez crisis hit hard, and before the last great period of famine the traffic had again come to a standstill. Future plans for harbour development in Port Sudan and Suakin are based on the RoRo-principle, and the container revolution will make the Beja stevedore superfluous.

In the 1970s and 1980s Port Sudan city expanded substantially due to the war in Eritrea and the famine of 1984-86. It is now surrounded by vast villages, many containing all kinds of buildings from simple cardboard and ironsheet shacks to concrete brick houses at all stages of construction and abandonment.

Conclusion

In this chapter we have tried to provide a summary of the larger political and economic framework within which Beja livelihood has operated over a rather extended timespan. Some elements, such as the rearing of

---

[1]See for example Kassala Province Monthly Diary, August 1941. This year, "...want among the Arabs /Beja/ kept the supply of labour in Sinkat surplus to all demands which are themselves exceptional"... In Port Sudan "the labour position is satisfactory for the moment but the falling of rains in the hills and the advent of Ramadhan may easily create a serious situation"... As it had rained in Gedaref "many men who ordinarily come to the Gash for the sowing have already earned more money than in normal years in work for troops and nothing but prospects of bad harvests at home will now make them move...".

camels, cattle, sheep and goats, can be shown to have existed for at least two millenia; others, like durra and dukhn cultivation, can be hypothesized as being of equally ancient origin, but are more difficult to substantiate. For these activities, droughts, locust attacks and rains are as important historical events as the political ones. Our sources offer very little information on such issues before the Mahdiya period, and for reasons which will become clear later, the local value system influences what kind of oral data we can get on past famines, and creates methodological problems for historical reconstruction. Some of these issues are dealt with in Chapter 8, where we offer a chronology of more recent droughts.

The macropolitical situation, where the Beja have for most of the time occupied peripheral spaces in between centres of commerce and political power, can however be postulated to have been decisive for the degree to which foraging of forest products and pastoralism have been commercially oriented, and to what extent trade has offered opportunities to and placed constraints on Beja life. Changes in the relative importance of subsistence or commercial production can not be new phenomena but have existed for millenia. As environmental and politico-economic conditions changed, the emphasis on the various activities, on rearing camels or cattle, sheep or goats, on cultivating, foraging or caravaneering, is likely to have been in flux. The viability of any temporary form of adaptation from the point of view of human survival cannot be taken for granted. If pastoral societies are characterized by some common trait, that trait is possibly the flexibility of resource use, their way of making use of new possibilities in a diversified economy in an opportunistic fashion. The Beja fit well with this description.

In our concluding chapter, we will be concerned with the present-century threats against Beja survival as pastoralists. Looking at the Beja economy over the time span of a couple of millenia, however, brings to the fore a question which is not likely to be raised by contemplating contemporary issues. This is the question of the importance of caravaneering and of its consequences for the rural Beja during past centuries. What remains of the old trading patterns today are only very vague memories (if we disregard a good deal of smuggling of live animals driven on the hoof through the desert in order to be shipped by sambuk to Saudi Arabia).

Although we can with some certainty point to periods in Beja history when the caravan trade has been more or less brisk, and also follow the changes in the point of gravity of the trade from the Aydhab hinterland to the Atbara-Suakin route, it is difficult to say what the impact of the trade on the Beja economy and daily life was. Were the caravan routes lines of attraction, or did they rather repel the population? Perhaps it was both attraction and repulsion; they did on one hand act as a focus for the activities of adult and active men, while on the other hand the families were as far as possible safeguarded in the mountain glens. From a social point of view there were few positive values to be expected from these caravans of slave-traders and alien merchants, if we set aside the necessity they caused for the Beja to be well enough organized to be able to maintain the control over wells en route and over the information about how to manage the difficult journey.[1]

Apart from the "protection fees" that we know of at least from the Ababda in the 19th century, profits could be made from the supply of camels and camel sykes. Each caravan would consist of between 500 and 1,500 camels (Bloss 1938:253, Burckhardt 1819:307-8).[2] To engage in loading, unloading and drawing water from deep wells, a caravan would normally require one man for every four or five camels, so that between 120 and 250 people would be used to manage a caravan of the size mentioned (Khogali 1963 quoted by Amin 1968:59).

The impact that these caravans had on the local Beja economy is not fully clear. Christiansson (1981:159ff) writes about caravaneering through Tanzania that each major foreign trade expedition hit the local population as a major crop failure would have done, since the personnel of the caravan, including the slaves it brought, had to be fed on provisions supplied locally. The risk of such exploitation, or of treachery and misuse of hospitality, could be partly avoided by the Beja, thanks to the roughness of the country, which was inaccessible without their knowledge and goodwill.

It is impossible to get a quantified answer on the economic importance of the caravans; they might have been the pitprops of Beja existence from a material point of view. Socially, however, it is most

---

[1] According to both Hassan (1967:32) and Kheir (1982) the reason why Ibrahim Al-Qifti, the headman of Quft, was led astray by the Beja in 819 and left in the desert to perish was that he knew their area too well.

2David Reubeni, a Jewish traveller in the 16th Century, went from Suakin to the Nile with a caravan counting 3,000 camels (Hillelson 1933).

likely that they were a great burden. There was clearly a need for cultural devices maintaining distance to strangers and at the same time forcing them into reciprocal obligations of gratitude. The maintenance of the Beja language, the reserve and suspiciousness, the development of mediatory roles, the extravagant hospitality and the careful guarding of Beja women are striking cultural traits, which all appear logical in this context.

3

Territory, resource control and solidarity among the Atmaan

The traditional Amar'ar area, roughly 60,000 square km, covers the coast north of Port Sudan up to Mohamed Qol (Gunob), the hills running parallel to it, Khor Arbaat and the inland plains (Atbai and Aulib) around the upper khors of the Oko and Amur basins.[1] Within this area there are also Bishariin and Hadendowa, getting rights of grazing and cultivation through the Amar'ar. We also find Amar'ar just beyond the periphery of this region, who themselves acquire rights from the above-mentioned groups. Some groups who from a point of

---

[1] The text gives approximate locations of the main settlements in 1980. It should not be taken as signifying ownership rights.

view of genealogy identify themselves as Amar'ar live in more distant locations: for example the Nurab at Tokar and Gash, and the Nahadab who live close to Atbara.

We have used the name "Amar'ar" mainly because most of the traditional ethnographic literature refers to the people by this term. However, the Amar'ar mentioned in colonial sources embraces two major sections, the "Amar'ar proper" and the Atmaan, the Amar'ar presumably dominating in numbers at some time long ago. The Atmaan, who are today in an absolute majority, nowadays rarely use the expression "Amar'ar" to talk about themselves.[1] This study is also primarily concerned with the Atmaan.

According to Sandars (1935:39) the eponymical lineage ancestor Amar had five sons and one daughter. In today's genealogy only four sons are remembered: Muhamed (giving rise to the Homadab), Sheib (Ishebab), Fadil (Fadlab) and Amil (Amlab). The daughter, Nahad, has given her name to the Nahadab. The Homadab were in 1980 a group living around Sallom Station, the third railway station from Port Sudan. The Ishebab lived on the western side of Erba Sarara Wario (Mount "The well of Wario") in an area not fit for any farming but with camel and goat husbandry. The Fadlab lived in the Agwampt area north of Musmar, intermixed with the Musayab and some Hadendowa groups (Ashumab, Alaishigoiab and Malatinab). The Nahadab were said to be found at Gebeit, living apart from the Atbara, and the Amlab lived in Khors Amur and Agwampt.

It is estimated that of the Amar'ar living today 85% belong to the Atmaan branch. Atmaan is assumed to have been a historical person, a son of Ajib, an Abdullab ruler or sub-ruler under the Funj.[2] The kinship with the other Amar'ar is traced through a female link. The

---

[1] There is a superficial similarity between Amar'ar (TuB: The children of 'Amar) and Beni Amer (Ar: the children of 'Amer). The two names 'Amaar (Omar) and 'Amer (Amir) are different. However, although generally the Amar'ar are reluctant to suggest any close kinship with the Beni Amer, we did come across a myth stating that the two were brothers. According to a tradition recounted by Sandars (1935:198), Amar was the son of Kahil Walid b. Mugheira. The Seligmans, who did some research around Aqiq, recorded traditions that Kahil has a son called 'Amer, who in turn begot 'Amar, the ancestor of both Beni Amer and Amar'ar (Seligman and Seligman p. 85). Relying on a completely different tradition, Crawford 1951:112 and Paul (1950:224) identify Amer with Amer, son of Ali Abu el Kasim, a Shaadinab Ja'ali assumedly living in the early 17th century.

[2] We have not been able to ascertain whether this was Ajib the Great, who died in 1611 at the battle of Karkuj after having waged war against Ethiopia, Ajib II who ruled for a short time about 1659, or Ajib III who ruled about 1710. See O'Fahey and Spaulding (1974:36).

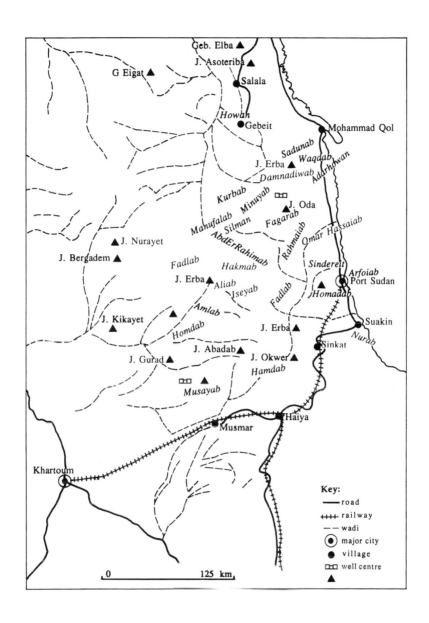

Key:
—— road
++++ railway
– – – wadi
◉ major city
● village
▱ well centre
▲

MAP 5: The core area of Atmaan traditional rights and settlements

47

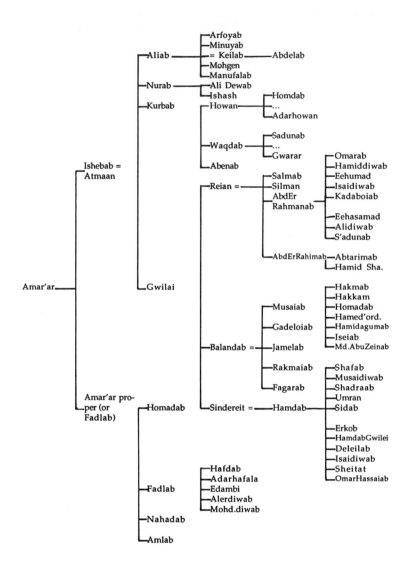

FIGURE 1: Amar'ar groups and subdivisions

48

popular reason given why the Atmaan were accepted into the ranks of the Amar'ar was the successful battle that Abu Ali Gwilai'or led against Osman Digna.

According to current genealogical claims, Atmaan had four sons who created significant genealogical lines, Ali, Nur, Kurub and Gwilai. These are the ancestors of the Aliab, Nurab, Kurbab and Gwilai respectively.[1]

The myth tells us that Gwilai was the youngest of the four brothers, but became superior to the other three.[2] He was loved by his father Atmaan and had many more children than his brothers. He married four wives. The first wife, Reianit, gave her name to the Reian line. She came from the Fadlab. Balandaba, the second wife, gave her name to the Balandab. She came from the Arteiga of the Tokar area. The third one was a Bishariin woman whose name is no longer remembered, and who is said to have gone mad. She killed her eight first-born sons before her madness was discovered so that the ninth child could be saved. He was breast-fed by Balandaba. The fourth wife, Sindiritor from Hadendowa, had only one son, Hamid. The name recurs in that of the Hamdab. However, Sandars (1935:201) calls this line the Sindereit after Hamid's mother. Hamid is claimed to have been a nervous boy when young. The good relations between the Musayab and the Hamdab which prevail today are mythically explained by the love felt for Hamid by his elder classificatory half-brother, Musa, who took responsibility for protecting him.

The lineage system, a folk model of historical links

The visual impression from Figure 1 is one of a segmentary structure, but the Amar'ar lineage system does not fit a conventional model of segmentary opposition. Names which are on the same structural level vary in the degree to which they actually function as economic and political groups, and to which degree they are used as terms of reference. Nurab, for example, is a name which is frequently referred to, whereas the Gwilai on the same level and even their subgroup the Balandab one step down in the structure are treated as united entities

---

[1] Sandars (1935:201) has reversed the seniority between the Nurab and the Kurbab. Our informants consistently claimed that this is the proper order.

[2] Crawford (1951:175) also mentions Hamid, another son of Atmaan's wife, but probably with another father.

49

mainly in the context of historical discussion. The Ishebab, who formally include the Atmaan, also exist as an entity of their own, separate from all the rest of the Atmaan.[1]

Like other models of its kind, the Amar'ar genealogy is not necessarily an "objective" mirror of historical realities, but rather a folk model of historical links, adapted to fit into present-day needs.[2] Links of alliance and lines of descent have been forgotten or telescoped when not offering points of disaggregation or conjunction of interest in the strife over subsistence resources or political influence. One such "omission" of irrelevant links can be seen when one compares Sandars' (1935:201) description of the Amar'ar genealogy from 1935 with that which we obtained in 1980. Sandars reports that the founder of the Aliab, Ali Atmaan, married a Hadendowa woman from the Sharaab. He had two sons by her. One was Atmaan Margub, and the other one Minni. The later gave his name to the Minniab (the Muniab of our chart). Atmaan Margub had five sons, Arfu, Manufal, Ali, Sayed and Moghen. According to Sandars, Arfu, Manufal and Mohgen gave their name to lineage groups. In diagrammatic form, Sandars' version and ours from 1980 look as Figure 2 shows (with the eponymical lineage founders underlined).

What has happened is essentially that some generational depth has been lost. The reason is obviously that it had no sociological importance; only the nodes connecting existing lineage groups need to be accounted for. This example therefore illustrates a continuous process of shifting the density of the lineage genealogy in response to its operational utility. Naming customs also make the telescoping of irrelevant links very likely, for it is common within Beja groups that a limited

---

[1] Today most diwab names end with -ab, and the alternative ending diwab appears to be used primarily when there is a risk for duplication of names - for example, within the Hamdab there is a Musaidiwab and an Isaidiwab which may have been named so to differentiate the groups from the Musayab and its subgroup the Iseiab. All groups ending with -diwab within the Amar'ar are however minimal units. Generally it can also be noted that a duplication of names within each larger tribal confederation is rare, although Aliab, for example, occurs both among the Bishariin and Amar'ar. Within the Amar'ar again Isaidiwab occurs twice, once as a Hamdab subgroup and once as an Abd er Rahmanab subgroup, and Homdab and Homadab may be difficult to differentiate. These seem to be the only concrete cases of duplication. Seligman (1913:631) uses the presence of "ab"-names among Kababish as a proof of Beja ancestry, but it appears that the practice is in fact common to the Beja and the Nubians. It would also appear that the practice has now spread more widely as a general Sudanese way of denoting an agnatic group.

[2] See Lobban (1980) for a discussion of the historical accuracy of genealogies. Since the Amar'ar are a relatively unhierarchical society, there is far less reason to expect accuracy from them than from the Nile Valley groups.

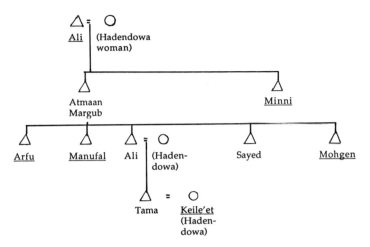

Ancestors of Ali Atmaan according to Sandars (1935) information

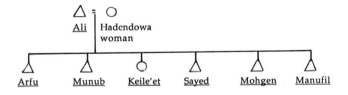

Ancestors of Ali Atmaan according to our 1980 information

FIGURE 2: Genealogies of the Atmaan recorded in 1935 and 1980

number of personal names are used in a particular group and especially that a person's direct descendants carry his name — as in the above example, where we find the name constellation Ali Atmaan occurring twice.

The genealogical charter departs in several ways from a "historical record" of the factual kinship structure that could be expected to arise from Beja social practice. We can note that despite the fact that Beja lineages are extremely endogamous in ideal and practice, many of the

51

nodes of differentiation relate to women marrying "in" to the diwab. The story associated with the genealogy usually does not tell whether the founding ancestresses were also in a spatial sense marrying in, or whether they were married to men who moved away from their area of origin in an uxorilocal marriage. In any case the number of exogamous marriages in the genealogy is very likely to exceed that of real life. Given the ordinary Beja practice of marrying "in", an exogamous marriage establishes a group of descendants within the diwab who in contrast to the offspring of an ordinary marriage have a latent alignment of solidarity with another group. Exogamous marriages will be remembered as historical points of fission, divisive forces within an ideally united kinship structure.

Diwab membership is basic to identity concepts for the Atmaan and for the Beja in general. The principles of recruitment to the diwab has two basic components: sharing descent and sharing affiliation to a territory and its productive resources. The appreciation of these two principles as being differentiated may be an expression of ethnocentrism. We have not been in a position to venture deeper into Beja concepts of the nature of the link that joins members in the diwab. A European understanding of kinship is that it refers only to biology. But there are many cultures where living together on the clan-owned land and consuming together what it produces conveys a communion of substance which cannot conceptually be differentiated from that which is conveyed by the transfer of semen, blood, etc, or whatever biological kinship is thought to be about (C. Pitt-Rivers 1973:92ff and Strathern 1973:28-9). It is tempting to interpret the Beja view in this way, particularly since it is actually men who symbolically dominate both the conveyance of kinship and of food. Although this as so many other things has to remain a hypothesis for further research, Beja symbolism contains various elements that have a potential bearing on this issue. There is, for example, the well-reported Beja custom of placing the placenta and umbilical cord of a male child in a bush and that of a girl at the hearth. Unfortunately there is no information on whether "the bush" is necessarily a bush in the territory of one's own diwab. Another symbolic link between fertility and soil is the smoke-bath arrangement, which will be described below.

H.M. Salih (1980:119) is of the opinion that the Hadendowa have a strict rule whereby women are excluded from collective inheritance of territorial rights, having no sorts of recognizable claims to land: "The

Hadendowa explain the exclusion of women from these rights by claiming that since a woman might be married outside the lineage any rights to land that she held must be claimed by the non-agnatic husband and his descendants".

When one considers access to membership generally and not to specific cultivation plots, actual practice among the Amar'ar, in relation to the position of an exogamously married woman's children, appears to be less rigid than in the Hadendowa case. When a person is of mixed descent, this is something which is frequently referred to in everyday conversation. The "mother's lineage" provides a kind of supplementary affiliation. The partners of the exogamous marriage do not gain membership in each other's diwab, but their sons and daughters will have a double affiliation and inalienable rights in both diwabs.

The children of an uxorilocally and exogamously married man have a good chance of being accepted — but not completely trusted — as members of their mother's diwab. They also have the option of turning back to their father's home area. It is, however, less likely that the children of an exogamously married man who have resided with their father's group during all their life will be able to claim rights in their mother's area. Descent is not traced back very far on the mother's side, so ambiguous claims to resources from the mother's side are not inherited from generation to generation when the wife has married exogamously and virilocally. Such claims must be backed by residence and acquaintance. In any case, these situations are not so common, because of the preference for very close diwab endogamy[1]. Usually, the mother's and the father's groups coincide not only on the diwab level but also on the level of the closest kindred of the individual. We will return to the Beja interpretation of this practice, and to its consequences, in the next chapter.

In any discussion of Beja principles of linearity it is impossible to avoid mention of matrilinearity. There is a very strong tradition among scholars of accepting that the Beja were once matrilinear.[2] This tradition goes back to among others Ibn-Selim al-Aswami, himself a resident of Aswan, who in his "Khitat" said of the Hadariba in quite

---

[1] When the founding ancestress of a tribal section was an uxorilocally married daughter, or one of several externally recruited wives, the clan affiliation of her husband or father respectively may be remembered in the tribal pedigree and so form a latent claim on membership in another diwab.

[2] This is a point which authors come back to over and again, notably Shaaban 1970:108-9, Clark 1938:3, Kheir 1977, Macmichael 1922:171, Murdock 1959:317 and others. The reader can also see Kheir (1977) and Zaborski (1965:306) for summaries of the various Arabic sources mentioning this.

53

explicit terms: "The inheritance is passed to the son of a sister, or to the son of a daughter, to the exclusion of the son of the deceased." (Vantini 1981:98,1975:619).

However, the Beja practice of close endogamy (see below) makes the question of the real outcome of matrilinearity or patrilinearity mainly a matter of interpretation and ideological emphasis. It is difficult to prove the time-depth of this endogamic system, but our understanding of Beja culture is that it gives an unusual emphasis to sibling (and by extension close cousin) solidarity at the relative expense of an evaluation of marriage as such.

Following Riches (1979:163), we do not wish to imply that Beja (or any) descent ideology is necessarily unambiguous. It is used "in so far as the strategy which [it] embodies is pertinent to the actor's current purposes and situations, as the actors perceive these purposes and situations" (*ibid:*147). We may have here a similar case to what is suggested for Melanesian cognatic structures, which embody "statements of group maximisation of manpower ... their emergence relates to situations of critical pressure on land, which make waging war, defending territory or simply inter-group tension highly probable ... In times of colonial peace ... one would expect an increasing relative emphasis on rules restricting individual movement" (*ibid:*163). In our case, of course, the issue at stake is not physical "movement" as such but nominal control over cultivation plots and full access to membership in the group that socially and politically dominate a particular area.[1]

The diwab as a unit is formed around the control of a composite set of material and symbolic resources. Among the first of these, collective title to grazing land is the most important, followed by the sharing of common interests in livestock, particularly camels. Harbour labour in Port Sudan is organized on the basis of registered work gangs, and many diwabs "have" such gangs which can be regarded as yet another form of corporate property (see for example Lewis 1962, Milne 1969). Among the more immaterial joint interests are the loyalty and solidarity of diwab members through the collective "honour" of the group. We will return to these interests in Chapter 5 below, and concentrate in the present chapter on the resources of livestock and land.

---

[1] Riches here leans on the transactionalist methodology of Holy (1976) and Stuhlick (1977).

Diwab ideology and livestock property

Despite the fact that recruitment to the diwab is ambilineal, dominant lineage ideology gives emphasis to patrilineal descent. It is the patrilineal links that are remembered. Also, in the actual practice of property devolution, when it comes to individualized property, there is an emphasis on patrilineal inheritance, even though this does not correspond to any absolute rule. In theory, Amar'ar inheritance follows Muslim Sharia laws, whereby all sons and daughters inherit at a rate of 2:1. In practice, much of the property transferred from generation to generation passes through pre-mortem allotments of stock or capital. These allotments, as in many pastoral cultures, are partly regulated by traditional norms stipulating gifts at certain life-cycle rites such as *ti'smaya*, namegiving, and partly by the wills and whims of the parents and other close relatives. In the case of livestock gifts, girls are not excluded, but tend to be disfavoured compared to boys. There is apart from this a differentiated evaluation of wealth which arises from the fact that cultivation plots are to a much higher degree carriers of the symbolic content of diwab membership than for example sheep and goats and trading assets. The same may apply to camels. Camels, like other stock, are held by individual title, but there are strong social sanctions against their disposal outside the clan. Camels are also branded with tribal marks. In the case of immigrating uxorilocally married men from other diwabs, the camels get two sets of marks (Salih 1976:56).

Such a corporate attitude towards the stock of camels, which the Beja share with many Arabic groups, is sometimes analytically explained by the fact that the payment of "blood compensation" was traditionally in the form of camels. Thus, corporate interest in camels is seen as related to the corporate interest in human members of the lineage or the clan. Sharing interest in livestock may however express itself not only in the pooling of livestock for compensation purposes, but also in a common responsibility to provide a basic core of animals to anybody who is unfortunate enough to loose his herd.

Both these practices appear now to be alien to the Beja. Gifts of stock are appropriate at name-giving and marriage, when the members of a man's closest clan section and perhaps some close affines outside the group will assist him with wealth. Since the 1980s camels have become such a rare wealth that the situation of a relative parting with

55

his camel for such a purpose is more or less out of question. When it comes to assisting a stock-less person, the present economic situation makes it difficult methodologically to assess whether Beja ever redistributed livestock capital to stock-less men — in contrast to food, which is commonly redistributed. There are simply too many stockless people around. *Diia* payment, that is, compensation paid to the relatives of a murdered person, is not an indigenous Beja custom. It was introduced and practiced during British colonial times, but it is against the Beja code of honour to accept animals as full compensation for a dead person.[1]

In olden days, when the Amar'ar still followed *o'slif*, customary law, women are said to never have inherited camels. Members of the late Nazir's family told us in 1980 that this dignitary, when settling cases of camel inheritance, had followed Sharia law. The same informants, however, had heard of cases from more peripheral groups, like the Tokar Nurab, where women had been refused camels in accordance with o'slif.

Because of the different degrees of symbolic evaluation of wealth, when a man's heritage consists of a variety of assets, items of a lesser symbolic value but of economic significance can be allotted to the daughters to ensure a fair Muslim distribution of wealth, while still adhering to the traditional notion that "camels and land should not be given to women, because then they may pass out of the diwab" (for the Hadendowa, see Salih 1976:79, 1980:119; cf. Wilson 1984:57ff). Given an absence of brothers, or in the case of various idiosyncratic circumstances, e.g. when there is a public recognition that the brothers are careless squanderers of wealth, inheritance of such wealth may still enter female hands. The Beja claim that such cases are becoming more and more common. In the case of land, this means that an area which is generally known as belonging to a particular diwab may contain islands of plots individually owned by members with an ambiguous membership (cf. Mohamed 1980:52). While practice is flexible, the emic view of the diwab's stock of wealth is however that of one which has been, and should have been, largely patrilineally transmitted.

---

[1] Pro primo: the relative's obligation of honour should not be cancelled by money or wealth. Pro secundo: A freeborn person should not be exchangeable for wealth, a principle which also appears vital in the context of Beja's rather limited marriage transactions. This has to be seen in the context of Beja lands having been constantly traversed by slave traders.

Whereas the rights to livestock as capital, as in other East African groups, appear to combine notions of individual property with notions of a common, corporately held body of inheritance, it should be emphasized that management decisions are independently taken by each household head. In making arrangements for watering and herding, the senior man also acts on behalf of the individual junior stockholders that are included in his family, be they wives, children, siblings or other dependants. Taking decisions on such issues is not a collective task, despite the strong corporate identity of the diwab. Individual ownership does not mean individual control over products; it is not even the case that a particular wife has the exclusive right to get the milk from any particular animal. It is not so common that a man has two wives, but in such a case, they share whatever milk there is. Generally, food is shared between all members of the household, and, as we shall see, even outside the household.

Physical and social territory

The primary resource base of the diwab is the *kurai*, the grazing territory to which it claims customary rights. From a national point of view, all Beja lands belong to the state, but in Beja minds the area is parcelled into tracts with definite local owners. Although there is a general agreement between different Beja groups on which territory presently belongs to which group, some overlapping may still occur, so that there are conflict zones to which two different diwabs claim customary rights.

Within their territory, diwab members have certain prerogatives. They are the only ones to be allowed to dig wells, cut branches for fodder or firewood, and, above all, they have a priority in cultivating plots. In old times, it was their prerogative to escort strangers through the area (Jennings-Bramly 1901). Members of other territorial groups may ask permission to use such resources but the open recognition of ownership is very important and a symbolic token — *gwadabb* — should always be given.[1]

---

[1] Salih (1976:103) refers to the rights obtained in exchange for the gwadabb as *i'mara* rights, but this expression was not used by our Amar'ar or Hadendowa informants. According to Hassan (1980:119) the two concepts *asl* (origin) and *a'mara* are two Arabic words which have been incorporated into the Tu-Bedawie language and become the principal legal terms used by the Beja in relation to the question of land. Morton and Fre (1986:32) express doubts as to the extent to which these words are used.

Politically there is also a great difference between being on one's own land and being an "immigrant", and it is usually only the "owners" who take part in o'slif conflict settlements etc (cf. Morton and Fre 1986:20). Given this, and the nature of the terrain, Beja notions of territoriality emphasize land as a social and symbolic resource rather than strict resource control in a physical sense (cf. Myers 1982:185, 191). These territories were traditionally probably not to be seen as defined in the way of discrete entities with fixed boundaries, but rather as the territory extending out from certain core features and landmarks. Such landmarks would be the river valleys (cf. Haaland and al Hassan n.d.:16-18), passes, mountains and stones of specific symbolic significance to particular groups. This implies an understanding of "territory" which deviates from conventional western thinking but which agrees with what is found, for example, among other Cushitic groups such as the Gabbra.[1]

Using resources without a proper demonstration of "respect" can be interpreted as a claim to ownership. Normally, the territorial boundaries do not pose very serious limits to the availability of pastures for a particular group (cf. Shaaban 1970:115). In principle, as long as there is enough pasture in a certain area, any herder has a right to go there, provided that he acknowledges the rights of the owners. This generally means that he has to contact and consult (o'mkir) an elder of one of the households belonging to the property-holding diwab, who will then check with his clan-mates, and perhaps receive the token of respect. Such rights of admission to plentiful grazing are not limited to members of the larger ethnic confederation, nor even only to other Beja herders; they are open to anybody. Between two neighbouring groups there will over time develop a tacit expectation of access to each other's territory. If the pasture one year is best in the area of the Musayab, next year it will be better with the Abdelrahmanab. It is when pasture is becoming scarce in the area that the guest grazer will be supposed to leave and conflicts may arise, the host group pushing away any intruders whose stay approaches permanency. Morton and Fre (1986:84) quote OXFAM data from the Shebodinab living at Khor Dirbab, which tend to support the view that a system which seems in good years to be largely about politics may assume a function of controlling resources when they become scarce.

---

[1] Oral communication from G Schlee; lecture on Ritual Topography and Ecological Use, EIDOS workshop SOAS, London, June 22-24 1989.

This means that in practice selective permission is exercised in favourable periods, exclusion in drought. Such a suggestion would probably be abhorrent to Beja values. Therefore, the ensuing conflicts do not usually openly concern grazing, despite the fact that ultimately the "owning" group has a recognized right to deny anybody the use of their territory. We will return to this issue below.

Beja land rights are not and have never been ratified by any central government, or any common tribal authority above the level of the Nazir, if we do not count the fact that the Arab invaders of the Sudan recognized the *sulh*-rights of the Beja (see Kheir 1982:233). By sulh, the property rights to land remained with the original owners. Sulh was granted to people who made peace with the invaders before they were overpowered.

It would also not be completely correct to classify Beja land rights as "usufruct rights", since at any point of time an area is likely to be grazed both by "owners" and "guests" gaining admission in exchange for "respect". More correct would be to say that these rights are continuously maintained by their formal and informal symbolic recognition in everyday social intercourse. The diwab is a collective owner as long as members are treated as owners by others. This is a matter which of course does not solely grow out of politeness but is also derived from how the relative military strength of the group is evaluated by the guests. The Beja are aware of the risk of a situation such as the one described by Mohamed (1980:85) from the culturally affiliated Kawahla Arabs of the White Nile. When the Hassaniya Kawahla arrived at the White Nile, they were allowed to rent land from the original settlers: "They seem to have been a submissive, poor and disorganized people, who did not seem to be related to one another. As they grew in power, however, through their increasing numbers and further immigration from the north, they rebelled against their host tribes by refusing to pay tribute and by claiming ownership of the land".

Yet in reality it is almost inconceivable to the Beja that a situation such as this could arise; territorial rights on such a level are seen as essentially undisputable, although some Beja diwabs trace their territorial claims to a historical conquest.

Sandars (1935) describes the Atmaan 18th century expansion in terms which suggest a conscious use of matrimonial links for the purpose of taking over areas from a group whose power was on the decline. This is probably a realistic assessment of what has actually happened historically, but rather as a matter of effects than as one of conscious intent.

In principle, non-Beja users of Beja resources are expected to "show respect" in the same way as Beja guests, and the failure to accept such rules is a source of tension which actualizes the ambiguous property status of Beja lands as both customary diwab territory and modern state property. According to Salih (1976:111-3) the Rashaida who in the 1970s were competing with Hadendowa over their traditional southern pastures were reluctant to pay gwadabb to the latter, paying their taxes to the Sudanese state and thereby, as they claimed, fulfilling their dues.

Gwadabb should always be paid to the tribe that has the original rights to an area, even if they are no longer using it (cf. Haaland and al Hassan n.d.:20). Jennings Bramly (1911) writes a note about a case of Hadendowa Kalolai who after 100 years of absence from what was for practical purposes counted as the Gemilab core land, still claimed the right to be consulted about the lining of a well, and to supply an agent for contracting labour. In a letter from 1901, the same author recounts a story about how the Eshebab Ababda in about 1870 after a long absence returned to claim the Abu Tabaj wells from the Aliaab Bishariin (Dakhlia 112/11/75). Recently, an Atmaan diwab who maintained the rights to a particular strip of coast heard that some non-Beja smugglers were out of ignorance paying gwadabb to another Beja group who were using their land in their absence. The first group decided to keep silent until the smugglers had landed 14 loads of contraband on the shore, whereafter they took the smugglers by surprise and forced the latter to acknowledge their right to a gwadabb by threatening them with the police.

The grazing territory is a collective resource in the sense that it is not divided into individual pasture plots. It should also be noted that Beja concepts of land rights were traditionally concerned not with the land as such but rather with the resources found at its surface, primarily the vegetation. The idea that resources hidden in the soil should be part of the heritage is relatively new but gaining a foothold among educated Beja — a fact of possible future significance, as the mineral deposits that were exploited in antiquity in the Red Sea Hills are expected to offer opportunities for future development of the mineral industry. On the other hand, to move stones lying on the ground is seen as a symbolic manifestation of land claims, so nobody can actually get at the underground resources without essentially violating traditional Beja rights. (It should perhaps be added that this is absolutely in no way a guarantee that it does not occur.)

Shaaban (1970:115) claims for the Hadendowa that a Beja territory always contains one particular mountain to which the diwab group believes itself to have a particular relationship. Apart from the importance of Jebel Elba to the Bishariin, Erkowit to the Balawyab Hadendowa (Murray 1935:308) and the traditional affiliation of ancestral Atmaan to Jebel Akereiribai (Sandars 1935:198), we have not found enough support for this. But undoubtedly, Beja are generally strongly emotionally attached to their home territory in its entirety, and the notion "in the mountains" is a metaphor for the idealized rural paradise. The mountains are also regarded as a refuge to which one can escape from drought, disease and war, hiding in the inaccessible glens and using the grass that is frequently available in the mountain heights.

For the purpose of cultivation, plots are allocated on an individual basis, either in the form of plots for rainfed cultivation in places where abundant water from wells allows permanent settlement, or in the seasonally flooded khors (Musa 1971:16). New plots are allocated by the diwab sheikhs, and shares are generally inherited from father to son.

The diwab land generally contains a number of individually or family-owned wells (Fawzy 1978:32, Salih 1976:124). Furthermore, as has been mentioned above, no foreigner is allowed to open up a new well on his own without asking for explicit permission. Again, it is the right of the holder of a well to ask any guest for a token of respect, which in the case of neighbouring Beja on the basis of reciprocity will be little more than a moral symbol. In the era of caravans, however, many more foreigners than now depended upon the Beja wells. Talhami (1974:162) describes how in 1866 "...the Amar'ar and Bishariin as well as some Hadendowa seized the opportunity to assert their rights to collect dues on the use of water holes in their respective territories...Whenever caravans stopped to water their animals...armed tribesmen burst out from their hiding places and demanded tribute, usually five piastres per cameleer". In more peaceful periods, the safety of caravans was frequently entrusted to influential diwab leaders who offered services of guarding the caravans and supplying camels to them. It is likely that the conditions on which these Beja leaders mediated peace for their customers still included providing for a

61

regular gwadabb payment and that this was of economic significance to them. However, even though historical records suggest that the Beja were paid for their hostship in the desert, the idea is clearly contrary to present-day Beja ideals. Caravans belong to a past which for the Beja appears both shadowy and irrelevant. It is therefore difficult to get information on this topic.

Urban resources and diwab structure

Although the home territories and "the mountains" mean more from an ideological point of view to the Atmaan than their city settlements at Port Sudan, or the rural centres such as Sinkat or Musmar, urban resources are very important to them from an economic point of view. Though many people have individual ties to the urban economy, the attachment particularly to Port Sudan is partly mediated by the diwab: urban residence is mainly by diwab, with a number of neighbouring blocks occupied by relatives, clustering around a shop owned by a diwab member. Harbour work is organized on the same principle.

Atbara also has an important role in supplying Amar'ar households with wage opportunities, but it is the harbour of Port Sudan that provides the backbone of the Atmaan non-pastoral and non-farm income. Without the port, the Atmaan would probably have been even worse off after the droughts in the 1940s, and perhaps not been able to maintain themselves as a distinct unit. To estimate the number of Atmaan in town over a number of years is difficult, not least because it has fluctuated wildly by year and season. Lewis (1962:16) gave the population of Deim el Arab in Port Sudan, the then most important Beja settlement there, as between 3,000 and 10,000. Comparing guestimates given to us by Beja leaders in 1980 with information given by Milne (1974), we would suggest that there were more than 20,000 Amar'ar living more or less permanently in Port Sudan in 1980. No fresh and reliable data on the total size of the population was available then, but the Sudan Government Census of 1956 had counted 45,000 Amar'ar altogether. The backbone of the economy of the Atmaan in town was the port, which offered over 1,500 jobs to them. Other Atmaan specialized in town-based animal husbandry based on commercially bought fodder. Of the two occupations, the latter was in 1980 considered the more secure by, for example, credit-giving shopowners. "The man who works in the port may break his back tomorrow". Men able to save a little money by dock work invested it in animals. The port work is physically very hard. Most port workers are men between twenty and thirty years old; it should be noted that this is also a category of labour which is very important to traditional pastoralism.

The port workers fall into two categories, the registered stevedores who are registered in work groups by the Labour Office, and the warehouse labourers working for different companies in the port. The stevedoring was to begin with dominated by Amar'ar. Lewis (1962:17) reports 60 registered gangs in 1954, each consisting of twelve workers. Of these gangs, 50 were predominantly Amar'ar — mainly Atmaan — while two were Beni Amer and eight Hadendowa. Later, the number of registered gangs increased to 119 in 1964, 124 in 1969 and 141 in 1973 (Milne 1974:77 and Hejazi 1975:317). The gangs were still dominated by Beja workers but also included a few groups of people from the southern and northern parts of Sudan. Tahir (1972) quoted by Musa (n.d.) listed the distribution of work groups per sub-tribe in 1968:

Atmaan		Others	
Musaiab	16	Fadlab	10
Nurab	15	Other Amar'ar	1
Kurbab	12		
Shafa'ab	10	Hadendowa	10
Abdel Rahmanab	10	Beni Amer	4
Arfoiab	9	Arteiga	4
Aliab	5	Bishariin	6
Salmab	5		
Omerab	4		
SUBTOTAL:	86		

This means that out of a total of 124 work gangs 97 were from the Amar'ar. In the period between Tahir's survey and 1980, the additional work gangs created were registered from Hadendowa and Beni Amer groups. Such gangs (qalla) ideally consist of twelve members including the leader. However, the Atmaan treat these job opportunities much as if they were corporate property, and the leaders allocate jobs on a temporary basis, normally to diwab members, so that there has at times been a substantial "reserve labour force" attached to each qalla, lessening the average number of days per month that any particular member would get job (Abu Sin 1975:409). The gang leader formally decides upon the allocation of jobs and persons but consults with other clan leaders. If a kinsman arrives from Aulib, he can thus aspire to get access to the "tribal resource" that membership of a qalla represents.[1]

Territoriality, kinship and neighbourhood

In traditional Beja society, as it is presented to us in the idealized picture of the good old past, a rural family's neighbours were usually their closest kinsmen. It was felt that diwab members should be trusted and well-known to each other, and have a shared close link to a common territory. They would traditionally be expected to be "neighbours", allowing for the fact that the settlement pattern in the mountains and desert was one where the distance between neighbours could be half a kilometre or more even when people lived in the same khor. Camps consisted of only two, three or four tents clustered either in a small khor feeding one of the main watercourses or at a permanent water-hole (cf. Newbold 1935:142, Salih 1976:81, Musa 1971, Seligmann 1913:597; Crossland 1913:50). Neighbours were expected to visit each other daily, if not for other purposes then at least in order to exchange milk. The men sometimes herded together and the women exchanged visits. In this way, the home area was impregnated with social significance, associated with well-known and trusted people. Contacts with people from other groups would be maintained only by the men, travelling with the herds or moving with the caravans.

Despite individual holdings of cultivation plots and livestock, the local community would be characterized by a common sharing of resources. Beja neighbours share a right to each other's milk, providing a case parallel to the Afar described by Ayele (1986:73ff), with their a strong feeling for the local community as a basis for sharing. Labour is pooled primarily with one's closest kinsmen but food should in principle be distributed out of the household as signified by the milk offering ritual (see below). This is not to say that food is always

---

[1]Registered workers earn each SL 2.50 or SL 1.40 per day, depending on whether they work inside the ship or outside, as a basic salary, whether there is any work or not. Each day's work, a *yomiia*, is paid SL 5.00, and so the normal payment is SL7.50 per day. A captain may offer 1.5 or 2.00 yomiia if the work is to be done quickly. Such negotiations seem to be normal, judging from the discontent with Sudan Shipping Lines, which never enters into them. There are no pensions and no insurances for the workers.

equally divided in the neighbourhood, but that ideologically, it can hardly be denied to anyone. Some of it should always be symbolically distributed. The same, as John Morton (1988) has emphasized, goes for the circulation of information of vital importance for subsistence.

In this context, we would like to raise some suggestions about how Beja principles of sharing should be addressed from an analytical point of view. Ingold (1987:233) has recently called for a clarification of the concept of sharing. He notes that it can be understood in two very different ways: "first as a principle of generalized or unrestricted access, whereby means of subsistence are enjoyed in common; secondly as a distributive movement whereby stuff held at the outset by a single person is divided up, so as to be available for use by an aggregate of beneficiaries". Generalized reciprocity is in the latter case conceived of as "a relation between economic identities, autonomous and discrete" (Ingold 1987:231, quoting Sahlins 1972:94). An analysis of the flow of material values is likely to put emphasis on this latter way of looking at the issue. However, we would like to suggest that in the case of Beja, the emic view of food-sharing principles is not based upon a transactional paradigm, but on identity rather than distinction. Sharing in the life-sustaining substances emanating from the common territory is both a way of acting-out membership and recreating this shared identity.[1]

In retrospect, one cannot prove to what extent the idealized picture of a near-total congruence between kinship and locality[2] would fit with statistical reality. The practices of allowing guest groups to come and graze, and of allowing back matrilateral descendants, would in any case have led to a certain mixture of non-diwab relatives. This was certainly so in the relatively settled villages and along the caravan routes for a long time, as well as in "urban" settlements such as Aydhab, Suakin or Tokar. Hence, there is room for a certain external influence along with diwab solidarity. It is in any event clear that today's neighbourliness is a very important principle for cooperation in its own right. At present people are obviously brought into pretty close contact with members of

---

[1] Ayele (op.cit.:79) in this context quotes a popular saying of the Afar with a striking similarity to the well-known Beja phrase "o'hash hashoun, balad baladoun" (this soil is our soil, this land is our land). Noting that sharing is fundamental to local community members, Ayele recounts an episode when he hired an Afar camp attendant and told him to bring his food. The guard responded "this is our land" ("baro no baro"). This statement implies that wherever an Afar goes, even outside his local community, he faces no problem in getting food. We have not heard of a similar interpretation of the Beja saying, but it might have a related connotation.

[2] Haaland and al Hassan (n.d.:17) suggest that the Hadendowa rarely migrate further than a camel can walk in one or two days, and that their grazing therefore is normally confined to the own territory.

quite unrelated clan groups in Port Sudan, Atbara and Suakin, and in the famine camps. As stated above, places like the suburbs of Port Sudan are usually numerically dominated by one ethnic group, and diwab members tend to congregate in specific quarters. Still, a certain mixture always exists and the quarter across the street may be dominated by one's traditional enemies or by totally unknown persons. The urban Beja lives in a network whose central nexus consists of nephews and cousins. In the periphery of this network there are a large number of indirect relationships with neighbours mediated through each of these kinsmen. These are relationships that may become intensified or remain distant.

Amongst the Beja, some of one's clansmen are inevitably living in other villages or towns and in relatively distant places. Among people who are close enough to share grandparents or great-grandparents, there is a substantial amount of travelling back and forth, even over long distances. For example, when there is a message of a death, failure to visit the bereaved is considered a serious breach of the relationship, and a related family in Atbara will send a member to carry the condolences to people in Port Sudan.[1] Among less closely related diwab members, there is certainly a sense of identity and hence solidarity, but this is not strong enough to override a certain scepticism and create friendly intimacy between the households unless they "have learnt to know each other".

In the Beja's own models of what causes and legitimates close social relations, acquaintance is prominent. In the introduction, we touched upon the sensitivity of social information handling for the Beja. Much of the practice corresponding to ideals of honour relates to the keeping up of a facade, and there is a general fear that if you give information about others, they will accuse you, and if you admit information about yourself, it will be misused. Paradoxically, however, close acquaintance and knowledge of each other is generally seen to generate respect and solidarity. Or perhaps, people who accept you even when the facade has been dropped, are people whom you can trust. Where suspicion reigns, trust is also a scarce and highly valued resource. But the road to trust is long and risky for the Beja; the opportunity to live together with people whom you already know is explicitly highly

---

[1] During the famine, this was of course not possible, and at times people in the worst hit areas are said to have had to compromise even with assisting their neighbours in burials.

valued. For example, allowing the women the comfort of continued close association with the same narrow circle of women is usually given as the legitimating argument for endogamy.

Because of this, what matters is neighbourliness rather than proximity, for just as the guest grazer has to continually symbolically assert the rights of the land-owning hosts, the neighbour who wants to claim neighbourly status has to continually assert it, irrespective of whether the neighbour is a diwab relative or not. If two households are in a neighbour relationship to each other, they have definite claims and responsibilities towards each other. If one of them is in some kind of a difficulty — for example if somebody has died, is sick or convalescent — a daily visit is expected. Neighbours contribute to funds for celebrating marriages or job advancement and funds for mourning. They assist in digging a grave when needed. They run to your succour if the house is attacked by burglars. They see to it that nobody is left alone. They welcome you on the very day you return from a journey. Even in an urban context such as Deim el Waheda outside Port Sudan, greeting and offering assistance are not just things done if you happen to meet in the street but rather compelling norms to respond to. If a person fails to follow these norms, it is commented upon and he risks that risk the failure being interpreted as a formal break of neighbourly relations. When there is no diwab base for solidarity, there is with the Beja, to borrow Pitt Rivers' words (1973:97), "no other way to demonstrate one's sentiments than through actions which speak plainer than words".

Once a relationship of trust and neighbourliness has been established between neighbours, the relationship may outlast the relationship of physical neighbourhood. People live separately, and they do not have to affirm their relationship all the time. Yet, we came across cases of ex-"neighbours" coming to Port Sudan from the Gezira to express their condolences, and explaining their relationship to the bereaved in terms of having once been neighbours. The Beja themselves emphasize that they are suspicious of strangers, but that once you have obtained their confidence you will be friends for life.

As neighbourhood is an "excuse" for exogamy, and as an exogamous marriage gives rise to double claims of affiliation, one marriage between two Beja diwabs tends to lead to more in its wake. The maternal diwab of a man is the natural first choice of a man who wants to stop living with his father's group. Whereas he cannot by marriage establish new rights for himself in another territory (only for his children, see Chapter 5), he can strengthen matrilateral claims with such a move. In the next generation such immigrants already have the status of "well-known neighbours". A high incidence of inter-diwab marriages, the Beja say, is a first step towards a merger between the diwabs. When there are many such links, it becomes impossible to maintain the distinction between the groups. If a group becomes too small to guarantee an even demographic access of marriageable partners, it is likely to become absorbed over time into a larger unit; then territoriality and diwab-ship again merge.

4

The responsible man

In Chapter 3 we considered some aspects of lineage corporativity, basically those relating to land and livestock. In the present chapter we will deal with a lineage's non-material essence, its honour or reputation. The honour of a diwab is to a large extent an aggregate of the honour of individual men, which in turn depends upon a number of personal characteristics and modes of behaviour. These can be summarized under the concept "the Responsible Man". Strong identification with the collective values of the diwab is an integral part of this concept. In order to understand collective honour, one therefore has to proceed by an analysis of individual honour and what it comprises.

Key male virtues

The Beja have been described as an extremely male-oriented society (Morton and Fre 1986:6). This is true to the extent that their concepts of honour appear much more oriented towards a description of the ideal man rather than towards ideals of female virtue. The concept which we will translate here as "honour" is *Tu'Durarey* or synonymously *o'rya*. This quality has the following components:

a: The man of *durareit* should show self-control and willingness to subject individual wishes and needs to the interests of the collective. Self-control as well as resistance to pain are themes central to the male values of several pastoral groups.[1]

b: The responsible man should have the ability and preparedness to take responsibility for the protection of minors, dependants, women and guests in the sense of guarding them against suffering, whether by hunger or physical harm (*dameini* — to cover). By implication he must be strong, physically brave, able to withstand pain, kind, and able to provide food for his dependants.

c: From (b) follows also a preoccupation with the control of information and the maintenance of the diwab's facade. An honourable man is straight-forward in expressing his opinions, but cautious with giving information that may harm the diwab. This is a matter both of maintaining the facade of the diwab and of not saying things that might threaten the access they have to resources, e.g. by provoking open conflicts over ambiguous claims to land. A man should also avoid talking about matters concerning which he has only hearsay information.

d: The honourable man must be prepared to respect (*hamoisin*) the prerogatives of others when they are on their own territory.

e: While there is nothing shameful in the weakness of stranger-hood, on his own territory a grown man should not put himself in a position of being the weak receiver of protection. Thus he should never ask for anything, except from very close relatives, and even in that case only if he is sure that they are capable of offering help, so that he does not embarrass their durareit. The honour of an individual, when given public recognition, is expressed as *sumatu* or individual reputation.

---

[1] See for example Paul Riesman (1977) on Fulani concepts of self-control and Dahl (1979:176) for the Boran evaluation of a subsumption of individual desires to the benefit of capital care. See also Jackson (1991).

The idea that durareit implies avoiding to put oneself in the position of recipient dependant as well as keeping up the facade has as a consequence that it is against durareit to admit any flaws in the wealth or physical endowments of the tribal group or family. The Beja do not like to talk about drought and poverty. In front of strangers they prefer to play down the hardships they face, although there are nowadays those who gain local political credit by mediating foreign assistance and who therefore have to present the Beja as in need of help. Generally it is difficult to interview people about, for example, things like traditional emergency food. Many available practices of feeding oneself or getting cash were originally considered somewhat degrading, because they communicate poverty: practices such as selling milk or, worse, camels, or eating for example *senab* (colocynth) or rabbits (*helai*). In normal (pre-famine) times, and perhaps even now, Beja would not be likely to volunteer information about themselves following such practices. On the other hand, when talking about other people, most Beja show a considerable pragmatic tolerance towards practices which would in good times be considered reprehensible. Necessity overrides morals when it comes to cutting trees for charcoal, or selling milk or camels, or allowing women to work hard. But there is no doubt that the cultural preference is for Beja to show stamina, to "manage somehow" and to do so independently.

As stated above, Beja concepts of honour are male-oriented. Many ideas regarding the proper behaviour of women seem to gain force more from the symbolical challenge that women can pose to men's durareit by showing themselves "unprotected" than from an evaluation of female virtue by itself. Self-control is a highly valued personal trait in a woman as well as in a man, but it is not normally expected from her. One can compare this, for example, with Latin American honour and gender concepts, which attribute lack of restraint, particularly in sexual matters, to men rather than to women, and thus place the responsibility for honour somewhat differently. If a Beja woman is promiscuous, or earns her own living, this is a bad reflection on the capacity and willingness of her brothers in particular to live up to the standards of durareit. Similarly, if a man is insulted or damaged, it touches on the honour of all men of his group, as the insult is a symbolic message challenging the capacity and willingness of each individual male to protect his clan-mates. All clan members, whether male or female, can expect protection in this way, but women act as "the archetypal weak".

The self-control that is implied by several of these aspects is also assumed to be part of a man's personal behaviour. Among the things that people mention in relation to how a person of durareit behaves is the point that such a person is a *m'tarim*, expected to be able to withstand pain. Furthermore, although the ideal is to be a cheerful, witty and charming person (*o'nifsia*), he should avoid laughing on the wrong occasion. He should not go to prostitutes, and in this culture drinking is not regarded as an excuse for relaxation of self-control.

One important aspect of Beja concepts of honour is the notion of the worthy adversary. Whereas a man should not take an insult (*suganneit*) lightly, if it comes from his equal, he should also not let himself be challenged by an unworthy adversary. There is a saying which goes: "*Tu'Durarei wahfoko orya walyok shibobo afal ossabite hassy arwadorate rebandy*" (People always assume that your behaviour is durareit. Therefore, choose the right time to show orya and forgive worthless people talking rubbish!) Hence there is a delicate problem of whether to respond to the insult, acknowledging a degree of honour to one's opponent, and proving that one is prepared to defend oneself — or whether to ignore it, thereby reducing the value of the opponent and at the same time taking the risk that one will be suspected cowardly. The concept of tolerance of insults from unworthy adversaries is very close to that of offering protection to the weak.

To be hospitable (*hadarenini*) is an important part of durareit. Although strongly attached to their home territories Beja men, as herdsmen and caravaneers, have for centuries been obliged to travel extensively over the Beja area, and also to receive all kinds of strangers, as we have seen in Chapter 2. To them, as individuals as well as parts of larger kinship groupings, their "symbolic capital" depends to a very high degree on their ability to prove themselves as very hospitable people (*hedareb*). Any traveller through their country is bound to have observed that hospitality is a prime value with the Beja, for hospitality is a virtue which not only figures in their own idealized picture of what it is and should be to be a good Beja, but which is also put into practice. Ibn Sulaym[1] was one of the first to describe this: "...they are very hospitable. [The host] on the arrival of a guest will slaughter [a sheep] and if they are more than three [the host] will stab

---

[1] Kheir (1977:38), quoting Accounts of the Cataracts and Glimpses of the Land of Al-Nuba, in Wiet's edition of Ibn Sulaym IVXXXII - 16 p 267-8, Buqas edition I:194-6.

the nearest camel. It may happen that it is the guest's camel but he compensates with something more precious..."[1]

A man who is hedareb is said to be like a moist place (*o'darur*) with water and grass to which any animal will travel. Or: "*O'haddai gawib mi tat takutta*" ('in the house of a lion, you can find the bone of a sheep'; that is, the hospitable man's house will have something for everybody). Such a cultural emphasis on hospitality is not unique to the Beja, but is a generally pervasive theme in Northern Sudanese culture[2] and, indeed, in Islam (Ahmed 1976:58-9). To the Atmaan, however, hospitality is part of their ethnic distinction. The Beni Amer, for example, are not liked by the Atmaan because they are considered not to be truly hedareb.

Hospitality for the Atmaan means the free and generous provision of subsistence necessities to the guest, which on the small scale this might mean offering him a bowl of water on his arrival at your home, or later some Turkish coffee (*jabana*). On the large scale it could mean that he is allowed to graze his animals on your grounds. In relation to the individual guest, rules of decorum are elaborate. The host will all the time check closely that the individual guest is eating, and that he is not subject to any discomforts, however small. In order to make the guest *reihab* (at ease) the host will repeatedly encourage him to rest on the rope bed (*angareb*), assist him with cushions, tell him not to sit in the sun, etc. When he is about to leave, he should be repeatedly impressed that it is not yet time to depart.

The perfect Beja host is supposed to offer food even to a murderer who arrives in his tent during the night. Whether that has ever happened is perhaps more doubtful. Paradoxically, the host gains prestige by showing that his willingness to humiliate himself for the guest shows no limit (see Abou Zeid 1965:258-9). This is a well-known trait in Middle Eastern notions of hospitality. Peristiany (1965:16), in discussing this on a general level, notes that a very good example of this is the obligation of honour to grant sanctuary (Beja: *o'hiwa*) to an enemy, a theme which also appears in Beja story-telling for example in the tale of Gwilai'or, the Amar'ar hero who on one occasion showed this kind of mercy to a killer jackal who had ravaged his herds (Clark 1938:27).

---

[1] A contrary view can however be quoted as well. Burckhardt (1819:372) describes the inhospitality of the Bishariin.

[2] See Nordenstam (1968:85 ff), Asad (1970:39), Mohamed (1980:79-80).

Nordenstam (1968:158) quotes one of his informants reporting on a Sudanese Arabic custom to "swear on the divorce" ('*alay al-talaq*, Ar.). This means that the host insists on the guest accepting more of his hospitality or he will divorce his wife or abstain from sleeping with her ('*alay al-haram*). This oath is not to be taken literally, but as a way of emphasizing his willingness to sacrifice himself.[1] This custom is also known among the Beja, although we do not know whether it is ever carried out to its logical conclusion.

Older sources hint that in earlier periods, the provision of sexual favours from the wife or daughters of a man might have been part of Beja hospitality. Such practices are known from other East African societies, but we have not come across any evidence that they are presently found with the Beja. We mention it only because it is such a recurrent theme in the old literature (see Clark 1938:5; Murray 1927:45; Crossland 1913:20; Hartmann 1865:256; Lane 1860:297). The evidence is extremely difficult to evaluate in a case like this because one can never know whether the information was first-hand or based upon "neighbours' slander". The stated Beja norm is that the rural host should place the stranger at definite distance from his wife's house, and carry food and other provisions to the guest himself if he cannot send a child.

Beja women are of course supposed to treat their closest kin hospitably, but the social world within which they operate does not give much room for elaborating the virtue of hospitality further than that. Also, while a man is expected to be hedareb, the phrase hedaret is not positive when used about women, but carries a slight connotation of promiscuity. Among the Beja, man is the provider of food, woman the source of human warmth, sexuality and children. In so far as she cooks for the guest, she is is just mediating the resources offered by her husband, and her own resources are not supposed to be shared out.[2]

An act of humility towards the guest is that the guest has a right to literally be offered the gwadabb, the front meat. Another aspect is that it is normally taboo (*ayb*) among the Beja for a man to build a house, but the context of hospitality to a guest allows for exceptions to this rule. However, at the same time as the host is honouring his guest by

---

[1] For a literary example, see Tayib Saleh's "Season of Migration to the North" and "The Wedding of Zein".

[2] This contrasts with for example the situation found among the Borana, where a woman hospitable with food is a political asset to her husband.

prostrating himself, he does so on the basis of his status as land-owner rather than house-owner. The guest is obliged too, to accept hospitality, and thereby in a wide sense, to recognize his host's territorial authority. By doing so, the Beja guest pays respect to the host and also proves to be a person of durareit. The complementary rights and obligations involved in the guest-host relation have been discussed on a general level by Pitt-Rivers (1968) and in the specific context of Sudanese ethics by Nordenstam (1968). Both authors emphasize that offering hospitality and graciously receiving it as a guest equally involve rights and moral obligations, which are closely tied up with the symbolic expressions of honour. Pitt-Rivers formulates the territorial aspects of the mutual obligations rather nicely (ibid:26-7): "The roles of host and guest have territorial limitations. A host is host only on the territory over which on a particular occasion he claims authority. Outside it he cannot maintain the role. A guest cannot be guest on ground where he has rights and responsibilities...The range within which their complementary relationship holds good coincides with the territory where their mutual status is unequal. Where neither has a greater claim to authority than the other, the complementarity lapses."

Honour as a collective resource

Although each man is ultimately responsible for his own honour, he also shares in the collective honour of the diwab and should be prepared to defend the honour and physical safety of any other member, as well as the collective name of the diwab. The Beja situation is thus in contrast with what is suggested by both Barth (1965:79-81) and Black-Michaud (1975:76), that honour is part of an individual power game. A man's individual renown is important to him, but competition for honour does not take place so much between individuals of the same diwab, but rather between diwabs. Thus the diwab gains in honour when its members are recognized to include efficient and well-respected arbitrators and leaders, hospitable men and beautiful but well-protected (rather than virtuous) women (see Abou Zeid 1965:252). The quality of the material collective resources is also important. Insulting descriptions of the relative merits of the vegetation and topography of the lineage territory were mentioned to us as typical assaults on lineage honour, even if these were not always taken seriously.

The most important provocations (*suganneit*) against the collective honour of the diwab were demonstrations of lack of respect through actions questioning the rightful claim of the diwab members to their property. Other actions found provocative were those which challenged the diwab's capacity or willingness to maintain control over this property. Refusal to pay gwadabb was the most blatant case, but other types of action may also be seen as highly provocative.

There are a number of acts which have a recognized meaning of such a collective challenge, because they refer to things which only owners of the land are supposed to do. Cutting branches for charcoal or digging a well belong to this category. Manger (n.d.) quotes a Hadendowa case where a feud broke out when a visitor cut firewood for himself. In the rather drab landscape, stones that mark graves, plot boundaries, old goat sheds or underground grain pits do not always stand out clearly to the stranger as having significance, but as mentioned previously, there is in fact a general rule that stones should not be moved in another diwab's area. The "hosts" have to decide whether to regard the insult as a childish mistake by an unworthy person, thereby scoring points of moral merit by being tolerant to the weak one, or whether to respond to the act as a serious provocation. This implies that the meaning of such an act is always judged from its context.

The Beja are marked by a flexible pragmatism that make them tolerant to deviations from the stated norms in the face of necessity. Cutting a branch to feed one's livestock if fodder is scarce is thus not necessarily always taken badly (see Jennings-Bramly 1911). On the other hand, it is likely that serious competition for grass or water will make a host group less tolerant against insults. Generally, relations between visiting groups (*mafanab*) and the owners of a kurai are regulated by the standards of hospitality, even if these are formulated less strictly than those which regulate the relationship between individual guests and individual hosts. It is thought very inhospitable indeed to deny grazing or water to any fellow pastoralist, and the only condition under which the normative system sanctions open fight against intruders is when they challenge the owners' status of hosts or insult their honour. Perhaps the Beja are a good case in support of Black-Michaud (1975:189) who, paraphrasing Coser's (1965) discussion of realistic and non-realistic conflicts, notes that where scarcity prevails, the less it is possible, for reasons connected with the survival of the community at large, to indulge in aggressive interaction for the control of material resources, and the more honour will be invoked as a symbolic pretext for conflict.

As we shall see later in the context of Beja attitudes to resource competition, the same general principle of normative hospitality towards guests in need colours the attitude that the Beja have towards the large group of Ethiopian and Eritrean refugees who now live in Beja areas, particularly in Port Sudan. However, in late 1986 strong feelings of resentment were voiced against "the Balawiet" or "the Sudanese" of Port Sudan, who in Beja terms did not behave according to the norms of guests, but rather took on the role of masters in what was traditionally Beja land. The economic elite of Port Sudan, with positions of power and wealth based upon the harbour and the official grain and livestock trades, are with few exceptions not Beja. They are either of families belonging to old or international trading diasporas, or to successful northern Sudanese, particularly Dongolawi. The people who contemporary Beja classify as Balawiet are urbanized and Arabized Sudanese originating from the Nile Valley. This category is also conceptually closely related to the national power holders. In reaction against this group, and for the first time since the 1950s, there was a large Beja demonstration in front of the Mudiriya, the main government building, and feelings were hot for a number of days.[1] The incident that triggered off this riot was what the Beja saw as a symbolic insult — somebody, presumably an iconoclast from the Muslim Brothers, had cut off the hands and head of the statue of Osman Digna.

Despite the traditional division for and against Osman Digna, he was in 1986 seen by all Beja as an important pan-Beja symbol, the epitome of the brave Beja warrior, and old oppositions between various Beja groups were played down. When the statue had been mutilated, loud-speaker cars toured the poor suburban areas around Port Sudan, playing traditional war songs and drum rhythms, and thus instigating the Beja to show their readiness to defend their emblems. Thousands of traditionally dressed Beja turned up, equipped with knives, swords and knobkerries. Cars and buses were turned over, and one bus driver was hit by a stone and died.

---

[1] If one goes back in history to look for a similar episode, it is necessary to refer to 1956 when during severe drought there were strikes among the railway workers and among the newly organized dock workers of Port Sudan.

That the Beja concept of honour can be transposed to a yet higher level was illustrated by another incident which symbolically challenged their nationality. This occurred when an Eritrean visitor was brought to the police station of Suakin by some infuriated Beja, after having torn a Sudanese pound-note into pieces.

When physical harm is done to any one of the diwab members, or when his or her rights are infringed upon, this is not only seen as bad in itself, but it also obviously seriously puts in question the preparedness of the diwab to protect its members. This is the case for instance when somebody has sexual intercourse with the unmarried girls of the diwab, or when a man is killed or assaulted. In fact, even intra-marital violence from a man against his exogamously recruited wife could be interpreted in this way.

Not just any offence or display of disrespect against an individual member of the diwab is necessarily seen as a collective insult. Obviously, theft of camels is something which is provoking not only because it brings an actual loss of an important material asset, but also because of its symbolic value. However, a theft of camels is only considered a serious crime if it concerns a number which is large enough for it to be judged as a collective issue rather than an individual one. So, the diwab will not feel affronted when one or two camels are stolen, but will if a man loses 50 camels to a thief.

The general attitude between Beja diwabs is mistrust, and whatever the objective statistical incident of feud is, there is no doubt that the subjectively experienced world of the Beja is a hostile one, where the constant risk of a severe feud is perceived as very real. The risk of a revenge action relating to a not-yet-known or presently dormant feud is what is constantly mentioned when Beja are asked why it is considered such a blatant breach of etiquette to ask somebody for their family affiliation. Women and children are equally regarded as irresponsible hazards to peace. Adults prefer not to see the children of their own group playing with children from another diwab, and they will break up even a relatively peaceful game in order to chase away the strange children. The reason is that tensions between kin groups are felt to be so great that even small conflicts of the type that children can cause may be taken as an excuse for letting an old feud flare up. Another expression of the constant preparedness for conflict is that no Beja man will move outside his compound without his dagger. In fact, the knife is used for various mundane purposes, but it is always legitimised by the reference to fights.

In some cases, inter-diwab conflicts emanate from spontaneous out-breaks of violence of a more personal nature, arising from brawls about girl-friends, jealousy over an adulterous wife, or mental disturbances. But conflicts do not of course only develop from occasional brawls caused by insults, even if these appear to play a prominent role. As we have suggested above, they may also emanate from a growing feeling of tension over resources such as water and pasture, in which case, however, the "legitimising spark" of conflict still may take the shape of a more trivial, personal quarrel. Slander and offensive talk about the diwab's women, or criticism of its leaders, will be less easily tolerated when there is already an accepted view that it is now high time that the intruders on the diwab's pastures turned back to where they came from. Members of opposing groups will joke and write songs about the beauty and usefulness and other relative merits of their own tribal territory versus that of the opponent, and the level of tolerance in such a situation depends much upon the availability of grass and water.

Conflicts also concern more tangible issues, such as adultery, broken business agreements, and ambiguous property claims. Morton and Fre (1986:26) note that "*asl* rights [i.e. customary title to land based on original occupancy; AH and GD] are not normally a strict control over economic resources but are of considerable ideological importance, being linked with diwab membership and the inheritance of personal identity in the male line. For this reason, disputes over land can occur when no economic advantage is at stake. One's chances of gaining political influence are far higher on one's own lineage land." When tensions rise and are concretely expressed in an interpersonal conflict, say between two men of different diwabs, it is mandatory for all male members of their respective diwabs to demonstrate that they are prepared to fight for their brothers. At the same time, nobody normally wants a conflict to turn into armed battle unless tribal resources are really threatened. If there are people with neighbour or kinship links to both of the groups they will encourage arbitration.

In the case of murder, when the risk of a conflict flaring up is obvious, one immediate action that is taken by the diwab of the offender is to bring him to the police. This method of externalizing the conflict is seen as the best way to avoid further bloodshed. It is not dishonourable in any way to be imprisoned.

One evening in one of the lineage-dominated quarters in Deim el Waheda, we came upon a meeting between some 30 elders. Muhamed Omer[1] of diwab (A) was accusing Musa Abdalla of a related diwab (B) of having cheated him of three sacks of durra. The background proved to be as follows. Three months earlier Mohamed had asked Musa to take three sacks of durra on his lorry to the family of Mohamed Omer in Aulib. Musa Abdalla usually carries out such services for Waheda inhabitants at a fee of SL. 1.00 per bag. In this case Musa Abdalla did not find the family of Mohamed Omer and instead left the sacks with Nur, another person from diwab A and a distant relative to Mohamed. When Mohamed Omer returned home three months later and asked his wife about the three sacks, it turned out that they had never reached her. Mohamed Omer then went to Musa Abdalla to inquire about the circumstances and was told to ask for the sacks from Nur. Mohamed refused to contact Nur, since he considered this to be the duty of Musa. Musa asked for two months to do so, to which his adversaries agreed. He then discovered that Nur had left the sacks with yet another member of diwab A, a distant relative in turn to Nur. This person however denied all knowledge about any sacks of durra. When Mohamed Omer was informed accordingly, he was upset and arrived early in the morning at Musa Abdalla's place in order to kill the latter, his stick and knife ready. Musa was agonized and prepared to fight. Neighbours went between the contestants and managed to persuade them to bring their case before the elders of diwab A and diwab B, forming a jury led by Sheikh Adorob, a well-respected member of diwab A, trusted also among the members of diwab B and other related groups. The meeting had to be postponed until evening, when Sheikh Adorob had finished his work in the port. During the day tension grew between the members of diwab A and those of diwab B. Both Mohamed and Musa had been discussing their case with friends and relatives. When Sheikh Adorob was informed of the situation after the end of the working day he demanded that all elders should meet within two hours.

So, in the evening the 30 elders were sitting in a wide circle, members of diwab A on one side and members of diwab B on the other. Sheikh Adorob chaired the meeting authoritatively, insisting on quiet speeches, first by Mohamed Omer and Musa Abdalla and then by their

---

[1]Names are fictive.

80

respective supporters. Although several of the men present were upset, most of them managed to discipline themselves. Those who did not were silenced by Sheikh Adorob. After the debate, his conclusion was that Musa, being a sheikh himself and a rich man, should adopt a generous attitude. Sheikh Adorob was of the opinion that it was Musa's responsibility to find the sacks, but if he could not, he should instead pay Mohamed Omer the equivalent value in cash. The Sheikh hinted that it was conceivable that if Musa refused to do so, he might himself pay the required amount in order to keep the lineage group united, but that he would then ever after be angry with Musa Abdalla. The meeting ended and was postponed to the following evening. Musa Abdalla had not agreed to pay.

The discussions the following day concerned two issues, the importance of the whole lineage group's unity against the outsider, and the fact that Sheikh Adorob, himself a member of diwab A, had sided with a member of diwab A against one of diwab B. When the evening came Sheikh Adorob revised his proposition to pay in case Musa refused to do so. He now suggested that diwab A should compensate Mohamed Omer collectively. Since Musa Abdalla continued to refuse to assume any responsibility, all diwab A households were later forced to contribute some cash for Mohamed Omer. The issue was thus settled peacefully but with a bitter taste. Individual diwab A members claimed that those of diwab B ought to be generous in the future if some member of diwab A slighted them. Until then, however, tension would remain between the two groups, and if diwab B members failed to show reciprocal generosity, that tension might easily grow instead of diminish.

When immediate arbitration fails, there is a conventional, traditional form of tribal clash. To prepare for a fight, the two parties form two opposite lines, arming themselves with heaps of stones (see for example Kassala Prov. Ann. Rep. 1952-3). To avoid an evolution of a smaller conflict into a more permanent state of feud, various tactics are used. A British colonial report from 1957 (Kassala Prov. Rep., Monthly Diary, Aug 1957) describes how 1,000 Beja men had gathered in Deim el Arab as the result of a conflict arising from two small boys fighting. "The Beja women were wise enough, for when seeing their men were about to kill each other they got ardently into the arena with unveiled heads". Another form of breaking up the fight with a surprise effect took place in November 1980 when a fight had broken out between a group of Hamdab (an Atmaan diwab) and a group of Kurbab (Amar'ar proper) in Deim el Arab. One man had beaten another man almost to death. People lined up with stones and beating sticks, and the police who came to the place of the fight were unable to stop it. A prominent Musayab leader decided that he should intervene. After having informed other Musaiab in order to avoid misunderstandings with serious implications, he went into the battle-field and pretended to fall down dead. The skirmish ended as if by magic when everybody started asking themselves who had murdered the well-respected elder, anticipating a long-lasting and bloody feud with a third party to emanate from the conflict.

Leadership and arbitration

Arbitration is preferred to fighting. The emphasis in the process lies rather on the merits of negotiated settlement than on the superior honour of a revenge carried through to its ultimate end. The corporate honour of having an efficient leader who masters his people despite their hot feelings here balances to some extent the obligation to retaliate.

Beja culture in itself puts no great emphasis on the inherent power of positions. Just as the settlement of jural cases is based on reaching a consensus, leadership is achieved by being accepted as a leader through consensus. This acceptance is in essence legitimised by reference to the general qualities of an honourable man, a man with reputation (*sumatu*), and is expressed in the degree to which a man is consulted (*o'mkir*); (see Haaland and al Hassan n.d.:16).

This is well expressed by Haaland and al Hassan (*ibid.*) describing the Hadendowa; they say they "are very sensitive to decisions or activities which are undertaken in matters where they feel they should be consulted. ...To the extent that one finds local tribal leaders one should thus not assume that they can take decisions on behalf of any group. What they can do is to serve as a channel for consultation and articulation of group interests".

Anybody who is honourable may compete for leadership; the leader is primus inter pares, and his authority may be challenged by his equals. A strong position may be built up on the existence of a personal following, through assuming in direct or extended sense the roles of father, religious or secular teacher, or of general patron and protector — roles in regard to which there is much overlap in the expectations.

82

Being the leader among honourable men entails a hierarchical relationship which is not based upon being different but rather on the leader embodying to an even higher degree the values represented by the members of the group and the group itself as a collective.

Jacobsson (1990) writes on the relationship between individual and collective in Bakongo matri-lineages, that "Whenever two or more members of the same matrilineage are in company with people from some other clan they are supposed to regard each other as one single jural and moral person ... whoever belongs to the matrilineage of one of the two adversaries will have his intervention interpreted as an official statement on the part of his lineage and ... it is important for either side to make sure that it is represented by the ablest speakers...". Much the same goes for the Beja in their relation to their diwab.

But the very idea of shared honour and identity then also paradoxically carries the seed for developing a "royal blood" discourse that we have mentioned as particular to the Musayab. That this is an inherent ambiguity in the Beja concept of leadership is also evident when one considers the *omda* positions. Lower level "headmen" are referred to as omdas or "sheikhs". The latter term is used for leaders in the kinship system but also denotes a Quranic teacher. It is usually reserved for old men who have Quranic training, even when it is applied to leaders. Other leaders may be called "Omda". Although there are omdas who are officially appointed by the Government, the Beja culture in itself does not necessarily limit omda-ship to one person. Leaders of any particular group are often respected outside their own diwab and used as mediators and peace judges. Within the diwab they are chosen for preference from among the sons of a leader, or as second best, from his daughter's sons. Usually the father picks out his favourite as successor, the one he likes best or the assumedly most intelligent one, training him for his future role as a leader by bringing him along to meetings and so on. The less favoured brothers just have to accept their father's choice. Traits sought for in a leader and encouraged in a future one are, apart from general wisdom and political and legal experience, such values as hospitality, humour, outspokenness, charm, warmth, and skill in oratory. However, in terms of Beja culture, anybody from an omda's family may be referred to as an omda, and in the absence of the influential man himself, members of his family are approached to mediate in conflicts. An omda need neither be old nor religiously learned, but the term may even be

83

jokingly and affectionately used to address children of the omda's family.

The idea of a common "omda-ship" resting in the family or diwab, in its extreme form presented as "royal blood", has close affinity in structural form with the idea of *baraka*, Divine Grace, as this is presented in Sudanese varieties of Sufism, for example in the sect which is most dominant in Eastern Sudan, the Khatmiya-Mirghaniyya. Divine Grace is a value residing in the founder of the sect and in his successors, transmitted to his disciples in a lineal chain of succession referred to as *silsila*, but present also in all his family members (see for example Voll 1969:128). This inherited competence is concretely expressed in various powers, such as healing and miracle-making baraka; like the suitability as a leader, it is expected in the family of people who have demonstrated such capacities, but is not absolutely restricted to them.

As emphasized earlier, one of the most important qualities in a Beja leader is to be a good mediator in the sense of negotiator and peacemaker. The presence of a strong leader who can represent the diwab externally as its spokesman, and who will also be asked for as a mediator by other groups, reflects positively on the cultural capital of the diwab as a whole (see Mohamed 1980:81, Fawzy 1978:122). A leader who is able to negotiate a settlement in a conflict gives the tribal group prestige through his capacity, so that even a compromise may not necessarily be seen as demeaning.

The collective facade-maintenance of the diwab is therefore in several ways the responsibility of the lineage leaders, who stand in the same position in relation to their diwab as the household head does in relation to his family.

Management of honour in a mixed cultural environment

When a person lives close to other people for a long time, he or she is able not only to learn about their neighbours' habits and general trustworthiness, but also to judge the extent to which such people will treat his or her household with respect despite getting access to their "backstage", to everyday life behind the facade. As long as this type of relationship between the households has not been established, ideally, if not always in reality, a person's relations with neighbours should be channelled and managed through the senior males of the household.

The latter should be the ones to regulate access to the person's back-stage domain. Handling strangers whom one meets only temporarily is far more difficult and risky, and by extension should be left to the senior people of the kinship group. They should be people whose own behaviour is characterized by integrity and honour, so as not to compromise the group. At the same time they should know the codes of diplomacy and, where necessary, the code according to which the stranger operates and communicates.

As long as a person is only involved in arbitration between two Beja diwabs, he or she is negotiating with people who share the same essential values, people who are in principle each other's equals. Negotiation like fights rests upon mutual recognition of each other as honourable people. Aiming at restoring peace, the object of this negotiation is not necessarily directly concerned with channelling material resources into the Beja group. Nevertheless, the group would in the long run depend for its survival both upon having peaceful access to other groups' pastures and convincing the others that they themselves are strong and brave enough to withstand attacks.

However, as should be clear from Chapter 2, a niche for another kind of mediator has existed for centuries. That is the mediator who goes outside the internal Beja system of structurally egalitarian units, and handles relations with non-Beja political power-holders and foreign merchants, drawing to his Beja group economic resources when possible, and protecting his diwab from depredation as well as notoriety. Seen from inside the diwab community, this position as a mediator between on the one hand the diwab, or the Beja rural people, and on the other urban or foreign resources, again has many structural similarities with the protective position of the male household head. Externally, the mediator acts as the hospitable host and facade keeper towards the strangers. Such positions were probably held in old times by elders or other diwab members who regularly stayed in the towns, or at villages such as Ariaab, in order to trade. Today, as well as traders, teachers and people with government jobs have a similar function. In larger urban centres such people receive their rural relatives and act as patrons for the urban poor. In the village they serve as local gate-keepers, receiving any strangers that arrive on the scene.

Knowing the code of communicating and interacting with strangers is a special skill. It is part of Beja patterns of social discourse to exaggerate any particular traits in a person in which he or she excels over other people or over what could normally be expected. In many situations when diwab members praise each other, this can be seen as a way of furthering collective honour. Just as a territorial host has to be respected in his home area, and his host-ship symbolically confirmed, the expert should be praised in the field of his particular secular or religious knowledge. This demonstrates the rights he has in his particular niche. Knowledge of the external world, and contacts "outside", can in the same way become exaggerated, unchallenged merits which contribute to maintaining a niche as gate-keeper.

An urban or village patron is supposed to protect his rural followers and take an interest in them. He is trusted to be the sieve through which information on them can be channelled. Of course, the Beja regard the Bedawiye value system and way of life as dignified and honourable (as do indeed, we should hasten to emphasize, the present writers). However, they do not generally expect this attitude from strangers, and they do not appear to believe that their ethnic heritage could in any way constitute a cultural capital with which they could score points on the national or international arena. *Hadara* (civilization) and *gudamantib* (development) are conceptually linked rather with the negation of a Beja life-style. The expectation of being met with contempt from other Sudanese is well-founded in experiences of having been described as dirty and backward (see Morton and Fre 1986:6; see also Mohamed 1965 for an example). Seen in a longer time perspective, and in the context of caravan guidance, a strict control of the information on the Beja's internal conditions may have been a necessary condition for survival. After all, their most important marketable resource was knowledge of waterways, passages and ways of escaping raids from competing groups. Today's handling of external relations is also a matter of meeting prejudice, and of competing symbolically on the national scene with other Sudanese groups. So, just as the eldest male is the main person responsible for keeping up the facade of the family, the educated leader is responsible for keeping up the facade of the people, in terms both of the perceived value system of the external society, and of their own. The urban mediator-patron is in this way a person who protects his rural network against losses of honour, but also an important link for channelling material and economic resources. And, as mediation works both ways, he could act for foreigners as a *rafig* (Ar.), a sponsor to vouch for one's good faith before Beja "barriers" are down (Clark 1938:1).

86

Fawzy (1978:120) describes how this worked in the context of Bishariin merchants in Aswan during the seventies. The urban patron would have a *manakh* (shelter) where he would hospitably house any mountain guests from his tribal section and store their goods for them. He would be supposed to pay them an advance and market their goods for their next visit. As the settlements of these patrons had become more permanent, they were also gaining more and more influence as judiciators, religious advisers and ceremony leaders (*op.cit*:121).

Morton (1988:427) also describes for the Sufaya Bishariin how the ownership of a *dekab*, a "rough but sturdy shelter of unhewn timber for giving hospitality and holding councils", is an important medium and sign for high social standing in the community. Such shelters are maintained by sheikhs and shop-keepers in the Beja trading centres, and these take on the obligation to look after the guests and provide food and assistance in coffee-making. We have also seen modern shop-keepers for example in Waheda plant a shade tree (*nandab*) for the same purpose.

In older times, this mediation may have entailed providing links to the market for *semn*, skin or other products that the pastoralists marketed. There was a need for people who could negotiate the contacts with the caravans in a way which was materially profitable for the Beja and who could protect their resources of water, livestock and people from depredation. Market contacts for livestock trade, credit and basic "savings-bank" services, as well as provision of grain, are still important. Other contacting may be needed for getting jobs, passes and educational facilities, negotiation with the police etc. We have already mentioned the role of the urban "work-gang" leader. Sudan is very much a country where personal contacts with the administration matter. The personal involvement of prominent merchants and politicians in such mediation varies. During the international food redistribution to the Beja of 1984-86, a particular mediatory role was developed when the World Food Programme and OXFAM used appointed representatives for each diwab to hand out food, appropriately referring to them as "Responsible Men". The organizations expressed some worry about the way these individuals used their position in redistributing food for enhancing their own status.

The impact of the state and external economic resources upon ordinary Beja peoples' everyday lives is much greater today than it has ever been, but there has been a place for such "gate-keepers" for centuries. Mediation between Beja and non-Beja political and economic structures is probably a key issue for understanding both pre-colonial and colonial patterns of stratification and hierarchy within Beja society.

By the nature of the historical records, we are more likely to hear about the Beja leaders that interacted with the Nubians and Romans, the Arabs, Turks, Funj and British than about those who based their position solely on resources and values internal to the Beja society. The influence of such people — merchants, tribute gatherers — on the Beja themselves may at times perhaps have been exaggerated by the observers. Yet, it is conceivable that it was only in the context of such contacts that any Beja leader was able to assert himself above the level of the diwab.

Reflections on hospitality, alliance and hierarchy

Beja culture at many levels appears to de-emphasize principles of alliance built on an egalitarian exchange between two partners, in contrast to the inclusive relations of kinsmen who share assets because they are part of the same entity, not two different units. Relations based upon transactions instead denote hierarchy to the Beja, and that hierarchy is primarily defined by space. One of the reasons why Beja territorial rights are maintained, despite the fact that grazing is practically free, is possibly the importance of such guest-host distinctions for everyday interaction. As we shall see in the next chapter, this way of playing down transactional alliance is reflected in Beja views on marriage as being of limited importance as a basis for individual alliances or for alliances between groups. There is a striking contrast to the case of East African pastoral cultures such as the Cushitic Borana, who have a very elaborate system of stock-friendships and also a general preoccupation with marriage as an institutionalized means to alliance. In these systems, ideological emphasis is usually on equality between two partners, who give each other the same kinds of goods or services, even if the exchange may be delayed.

Various authors, most recently represented by Johnson and Anderson (1988:6 ff), have emphasized the importance of such networks of reciprocity for pastoral survival, and have seen in the breakdown of traditional forms of reciprocal exchange an important contribution to famine conditions. In the context of the Beja, this model of analysis would not appear to hold, for the above mentioned reasons. In the internal distribution of grazing resources and food, they rely more on a principle of generalized reciprocity than on mutual agreement or direct reciprocity. It is tempting to see Beja hospitality as having a rather simple economic basis in a context where most men are forced to travel and where they, when they travel, will be completely dependant on their fellow men for food and water. The value of hospitality, then, would represent a system of generalized reciprocity, from which all men can hope to gain in the long run. Its cultural implications are probably much more far-reaching than these immediate and utilitarian considerations. In fact, the Beja morality of food aid in distress and hospitality actually directly negates the principles of social affiliation and attachment based on such dyadic and directed reciprocity. Your best guest is not just a stranger (see Lindholm 1982:xxix) but even an enemy. Johnson and Anderson refer, however, not only to how resources were rechannelled within pastoral societies themselves, but also to how households engaged in pastoral subsistence were linked to cultivators and hunters on the basis of reciprocity. The forms of contacts that prevailed between the Beja and Nubian cultivators in the Nile Valley, or the traditional durra cultivators at Gash, is still a topic that needs to be researched. Our evidence, though, suggests that such contacts would be managed by specialist mediators, operating within a commercial framework, rather than being a matter of individual family friendships maintained by a majority.

Barth (1965:79-81) analyzes hospitality among the Swat Pathans as a strategy followed by aspiring leaders in order to gain loyal followers, and has been criticized for not recognizing that even in Swat the ethos also obliges the ordinary villager to be hospitable (Lindholm *loc.cit* and Ahmed 1976:58). For the Beja, it would be most appropriate to claim that hospitality is regarded as a necessary virtue in any man of value, regardless of wealth.

Yet there are, however, situations when hospitality can indeed be used as a political resource — when the hospitality offered by for example urban kinsmen to rural relatives implies a mediation to external resources, or a security in the hazardous interaction with the non-Beja world. In this case, however, even though it is hospitality as a norm of behaviour which governs the relationship between guest and host, political allegiance would appear to result from material patronage and concrete protection.

The urban kinsman may be in the position to offer this kind of hospitality to his rural relatives, helping them to get access to resources and protecting them against the hazardous non-Beja world. Within his own diwab, a man who distributes his wealth is only yielding to what is more or less the rights of the recipients to a share in corporate property. That is, the symbolic message of intra-diwab sharing is "I give you because you have the right" while the message of the urban host to the guest is "I give you because I have the right, and am your superior in this territory. I will respect you only if you accept my rights". In practical life, the distinction between those two situations is not so clear-cut, and what is seen as fair sharing from one side may look like a position of dominance from the other. In 1987 we met a few very old traders who were boastful of the assistance they had been able to offer to deprived kinsmen. One old man told about the very young wife that he had been offered from a non-relative who had been assisted with grain in the worst period of starvation. Such cases were also mentioned in retrospect when people commented upon the relations between rich and poor men in earlier droughts, and it appeared that this is one of the contexts when rules of exogamy are transgressed.

This discussion of collective honour, male responsibility and the hierarchical implications of support should bring us to a final reflection about the emic interpretation of the relationship between famine relief recipients and donors. These are obviously very sensitive topics, and we have not been able to pursue them in open discussion with the Beja. Nevertheless, we do think it is important that more attention is paid to the subjective meaning of the economic transformation processes impinging on people like the Beja in terms of their own concepts and values. Therefore, and hopefully without offending Beja values, we would like to ask what it means to the latter, apart from survival, to become dependant on strangers distributing food in their own home territory. Perhaps the tendency to reinterpret the role of "Responsible Men" (in OXFAM's sense) as being really instrumental in providing the grain is a way to ideologically neutralize the negative implications. We assume that the European and American groups involved in promoting and mediating this assistance in 1984-86 did it from the point of view of a humanitarian solidarity which was based on valuing all people equally (an extended "inclusion"), although such solidarity may in many cases come dangerously close to paternalism. But Beja value systems give even less room than Western value systems for such an egalitarian interpretation of generosity with food, except between kinsmen and neighbours.

5

Gender roles, marriage and brother-sister relations

Inside and outside

As a visitor to the Beja area one can, despite the extreme hospitality of the people, easily get an impression of a rather harsh social world. In fact, social space in Beja life is sharply divided. There is a rather un-friendly relationship with the outer world, characterized by distrust, fear of strangers and a constant alertness against provocations, betrayal and violence. In the inner world of the household and the close kinship group, relations are instead marked by affection, intimacy and human warmth. The contrast corresponds to the physical characteristics of the respective settings. There is on the one hand the outdoor world, where men dressed in drab grey cotton move in the dustiness of the rural landscape or the dirt and unpleasantness of the squatter town street armed with daggers or even swords and knobkerries. On the other hand, there are the bright colours of the women's dresses, the laughter, the pleasant fragrances of incense and the tempting smell of the eternal coffee-pot inside the homes. As a man enters through the compound gate, one can almost see how the tenseness of his face and body relaxes, and how relieved he is to be in an environment marked by comfort rather than alertness. Outside is front stage (cf. Goffman 1959). Inside is where everybody shares the knowledge of the individual's hardships and the burdens of this person's honour.

The social spaces in which men and women move are very different, as are their roles in society and their tasks in everyday life. In this chapter we will try to contrast the two domains of men and women, but also show how they are interlinked. When analysing the Atmaan Beja, this cannot be done just by looking at the marital institution per se, for relations between sisters and brothers are just as important as those between wives and husbands. In fact, it is only by integrating these two types of relations that the ideal Beja marriage can be achieved.

Brotherhood and marriage

As compared with the implications of marriage, the sibling bond as cultural construct has received relatively scant attention from anthropologists — perhaps, as some anthropologists[1] suggest, because of its relative lack of significance in Western culture. A Beja man has obligations to his wife, but also to his sisters, the cognatic duties being seen as more fundamental than the marital one. The situation where these duties conflict is preferably avoided, and the ideal situation is achieved by merging the two categories through close endogamy. When this is not done, other solutions may be found, as in the example of Taha, a man in his mid-twenties, who had responsibility for five or six young unmarried sisters. Taha had simply postponed his marriage to the lady of his dreams, a Nubian girl, in the hope that in nine years or so he would have married off his sisters.

---

[1] V. de Munck, 1990, quoting Bank and Kahn (1982:5) and Marsh (1985:iv).

From the point of view of loyalty, confidence and ease, and non-sexual intimacy, the sister, for her part, has a closer attachment to her brother than to her husband. This was noted by Crossland (1913:22) who also reflected that "it is common complaint that she is supporting able-bodied brothers in idleness on her husband's earnings, without his leave and so far as possible without his knowledge". A brother turns to his sister, as she does to him, for consolation and support, and they often talk highly of each other.

Given the ambilineal recruitment to the diwab, in spite of its patrilineal ideology, it is the endogamic practice which in reality maintains the distinctions between diwabs. In contrast to their Arab neighbours, the Beja state their preference rule for partner choice ambilaterally, including both parallel and cross cousins on each side. In order of preference, it is considered best for a man to marry FaBrDa, MoBrDa, FaSiDa and MoSiDa, and then "any girl of the diwab". This particular Beja custom is thought to be against the Quran, and the difference between the Beja and their neighbours is noted by both and often a topic of conversation. The Beja notion is that this practice makes the group stronger, and that it in some way enhances its fertility and makes it grow. In practice one may suspect that it frequently has an opposite effect on cohesion, for such close endogamy makes the range of possible marital partners limited and creates tension over hoped-for marriages within the closest circle of relatives which do not materialize. For it is closeness which is the purpose of the custom, going right up to the limit set by the taboo against marriage with true siblings. The order of preference is also considered to be an order of closeness. Many marriages are actually contracted with close relatives, who are cousins both patrilaterally and matrilaterally. Since all members are likely to be related in several cross-cutting ways in a narrowly endogamous group, it is not evident that the actual resulting pattern differs much from what is found among Arabic Sudanese groups; the difference is probably more a matter of how the resulting links are interpreted.

Whether in any particular case an intra-diwab marriage is labelled a marriage with FaBrDa by classificatory extension or seen as being a first-degree marriage with MoBrDa is probably a situational choice. Suffice it here to say that to the Atmaan Beja, lateral cognatic closeness may be seen as being important as an agnatic relationship.

In contrast with what is the case in many other pastoral groups, marital alliances made for the purpose of obtaining supplementary grazing concessions are not important. As stated above, everybody is allowed to graze anywhere except in periods of extreme scarcity. More fundamental rights of ownership are not gained by marriage, except in the succeeding generation, and it is not likely that marriage strategies are formed with such a time perspective.

Since marriage does not imply any collective alliance between groups, there are few transfers of value from group to group in the context of a wedding. Bridewealth transactions are limited to personal gifts to the girl's immediate family and the provision of a subsistence herd for the new couple. The rule of preferred endogamy also makes it more difficult for diwab members to use marriages in order to further their personal and individual interests at the expense of the common interests of the diwab. The contrast is striking when comparison is made with the case for an individual in a society where lineage exogamy is the rule.

By ensuring that his sisters and daughters are married within the diwab, and by choosing a wife from the diwab, a Beja man can demonstrate that he fulfils the important obligation to take responsibility for the protection of sisters and classificatory sisters. Only under two special sets of conditions do the Beja recognize acceptable excuses for marrying away the women of the diwab in an exogamic marriage. One is when there is a very long-standing relationship of neighbourhood, so that the prospective husband is very well known to the male relatives of the girl. The other situation has already been touched upon in Chapter 4. It applies when, in acute crisis, the prospective husband is a protective patron of the father of the girl. It is probably in relation to such protection that we have to understand the historical records of Arab-Beja intermarriages as well.

Adding to the considerations of honourable protection of diwab girls, but less expressly formulated in the emic explanations of endogamy, comes the fact that a close marriage for the husband implies that he has more control over his wife. He shares concern over her virtue with her brothers and does not have to worry about the possibility of a major tribal conflict arising from marital problems.

It is generally considered more important to avoid marrying out the diwab's girls than to stop diwab men from marrying exogamously. In fact, however, as we shall see, even such marriages are seen as having a number of disadvantages, and as not bringing much good in return. A virilocally married wife introduces into the family group of the husband various social contacts which are difficult to handle. The brother of a woman always has free access to her house, but if he comes from another group his contacts with the other ladies of the family must be restricted.

The Beja rule of marrying as close as possible, whether with parallel or cross- cousins, can at one level be seen as a way of integrating and encysting the descent group and its property. Such a "functionalist" explanation relates to emic models insofar as the ambiguities that follow upon exogamous marriages are apparent to any Beja. The ambiguities express themselves in conflicts about land, about the marriage of daughters, and about the personal allegiances of the offspring. The recognition of these problems certainly influences the general opinion about exogamous marriages as such. In the actual situation of matchmaking, such a long term perspective is not very relevant to family strategies. The questions that relate to the resources immediately available to the couple, and the implications of merging their personal networks, are more salient, apart from an evaluation of the personal traits of each of the partners. To begin with resources: neither a young man nor a young girl marrying "out" from their own diwab and moving out of its kurai area would be free to bring along substantial subsistence resources. An exogamous marriage (if not contracted as a politically strategic elite marriage) leaves the couple with one rather than two sources of subsistence assets. A man who wants to move away to another area in order to marry there may find difficulties in convincing his father to contribute to bridewealth. At the same time the demands from the bride's relatives are usually higher under such circumstances. Endogamy on the other hand enhances the young man's chances that his wife's inheritance claims can be realized.

The dominant emic explanation for endogamy, however, is never related to such material considerations. What matters in the view of the Beja is that an endogamous marriage is more socially auspicious. It implies less social awkwardness, and is seen to offer the girl more protection. The Beja think that a woman should ideally be given the benefit of living together with women who are close and known to her. Thus, while on the level of structural ideals the continuity of the diwab is seen by the Beja as a continuity of patrilineal links, the interpretation of continuity in the social organization of daily life emphasizes en-

95

during female links. In practice, many Beja women live all their lives within roughly the same group of women: women to whom they have multiple links, so that one woman is at the same time, for example, somebody else's mother's sister, father's sister and mother-in-law. Also, it is thought that a man who is not a member of the girl's lineage is unlikely to look after her properly after the birth of the first child when the thrill of first love has passed over. Sexual enchantment is not expected to be an appropriate basis of marriage; it has to be propped up by brotherly love if the marriage is to last. Furthermore, although individual honour is always partly shared, a foreign man's brothers and clan-mates are expected to be weak in looking after the well-being and virtue of one's sister. The woman remains a member of her natal group after marriage, and her brother's protective duties toward her never cease. Hence, should she be mistreated or not fed properly by her new relatives, there would be cause for conflict. Or, at least, a situation would arise which would require great diplomacy if the durareit of one or the other were not to be questioned.

Total avoidance is expected between mother-in-law and son-in-law. The latter is also not allowed to sit in the presence of his father in-law. If the husband lives in the wife's parents' camp, his wife will stay in their shared hut only during night-time and spend the days with her mother. The mother is not supposed to have anything to do with the relationship between the two partners: it is shameful for her to visit her daughter's hut, and she is not even supposed to have a bridal photograph of the two. It goes without saying that the resulting constraints on interaction are easier to handle when the groom is surrounded by his own relatives. Newly in-married young wives who have no children as yet appear strikingly isolated, particularly as the constraints imposed by the concepts of honour and virtue are strongest during the first year of marriage.

It is true that when a man marries exogamously, he adds to the claims that his children can raise in the future, and he relieves some of the competition for diwab girls. But he will be supposed to live uxori-locally during the first years of marriage. The implications of this in terms of personal awkwardness, and the loss of labour to his own family, are felt more negatively than when a close marriage is contracted. Educated Beja men more frequently marry "Balawiet" girls — Nubian or Arabic — which causes resentment. Their poorer, uneducated relatives complain that such men fail to fulfil Beja kinship obligations. Children of such alliances tend not to learn TuBedawiye, as a result of the Beja expectation that a child should learn its language and culture primarily from its mother.[1]

After the first years of the marriage, the Beja husband is free to take his wife with him and settle with his own relatives. However, a number of exogamously married men do not do so. One case is of course the elite men married to Balawiet girls, who tend to be contemptuous of their Beja relatives. Other cases concern men who have no claim to any inheritance within their own diwab, or, as mentioned by Salih (1976:56), people who have committed murder or adultery at home. Men who stay away from their own group for a long time, however, do not necessarily relinquish their rights of membership, as the following case will illustrate.

A 66-year-old man, Adan, who had been living with the Hadendowa since he was twelve, made contact with the leaders of the Amar'ar X-diwab. "He talked like a Hadendowa and looked like a Hadendowa. We were all surprised to hear that he was from X-diwab just like us," one of his clansmen told us. It turned out that since he left his original diwab he had never actively sought contact with it. He had been married twice to women from the Hadendowa Y-diwab, a rather small group, having daughters in both marriages. The reason why he now returned to the X-diwab was that his brother-in-law wanted to decide on the choice of husbands for his girls. Enraged, Adan had decided to turn to his own relatives for help. Despite the fact that the man was completely unknown to most of them, the X-diwab summoned a meeting on his behalf, where feelings of hurt family honour ran high. Some young men said that if they had to put up with things like this, they would go and take Hadendowa wives by force. The man got promises of assistance in terms of money or fighting strength, which-ever he wanted.

An eloquent Arabic-speaking X-diwab man was appointed to accompany him to the Kadhi's court, where the brother-in-law was the main opponent. Here, it was argued that the Hadendowa man had no reason to meddle in the business of Adan's daughters' marriages, not being his brother. In the latter's perspective, being a paternal uncle to the girls would legitimate such an interest, but being a maternal uncle

---

[1] When discussing their origin, Beja like to emphasize their patrilineal Arab descent, but are willing to admit that their mothers were "Africans", and that their culture is thus African, despite the fact that they themselves are essentially "Arabs".

did not. The in-law's counter-argument was that Adan had once killed a Hadendowa man from yet another diwab. The case had never been brought to the knowledge of the authorities, but had been settled by discrete negotiations between the two Hadendowa diwabs, that of the victim and that within which Adan was living as an assimilated member. Accepting responsibility to negotiate for Adan, the Hadendowa man claimed, was tantamount to accepting him as a full brother, with a brother's rights but also duties. But the X-diwab point of view was that they also would not have refused to come to their lost brother's help had they only been informed. The implication that they would have refused to assist him was another challenge to their collective honour. If the Y-diwab wanted to decide over the marital fate of X-diwab girls, it would not only be an infringement of the rights of a father to decide for the future of his daughters, but also of the diwab's rightful claim to decide in matters concerning its own resources of marriageable girls. It was by hinting that his ambition had been to seek X-diwab husbands for the girls that Adan had been able to raise support for his case.

The Kadhi found that Adan would be in his right to move away with the two elder daughters and decide over their future as he found best, while the younger girl, who was under seven, would stay with her mother and uncle. This also became Adan's decision. Under other circumstances, he might have opted for the choice of actually letting himself be assimilated into his hosts. The risk of such a loss of a male member is of course a concern to his diwab if he suggests an exogamous marriage.

Gender and work

In order to understand the pattern of division of labour among the Atmaan Beja, it is necessary to refer to the symbolic content of tasks as well as to the material constraints of pastoral subsistence. At a quick glance, the division of tasks follows a pattern well-known for pastoral societies all over the world. Male tasks relate to the public sphere of societal decision-making, cooperation and defence, and to the herding of camels and cattle, and frequently of the small stock. Women's work represents an extension of the nursing and sheltering implied by the maternal role; they are responsible for food preparation and for anything that has to do with the household equipment.

However, when we look more closely, particularly at the symbolic messages contained in the tasks, whatever their formal characteristics, we find a structure peculiar to the Beja. An anomaly which several authors have commented upon[1] and which the Beja themselves regard as ethnically distinctive to them is the fact that milking is taboo for women. Beja women are not allowed to milk sheep, goats, camels or cattle.[2] This taboo is shared with some neighbouring Arab groups who are historically quite closely related to the Atmaan Beja, such as the Hassaniya of the White Nile (Mohamed 1980:46). However, it does not occur among Arabs generally, neither in Arabia nor among other Sudanese Arabs. Among the Kababish, for instance, women milk the goats (Asad 1970:44). Among other Cushites women usually do the milking, with the exception of the Somali and related groups, where women are allowed to milk goats but not camels. In other East African societies, milking is usually a typically female task, but the Hima of Uganda constitute an exception. Here a cultural linkage of milk and semen justifies a taboo similar to that of the Beja.

Milk must be drawn by a male person. In the absence of an adult member of the household a male child or a neighbour will do it. The first sip must then be offered to another man, and according to present-day Atmaan Beja, a proper respect of this rule in the old days could mean that the milking male would have to walk several kilometres hunting for a potential recipient of the milk before the family's needs could be met. To say that somebody "milks and drinks" was a traditional expression of abuse (Crossland 1913:44). Milne (1976:106) reports a saying that "only animals drink from the udder". However, people assured us, it does occasionally happen that a woman whose men-folk are away sneaks up in the darkness of the night to milk for her children unseen. The important aspect here is of course not the statistical adherence to the norm, but rather the fact that female milking is still nothing that can be done publicly or by daylight.

Whether milk symbolically stands for semen among the Beja, as in the case of the Hima, is more than we want to speculate on. The female taboo on milking is in any case a custom which neatly summarizes the view that man is the essential provider of food.[3]

---

[1]Milne (1976:106); Jackson (1926:21); Fawzy (1978:55); Clark (1938:9); Keimer (1951:III:121); and Murray (1923:420f).

[2] According to Milne (1976:106) the same rule applied to slaves.

[3] A man will also always be needed for slaughtering, even if the animal in question belongs to a woman. This rule, however, is less often held forward as being ethnically distinctive.

Other tasks are specific to the male gender, but are not as symbolically loaded as milking. Some authors seem to hint that the drawing of water from the well (as opposed to bringing it home) would be prohibited for women, but as one informant said: "The difference between the milk taboo and the prohibition against drawing water is like that between heaven and earth." The allocation of this task to men rather reflects the idea that it is a point of honour to the Beja men to save women from hardship, suffering and heavy tasks. This norm is very explicit, which for example accounts for the standard answer to the enquirer's question on female tasks: "Beja women do not work". "Work" is invariably taken to mean heavy tasks, or work for cash. In practice, of course, some of the traditional tasks that women actually carry out, such as grain grinding, involve great expenditure of effort; and this is not to speak of the hardships of motherhood. The Beja are also well aware that practical circumstances and poverty will frequently force people to pragmatically dispose of their norms, and women are in fact drawn into herding as well as agricultural tasks as circumstances force them to do so. The cultivation of durra does not involve any tasks which are directly tabooed to women, whether in clearing, sowing, weeding or harvesting, although all these activities have the potential for providing material for symbolic elaboration.[1] These are tasks thought of as being usually carried out by men, with children and women assisting.[2]

Care of the flocks of sheep and goats pastured at a distance from the home is also mainly a male duty. Women are responsible for the care of small stock close to the camp and in the house, although they naturally delegate much of the practical work with this to small girls and boys. Both sexes in this way are well acquainted with the important aspects of being herds-people, and though a woman might for practical reasons and considerations of modesty make a pause in herding activities during her reproductive period, she would take it up again when past child-bearing.

Turning the perspective, there are also a few tasks that it would be shameful for a man to carry out. The most important of these is the

---

[1] Some people might like to take this as an indication that durra cultivation is relatively new and peripheral to the Beja.

[2] However, one of us spent a very pleasant afternoon drinking jabana in the shade with some male harvesters, while at a distance of 200 yards some women could be watched forcefully threshing durra cobs with big sticks - a heavy task.

preparation of butter, *o'la*. Milk is soured for a couple of days in a sack of goat skin, and then rhythmically "rolled" on a string. The product is much valued and symbolically linked to fertility and the survival and growth of children. A woman always gets milk from a man, and it is up to the senior male of the household to allocate milk fairly between women if there are several of them in the household. The woman has full control of the milk once it is allocated to her. This means that the Beja woman has a narrower sphere of "housekeeping" than most pastoral women, who normally have direct rights to particular animals.[1] Consequently, if milk is sold before being allocated to a woman, the proceeds belong to the man, but proceeds from butter always go to the woman. It is up to her to feed her husband and children with fresh milk, sour the remnants for *hamid'at*, or turn a surplus into butter. Fatness is inherently linked to "good" femininity and fertility.

Not only does the man as provisioner bring milk and meat to the women, but it is also he who stores and distributes grain and who does the shopping when food has to be bought. This last naturally relates to the general idea that women have to be kept isolated from public encounters and contacts with other menfolk. "Bringing home food to her" is also seen as the essential male part of the marital contract, and as the essential duty of a brother to a sister under his responsibility. For a woman to complain over failure in this respect would be seen as utterly shameful, and men say that they would rather stay away or die than return home without anything for the womenfolk to eat.

Once the food has been procured by the man, it is for the woman to prepare it. A very heavy task in this respect is the grinding. Urban families who can afford to do so bring the durra to the mechanical mill to be ground, but hand-grinding is still very common. Durra porridge (*o'tam*) is very popular even in the towns, and is the normal staple food in the countryside when milk is scarce. Other dishes may consist of beans or onions. It should be noted here that milk products, apart from the butter preparation which also gives some symbolic satisfaction, are much less energy-demanding to prepare than grains and pulses are. This goes for the fuel involved as well as for the work spent on grinding and on firewood-collection in places where fuel is not bought. Such work is definitely regarded as belonging to the

---

[1] Dahl (1979) describes the case of the Borana.

women's domain, although in practice as much as possible of such work is delegated to young girls, according to availability.

Men should not cook or build houses. These tasks are considered shameful or at least unworthy for them if they are carried out under most circumstances. Here, however — according to a very widespread cultural pattern (Friedl 1975:62f; Sacks 1974:216f) — the priorities of male hospitality can intervene. Roasting meat, preparing jabana coffee or building a shelter for the guests (Clark 1938:6) are therefore accepted male tasks if no woman is there, or if the women can be saved from contact with strangers by the practice. In contrast with many African cultures, fires can be lit by men as well as by women, "but the ones lit by women get hotter".

Most human action has a double character of being both instrumental and communicative, and this goes for household work as well. One set of constraints acting on the question of who does what tasks is given by purely practical considerations concerning convenience, availability, skill etc. Another set of constraints operates on the communicative level. For the Beja men and women, household organization has to be carried out within the limits governed by the idiom of durareit. There are thus many things that a woman is considered potentially capable of doing, but which she must not do in the presence of a man, lest she challenge his honour. The most important things relate to defence — such as chasing away a thief, killing a leopard etc. Similarly, there are things which the husband or brother should not do, and other things that they should not let the women do, in order not to compromise himself as a good protector. A Beja man is never expected to beat his wife (Clark 1938:9). "That would be to put himself on the same level as her" — i.e. taking to violence against an unworthy adversary, who should instead be seen as inherently weaker and thus in need of protection and tolerance.

Womanhood and marriage

On the whole, women of reproductive age take little part in the productive system of the Beja. Most of their time seems to be spent in supervising the work of children, caring for babies or preparing food. A woman in her non-reproductive periods seems to merit less consideration as a woman to be protected in order to maintain the honour of the male protectors. Old women and young girls are

102

brought more actively into the collection of firewood and water or into the various tasks of livestock care. In the period between their marriage and the menopause, however, women's roles and activities are directed towards motherhood and towards being sexually attractive for their husbands. For women of any age, the main themes of interaction with other women are on the one hand body care, and on the other the mobilization of necessary support for women about to marry or giving birth, including the celebration of such events. In relation to her husband, to her closest family of origin, and to other women, a woman should not be *lab*, that is "lazy, cold and sloppy".

The interaction between men and their wives is limited. This does not mean that Beja women live in a completely female world during daytime, as they are interacting with brothers, nephews and so on. A newly-married woman is rather constrained from receiving many visitors, and may feel lonely a good deal, but a woman of some age may be like a friendly spider in the network of relationships. Jokingly, we used to ask ourselves in the field whether *diratun* (an "auntie") was not an equally important concept for the Beja as durareit. Certainly, the demands for respectful attention and recurrent visits which are made by elder female relatives are a very pervasive factor in the everyday life of any Beja man. For a large part of the morning and afternoon, however, men are generally expected to stay away from their homes, in order to make it possible for women to socialize with each other. At this time, the separation of worlds is complete, and if broken by accident, so that men and women who are not very closely related happen to meet each other, both parties show signs of extreme embarassment. A wife will complain over a husband who shows too much interest in female matters. As a wife, she should normatively "only talk to her husband during the night". In practice, we have seen men expressing respect as well as affection for their wives at other times. Urban Beja men show notable consideration for their wives and their feelings. "Virtuous" behaviour is reciprocally demanded. A woman who has detected that her husband is having an extramarital affair — which is regarded as synonymous with his association with "bad women" — has the right to claim compensation (*tajjer*) in gold or money. Tajjer is also offered when a husband wants to make peace after having suggested a divorce. When the wife is adulterous, there have existed standards of fines (eight camels, divided equally between the two adulterers) according to older sources such as Clark (1938:6).

Just as is the case with diia being paid for murder, however, it is not seen as entirely honourable for a man to accept compensation in money. Receiving such compensation would not erase the moral obligation to take revenge.

When Beja women have the choice, very much time is spent on bodily embellishment, usually interpreted as preparation for marital intercourse. Attractiveness according to Beja ideals relates to fatness, "cleanness", fragrance and brightness, which are also seen as signs of fertility. The activities oriented towards these ideals have three foci. The first is the smoke-bath, *o'di* (cf. Keimer 1953:IV:162 and fig. p 165 for a sketch). Functionally similar smoke-baths of somewhat different construction are important to the Somali, Borana and Afar women (Ayele 1986:50). The Beja o'di is a hole in the ground, inside the hut. The name — which is masculine — may etymologically relate to *adi't*, the female genital organs. In the hole, which is about 30 cm. deep and 15 cm. wide, is placed aromatic charcoal and incense, preferably *talh,* (Acacia seyal) which has the effect of making the body lighter in colour, and *salf*, which has a pleasant smell.

The woman sits crouched for one or two hours over this hole, wrapped in blankets and so that her private parts may be penetrated by the smoke. This is done at least once a week and is the standard prescription for any female ailment, be it pain in the reproductive organs or a headache. Frequently two friends, sisters or a mother and daughter will keep each other company taking turns at the o'di.

Beja women are circumcised and infibulated. The Amar'ar do this at the time of name-giving (*ti'smaya*), that is at the age of only one week.[1] The operation (*bushub*) leaves only a very small opening for all bodily fluids and, according to Dareer (1982), creates conditions conducive to cysts and infections besides of making child-birth difficult and risky, as the midwife (*sefarana't*) must always come well in time to cut the opening with a knife. The o'di and the preoccupation with the potential pollution of the female organs that it represents is very much a symbolical and ritual complex. Nevertheless, they also have to be considered against the background of very real health problems.

The two other foci of the women's attention to her body are the head and the feet. The hair is for the Beja a central identity symbol, signi-

---

[1] This time is indicated both by Darar and by our Atmaan and Hadendowa informants. Shaban (1970.124) and Fawzy (1978:41 and 73) state that the operation is done at the age of 5-6 years among the Hadendowa, Ababda and Bishariin.

ficant to both men and women. Whereas the young Beja man is famous for his bushy Afro coiffure, the man being the more masculinely beautiful the bushier it is, the woman is proud to have long but strictly "controlled" hair. It is daubed with fat and braided in a large number of thin braids ending with a knot. The coiffure takes more or less one whole day to renew. This has to be done every ten days to one month.

The feet are blackened with henna. This process, if it is to be carried out properly, requires that the woman sits passive with the feet covered for three to four hours on three days consecutively, concluding with a session at the o'di. Henna stays on for a fortnight.

Preparing a smoke-bath and tending to hair and feet are things which women do together with their sisters, female cousins and best friends. Childbirth and the care for a new mother and her baby during their forty day's seclusion (when the father is not allowed to see the child) is another domain for female cooperation. In this context, the obligations sisters have to each other come to the fore. The norm that a husband's demands on his wife's presence should be subordinate to the demands of a sister in labour or convalescence is strongly sanctioned by Atmaan culture. There is little possibility for a husband to refuse to allow his wife to travel to her sister under such circumstances. The sister coming to help will assist in housekeeping, looking after other children and attending to the birth itself. During the seclusion, no male over 14 years of age is allowed to enter the room of the mother and child. Closely related women bring her food and cheer her up with visits. Lamps are not allowed to go out during the night, a knife may be kept under the pillow of the mother and incense is lit under her bed, all in order to ward off evil. Women of the closest family and neighbourhood take care of the *wahalas*, the afterbirth which has to be deposed in a tree if the baby is a boy, or dug into the earth floor of the hut if it is a girl. This is done in a small ceremony where women proceed chanting and with incense to the appropriate spot. The women surrounding the mother also run the celebration for the birth of the child, which ideally lasts for a week if it is a boy, during which time they sing and ululate. The father should slaughter an animal and give the child a name, although he does not actually see the child.

When a girl is going to marry, it is again a joint task for the most closely related women to prepare for the wedding by assisting in manufacturing whatever is needed for her dowry — things like ropes, woollen mats and, in locations where there are dome-palm stands, palm-leaf mats. (cf. Salih 1976:24). The Beja hut, *bidagao*, for which the woman has the total responsibility, consists of curved ribs, stretched between two main supports (*o'marr*) and covered with palm-leaf mats. The opening is away from the main wind direction. Inside, the house can have a ceiling of cloth (*ti'dallal*) and walls of goat hair blankets (*shamla*). A large central bed is surrounded by red cloth decorated with cowrie shells (*i't*).[1]

Weddings are usually held in the harvest season and are important occasions, both for socializing in preparation for the guests and for participation as a guest. In all these situations of female cooperation and rejoicing, it is the old and middle-aged women who take the lead. Compared to the usually shy and very quiet newly-wed or teenage girls, these women make a remarkably outspoken and fearless impression.

The Beja woman pleases and reproduces for her husband. The Beja man protects and provides for his wife. These are the ideals, but they are never thought of as being carried out by isolated individuals; rather, they are strived for within the context of a strongly collectivist ethos.

The fundamental link that ties men and women in an Atmaan Beja diwab together is cognation, sibling- and cousin-hood, rather than marriage. Marriage as such is all about sexuality and providing children. Since sexual attraction is seen as ephemeral, it is by motherhood that a woman can strengthen the stability of her marriage in the cases where marriage is not propped up by the classificatory brother/sister link.

Women are seen as inherently sexually irresponsible, and the whole burden of "protecting" them thus falls on their male relatives. Because of this, individuals are generally not left alone to decide upon their marriages, even though marriages are concerned with relationships between individuals rather than with alliances between larger kinship groups. Primarily, it is the father of a young boy or girl who is involved in making the choice of a suitable partner, but other close senior male relatives in the family usually have a word to say. Even a man who is 20 or 25 may have to yield to what his senior kinsmen propose. There is a notion that the mother of a girl should in principle have a veto right, and an expectation that she will in most cases support

---

[1] For further references on huts, see Clark (1938:6).

106

her brother's son as the most suitable candidate for the daughter. But in practice, this right is frequently regarded as negotiable and can be exchanged for a promise that the mother's preference will be given priority in the future choice of a partner for a younger sibling.

While the provision of honourable first marriages for the girls of the diwab is a central concern for the elder men — this being the basic reason why the young men also cannot be allowed to choose for themselves — the elders have few sanctions available with which to keep the marriage together in the long run. Sons who resent the choices made by their fathers or uncles consider it easier to accept the marriage and then break it after a year than to make effective resistance from the outset. The instability of these unions is a popular topic for discussion among the educated Beja, who are playing with ideas of modernity and love marriages.

Fulfilling the demands of beauty certainly requires that the woman is not bogged down by subsistence activities. The poor wife, who struggles to herd some few goats in the mountains while her husband roams the country hunting for jobs, does not spend so much time on these activities as the wealthier women, who have children or servants to do the more practical "women's tasks". Nevertheless they reflect the ideal, the general attitude that apart from child-birth, sexuality is the main female contribution in the marital contract. In offering her sexuality to her husband, the woman may subject herself to pains that are seen as a natural part of it. Unlike other pains, this is a sacrifice that the Atmaan man expects his wife to bear for his sake; this is her arena for showing herself a *ti'm'tarim*, a woman with stamina.

The limited significance of marriage

The theme of this chapter has been the division of the Beja world into a male and a female sphere, and a description of the interlinkage. We have argued that it is as much the brother-sister bond as the marriage which provides this interlinkeage. A basic conclusion is that marriage among the Beja is generally not consciously used in order to create alliances between clans (in fact, when such alliances are made, they are expected to lapse into common identity). Marriage is seen as a brittle institution, which has to be reinforced by brotherly solidarity. A man can play his role as protector and provider towards other weaker and poorer men, and towards children and old people. The archetypal counterpart for the "responsible man" is, however, the woman in her role as sister-cum-wife (and more as sister than wife!).

A crisis of economy and subsistence, which leaves the husband unable to fulfil his basic responsibilities, is bound to have far-reaching consequences for his own identity and for his relations with women. Perhaps these are consequences which do not seem to strike so hard in the immediate face of drought — a long-term God-given event beyond individual control. Rather, these consequences have a psychological dimension, affecting the community members in a culturally bound way with feelings of non-fulfilment of responsibilities. Even though change is experienced by each man and woman on their own, a disaster causes lasting internal effects for the community as a whole.

6

Getting Grain

In the earlier chapters we have attempted to put the Beja into a historical framework, and to give some indications of the central values of their culture. In this and the two following chapters, we will take a closer look at the conditions of Beja subsistence by examining their sources of grain, their form of pastoralism, and the way these resources have been threatened by more recent changes.

Grain is an essential element in Beja economy. Although observers like Salih (1976:77) have commented that milk is a more secure asset than durra, o'tam is almost as highly appreciated as milk. This is a thick durra porridge eaten with milk and/or clarified butter. The word stem, "tam", is identical to the verb "to eat", but as a substantive it refers to durra porridge and not to food in general. Arabic, too, has this word, *ta'am*, for "nutrition, food" and as an alternative for durra and sorghum (Stuhlman 1909:168). O'tam is a very ancient Beja term, and this food is highly valued.

The significance of homegrown durra in values such as identity and inclusion was brought home to us through the reaction of our hosts when we first proved willing to eat o'tam. O'tam is not what the Beja host considers as a suitable treat for his guest, and we had been lavishly entertained with foodstuffs that had a higher symbolic ranking in relation to urban culture and modernity. The porridge was somewhat apologetically brought to us, as there was nothing else in the house, but we did not mind eating it in the least, as porridge is also important in our Swedish diet. We had not expected the meal to become our "rite-de-passage" into being taken seriously by the Beja, but the enthusiasm demonstrated when we ate it was striking and completely transformed our relations with our Beja friends.

Eating o'tam is an important part of "being Beja"; it is regarded as an ethnic marker. Durra (sorghum) and *dukhn* (finger millet) are today obtained either by trade or by home production, and both grain trade and grain cultivation probably have a very long tradition in the area. Those living at the coast use dukhn, which grows better there, for their porridge, rather than durra. A similar high value is placed on that product. In Port Sudan, where the workers in the docks and other full-time employees find difficulties in affording the time needed to bring durra to the mill, maize-meal is gradually taking the place of durra as a staple food. But durra remains more highly valued than maize.

Apart from being a basic food crop, durra is also given as supplementary fodder to Beja animals in times of scarce pasture. This use has grown in importance in the towns, where urban livestock are fed partly on a sorghum diet, so that even if urban Beja eat maize themselves, they still need to buy durra for their animals. During the present century, the Beja have sometimes been able to store durra from year to year, exploiting the windfall of a good harvest in order to cover the animals' needs in a coming bad year. The extent to which rural people used to resort to this in earlier centuries is difficult to ascertain, but today we see practices which the Beja term traditional used to successfully store exogenous varieties of durra for several years in holes dug in the laterite soils found generally in Aulib. There is little reason to believe that the possibility of storing a sudden surplus of durra for future use has not been known for a long period. Unless such precautions are taken, drought in Beja areas results in a shortage of fodder prior to causing a shortage of water. Access to supplementary fodder is therefore a vital element in ensuring continuity in food production.

A likely, but so far unproved, increase in the human population, associated with a dwindling of particularly the camel herds, and the loss of drought resort pastures in the Gash and at Tokar, have during this century combined to increase Beja dependence on grains in traditional pastoral areas as well.

Durra and dukhn are cultivated in varying degrees of intensity by different Beja groups. At times, cultivation does not involve more effort than if natural grains were collected. In other cases a high degree of labour input is required. Many writers of earlier decades[1] appear to think that durra cultivation was generally new to the Beja when they observed them, and that it had accordingly been less extensive previously.[2] For example Sandars (1932) notes that the "Amar'ar are each year cultivating more land, for instance since 1919 the Nazir has not had to buy any grain at all for his own household; in 1931 he got 12 camel loads of grain from his own cultivation. In 1931 a party of Gadeloiab Musayab, a section which has never previously cultivated came across to Khor Arab and raised 72 ardeb".

Statements such as these can, however, be taken more as an expression of the stereotyping of Beja as essentially pastoralists, rather than as one of actual knowledge of the historical realities. Ibn Hawqal (Vantini 1975:151-2) wrote about the Beja in the 10th century that they "possessed neither villages, nor towns, nor cultivated fields". It is, however, likely that Beja groups for a long time cultivated when there was need and/or when easy facilities for doing so were at hand, and abstained from it when their herds were stable and healthy enough. Some sections have only limited access to cultivable land within their

---

[1] See Owen (1936): "Hadendowa have only recently developed the habit of regular grain eating" and "middle-aged [Hadendowa] men remember the time when cultivation was less than half its present proportions". Seligman (1913:599) appears also to regard cultivation as something new and alien to the Beja.

[2] Burckhardt (1819:370) writes about extensive Bishariin cultivation on the Atbara, but also (p. 450) on the absence of such activities among the norterhn Bishariin.

own territories, such as the Kurbab who, however, cultivate extensively in Khor Haiyet as guests in other diwabs' territory. Sandars (*loc.cit*) mentions them together with other Amar'ar groups such as the Omar Hassayab, Mohgen and Keilab who in his time did not cultivate at all. Among Bishariin, the Aliab for instance were reported to grow no durra in 1910 (Jennings-Bramly 1910-11:11).

Farm land and the question of ownership

Today durra cultivation is practised by members of all Beja groups.[1] The northern Bishariin, the Amar'ar and the northern Hadendowa are mainly restricted for cultivation to the river beds of some seasonal streams such as the Adiib, Oko, Haiyet, Amur and Arab, which are watered by flushes from the Red Sea Hills during the rainy season, July to September (see Maps 6 and 7).

In years of very good rainfall the Hadendowa, and other groups who come as guests, also cultivate the fertile Tibilol and Sinaaib plains. Some Hadendowa and southern Bishariin grow crops on the islands left after the main flooding of Atbara's river-bed. The zones of natural vegetation are shown on the following map.

Further to the south, the Hadendowa used to have access to the Gash. In good years the Gash Dai, an area outside the zone of modern irrigation schemes, still offers some possibilities for Hadendowa and Amar'ar farmers. The vast interior delta of the Gash river was once a reliable source of durra as well as of reserve grazing. The Gash river emanates from the Eritrean highlands, where it is called the Mareb. Once a year, from the beginning of July to the end of September, the river floods, making it possible to cultivate the naturally flooded river banks south of the delta and, by irrigation, areas in the delta itself. The delta was once controlled by other Beja groups such as the Halenga, Segolab and Melitkinab, but during the 19th century the Hadendowa became its owners. During the present century the Hadendowa have gradually lost control over it as it has been turned into an irrigation scheme, first for cotton plantations, then for plantations for castor cultivation (Salih 1976:709).

---

[1] See Fawzy (1978:81) for the Bishariin and Ababda, and Salih (1976:67) for the Hadendowa.

112

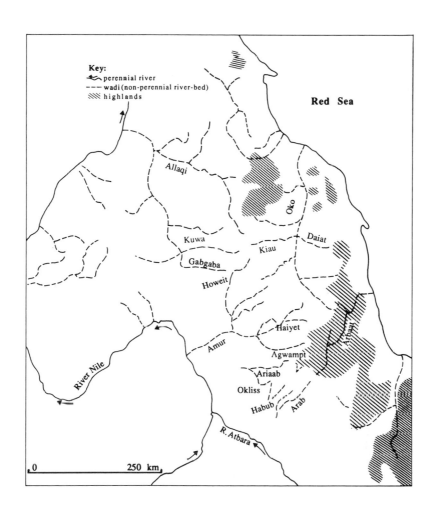

Key:
perennial river
wadi (non-perennial river-bed)
highlands

Red Sea

Allaqi

Oko

Kuwa

Kiau

Daiat

Gabgaba

Howeit

Haiyet

Amur

Agwampt

River Nile

Ariaab

Atbara

Okliss

Habub

Arab

R. Atbara

0   250 km

MAP 6: Catchment areas in Red Sea Province

113

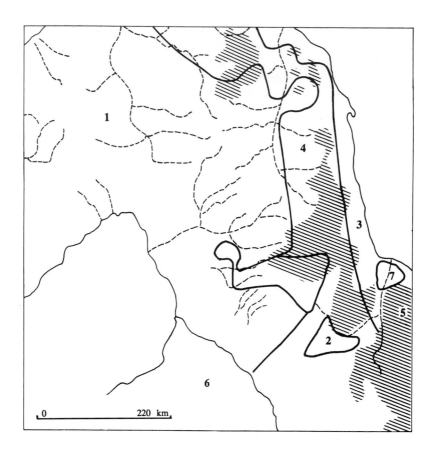

Key:
1. Desert
2. Desert scrub: Sparse woody cover with grass in drainage lines
3. Desert scrub: Medium woody cover (Acacia Tortilis, Maerua Crassifolia) with grassy patches
4. Desert scrub: Sparse woody cover (Acacia Tortilis, Maerua Crassifolia) with trees and some grass in drainage lines and wadi beds
5. Desert scrub: Sparse woody cover (Acacia Mellifera, Commiphora) and some grass in drainage lines and wadi beds
6. Semi-desert grassland on clay
7. Irrigated crops

MAP 7: Natural vegetation in north-eastern Sudan

The valley and delta of the Baraka river are also utilized by some cultivating Beja or semi-Beja groups, mainly of Hadendowa or Beni Amer extraction or — particularly in the valley — coming from a number of small independent groups such as the Ashraf, Arteiga and Shaiab. The source of the river is in Ethiopia. The Baraka delta, where Tokar town is situated, is 240,000 hectares in area. The yearly flood covers up to 80,000 hectares (Kaspar and Moll 1984:107). The delta is used mainly for cotton plantation, but the farmers are allowed to grow *dukhn* (see below) as a windbreak around the cotton fields.

The actual involvement of Beja tenants in everyday cultivation work is today limited. Most of the resident Beja are merchants and herders, and leave cultivation to Beni Amer and West African labourers. The latter are also increasingly establishing themselves as permanent tenants (Salih *op.cit*).

Both at Gash and Tokar the cash crop irrigation schemes have usually taken over the best-watered and most fertile areas, while durra and dukhn have been grown on the "left-overs". However, several authors (e.g. Owen 1936) note that the incentive for cultivating or taking jobs in the schemes has usually been to get access to cheap grain rather than any cash profits from the cotton or castor. As land rights and partnership systems in these schemes are very complicated and have been dealt with elsewhere by other authors, we will in the following concentrate on Beja cultivation as it is practised in the northern khors.

Rights to cultivate in a khor are individually held within the general area of the diwab. They are transmitted by patrilineal inheritance to sons.[1] If a man has both livestock and cultivation plots and several sons, it is common that all the land is given to one of the sons in order to avoid fragmentation. Another solution would be that the brothers take turns to use the farm, one per year, postponing the division until the next generation. Among farmers in the khors around Musmar fragmentation was, however, not seen as a very great problem in 1980. Concern was expressed at the thought of land being transferred out of the diwab. In older times at least, women did not as a rule inherit cultivation plots, because of this risk (Owen 1934; cf. Salih 1980:119, and also the previous chapter).

---

[1] For the rules of land use in Khor Baraka above the delta, see Morton and Fre (1986:84).

Clark (1938:9) wrote about the Bishariin and Amar'ar that women were not allowed to inherit land, but that some religious Amar'ar leaders, versed in the Sharia, had recently started to question this prohibition. It is said that sisters have recently inherited land according to the Sharia Law, and that this explains why, for example, some Bishariin families own land in areas that traditionally belonged to the Musayab Atmaan. On the whole, the right of women to get part of such land is weaker than that of their brothers. In the case that they actually inherit a title to land, they may leave it to their brothers to cultivate against a token of recognition (see for instance Haaland and al Hassan n.d.:19).

The plots are marked out on the ground with stones. People who have customary rights to more land than they can cultivate themselves rent out land, particularly to relatives. Such an arrangement may also be made with an immigrant to the lineage area by a lineage leader acting on behalf of the larger group. It is considered important that in any year all of the cultivable area in the khor is put to use. One big landowner in Khor Amur, for example, had more than 40 such tenants during the 1979 season. The tenant pays according to the size of the plot, measured in throws-of-a-stick parallel to the direction of the khor. Between two and three throws is a normal measure, each plot being thus 40 to 60 metres long. The expression *qole*, stick, is also used as an areal measure, where the width of the khor is disregarded.

A qole is the distance a land-owner can throw his walking stick along the khor. The width of the farm depends upon how much water the khor holds. As the measure cannot be precise, it to some extent reflects the social relations between the tenant and the landlord. A closely related and benevolent landlord may put a stronger effort into his throw than one who is indifferent to his client. Although people always talk about acreage in terms of qole, the measure cannot be used for comparison in the same way as real, quantified acreages, particularly not between khors of varying water amounts.

The payment, gwadabb, is not necessarily based on any actual evaluation of harvests. Most Beja are eager to stress that the amount given is much less important than the formal acknowledgement of respect that it conveys (see Haaland and al Hassan n.d.:19). The gwadabb may be given in the form of goats or the like.

A new notion of land-rights is implied by the Sharia Laws, a fact which in the long run may have far-reaching consequences for the total

116

social organization of the Beja. According to this body of law, land which you have used for 40 years is perpetually yours. There have accordingly been a number of successful cases whereby the tenant has been able to claim his plot by referring to Muslim Law. To this insecurity for land owning groups is added the complications of interpreting the status of government rights to land, a matter which relates to the articulation of Beja practices within a framework acceptable to the Sudanese state and its officials. According to one school of thought, land is owned by the Government and its correct distribution would be through local councils representing the Government. According to another set of ideas the Government only holds the land in trust on behalf of the community, and it is distributed for use by local leaders (see Euro Action Accord 1984:11). To the Atmaan, however, the idea which predominates is of course that there is an inalienable link between a diwab and its territory which no Government can really set aside, and that within that land area individual members of the diwab can have individual rights which they have obtained through inheritance.

The cultivation process

The Beja frequently build earth bunds across the khor beds to retain and redistribute the water when it comes rushing down from the mountains in heavy spates. Gleichen (1905:90) described in 1905 how this was done in Khor Arab near Talgwarab, where the Beja built "a number of horse-shoe shaped dams" over the fields and where he also saw "signs of the main channel having been dammed to divert the water over the flat earthy soil of the valley". The technique is largely unaltered since then. Haaland and al Hassan (n.d.:18), writing about the Hadendowa, describe it in more detail: "Large (often several hundred metres long) bunds are originally constructed by erecting a kind of dense fence made of usher or *tundub* in areas of good clay soil receiving sheetflow. These fences trap sand during the months of almost daily sandstorms before the rains in late July/August. In a short time a water catchment (*kirrab*) of sand is built up along the fence. By renewing and mending the fences large-scale catchments (2-3 metres hight) may build up".

The Euro Action Accord mission of 1984 noted however that "a scientific understanding of water flow appeared to be lacking, with the result that bunds were often built in the wrong places or to the wrong height" (*ibid*:11). The bunds are repaired in the early planting season, in the absence of any firm knowledge about the coming rain. Stern (1985:30) noted in 1985 after the long drought that people seemed to continuously maintain these bunds, and saw it as a sign that the Beja were expecting to take up cultivation at the first opportunity. Haaland and al Hassan (n.d.:19) also observed how the Hadendowa in Derudeb constructed diversion channels (*tarrit*) and dams with the help of branches, windblown sand and sandbags, though with some difficulty, as floods tended to wash these constructions away. Apart from this, no extensive preparation takes place. Sometimes the land is levelled with a wooden beam and clods are broken with a hoe (Milne 1976:108). Dry grass is cut and stored for the animals. Burning is never carried out as part of land preparation.

Sandars (1932), in describing the Amar'ar of 1932, lamented the low level of effort put into the cultivating venture by the Amar'ar by telling us that land was not prepared before sowing: "only clean bits of land are sown and if there is too much rain and grass springs up the sowing is often abandoned". The reason for this, thought Sandars, was partly that there was a shortage of hands, since men were absent with the herds, but also "laziness". Given the uncertainty of the outcome and the costs involved, this behaviour would be better termed "rational". In terms of water quantity and in terms of its areal distribution it is in many places difficult to predict where and with what force water is going to flow in any particular year. Water can be found at three metre's depth below ground in the khor at most seasons in a normal year, but there is only sufficient water for cultivation during three months. There is a chronic shortage of labour; labour must be hired and thus additional costs are involved. A low-investment profile seems well founded against this background of a high-risk undertaking. Improved water expectations for the farmer would alter this whole situation.

Durra is sown in July, making use of the spate in the khor or of the first good rain. One flush spate is enough to provide water for the crop, for the soil usually has a good capacity for retaining water. On rainfed fields, the first good shower starts off an intensive boom in work. The field must be quickly sown so that the crop can be established before the weeds take over. A second fall of rain, or a sudden spate, may wash away the seeds, so that one may have to sow the field

118

again. It is worth investing extra labour to combat weeds rather than loosing a couple of days, and many farmers who could afford to do so employed labourers in 1979.

In the traditional Beja division of labour, it was usually the senior men of the family who were in charge of organizing cultivating activities, as they were the ones to stay put permanently in the *damar* area (home base), while younger men were away herding. Cultivation itself did not entail very hard work, although it involved periods when an intensive amount of labour had to be put into it, and when extra labourers were recruited.

Clark (1938:20) describes how the Amar'ar and Bishariin used to make a sacrifice on the spot before sowing, slaughtering anything from a sheep to a she-camel, depending on the wealth of the farmer. This practice was still followed in 1980, we were told, although we did not see it ourselves. Poverty may put a serious constraint on the practice. The Beja sow with the help of a digging stick, *t'angash* (Ar. *saluka*). One person must go in front to dig out the row of holes and another has to follow planting the seeds, usually several per hole, then covering the holes with soil. The owner of the plot may undertake the digging himself; it is considered "hard work". He will then be followed by any available youngster, woman or child. There are no strict notions of who should and should not do this type of job, or ideas about proper or shameful tasks associated with men or women within the sphere of cultivation.

In chosing the durra type, it is important for the Beja to look for palatability, storing quality, depth of roots and length of the maturation period. It is possible in Aulib to cultivate different types of caudatum such as *shetariit* (or *el'harob*, white durra) and *akar*, which are hardy but comparatively less palatable, open-headed varieties of durra (Bacon 1948:305). Other types of sorghum are *adarharob* (red durra), *shafugan* and *hamash'nait*. Adarharob is preferred to shetariit, which the Beja do not like to eat and are reluctant to buy or grow if there are alternatives. There is also the "local durra", *balat'harob*, which appears to be identical with *himeisi*, Stapf variety.

Dukhn, Pennisetum vulgare, or bulrush millet (*billtub*) is grown after the coastal winter rains in certain places along the coast, such as Hushiri, Arba'at and especially at Tokar. The root system of millet

119

goes much deeper than that of sorghum, and hence it can thrive on sandy soils and withstand a certain degree of salinity.[5]

Depending upon the variety, the maturation of durra takes three to five months. *Shafugan, shetariit, adarharob* and *akar* ripen more quickly, while *hamash'nait* and *himeisi* need a longer time. Cultivators in Khor Amur stated that the first month after sowing is very demanding, as the ground has to be cleared of weeds between two and five times. The first weeding takes place in August, when the durra is between one and two decimetres high. For a field of three hectares, weeding represents six days' work for four or five persons. The most difficult weeds in this period are called *b'ab, sagwedd* and *balbal*.[1] In Musmar, the first weeding is generally sufficient treatment until November or December, when the field must be cleared from a grass called *i'qwajei*, as well as from some other weeds such as *hantut, hamim* and *tambalek* (Eragrostis tenella).

The second weeding is more easy, "almost a pleasure" say the Beja. Because of the importance placed on weeding, our informants told us in 1980, it was usually difficult to find workers in August. When found, they would be paid SL 2.50 per day, plus coffee and food, or paid according to work in line with the *mugawala* system. This is a system where the worker is paid for finishing a certain area. Four to five cultivators would also join in employing a watchman to keep out animals from the field after planting. Such a person would be paid on a monthly basis; 15-20 SL plus coffee and food in 1980.

Our informants were dependent upon the crop they could get, and invested time and money in safeguarding it. In other periods and places it appears, however, that Beja cultivation has been more haphazard, as seen from the quotation from Sandars above, where he stated that weed infestation was a cause for abandonment of fields. Fawzy (1978:53) also writes about the Ababda that they sometimes practice "seed-throwing" in vast wadis, coming back the next season to collect the harvest, but not putting much effort into weeding or guarding the crop against predating camels. In that case, cultivation was clearly subordinated to pastoralism, whereas even before the last devastating

---

[5] "Liking" dukhn rather than durra is frequently mentioned as an ethnic mark of distinction for the diwabs living in dukhn areas. Then it is presented not only as a reflection of ecology, but as a matter of preference. A Beja almost by definition "loves" whatever his home area offers.

[1] We have been unable to identify them.

famine many of the Amar'ar farmers were more or less sedentarized, even if they identified themselves as livestock people.

At the time for harvest, all neighbouring cultivators will agree on a certain day for reaping. The animals are let into the fields on the following day, so the person who is tardy with his harvest risks a loss. All people available are mobilized to cut the durra, which is guarded overnight in the field before being stored. Normally each stalk only gives one cob (*gangar*), but occasionally it may give two or even three. The cobs are threshed in the field by being forcefully beaten with sticks. When we saw this task undertaken, it was carried out by women.

The Officer for Traditional Crops in Port Sudan in 1980, Mr Abdulghadir, gave as a reasonable expectation for yields on rainfed fields 2-2.5 ardeb per *feddan*. But in practice yields are frequently less than "reasonable"; anything from nothing up to the above mentioned level. One man, who mentioned that his qole would yield twenty 90 kg sacks (*jawal*) under favourable conditions, had obtained only six sacks in 1978 and nothing whatsoever in 1979 and 1980. The low yields during this period were primarily blamed on lack of water. In 1986, however, when very good rains reoccurred after the long famine, grasshoppers and locusts (<u>Schistocerca gregaria</u>) consumed large parts of the longed-for and very promising harvest. Such attacks are one of the major threats to the Beja harvest. In this case, it appears that the problems were magnified by the scarcity of grazing animals caused by the drought. This left large parts of the durra stalks uneaten by livestock and welcoming to breeding grasshoppers. Haaland and al Hassan (n.d.:21), having considered the yields they had recorded for some Hadendowa families in Derudeb for 1985-7, come to the conclusion that "it is clear that even in a good year the yields would not be sufficient to satisfy the consumption needs of a family ... it is not possible to maintain a viable household on the basis of cultivation only. Unless the household can find sources of cash income from which grain can be bought it will not be able to survive".

If the Atmaan family should happen to grow more than its yearly need of sorghum, an option would be to sell the surplus, usually within their own area. But it could also be stored. Aulib suffers from few problems with termites, and it is not difficult to locate safe and dry places. Thus the grain can be stored in ground pits (*dayb*). The farmer digs a hole in the ground, some two by two metres in square, and places his durra sacks there. Then he covers the hole with sand and puts a stone marker on top of it to be able to locate it. The holes must be dug where the soil is strong enough for the walls not to collapse. If this is successful the durra can be stored for one to four years, if it is not destroyed by rain. The time that durra can be stored depends upon the variety, but generally it is said that whereas shetariit can be kept for several years, the more palatable types, such as *mugud* and balat'harob, keep less well (Bacon 1948:316). In other words, it is easier to keep those kinds of durra which are less suited for human consumption and better suited as fodder. Therefore, stored durra could ideally be used as a supplementary feed to camels which have been impregnated the year before and need excellent fodder, or to small stock.

The main purpose of Beja durra cultivation is, however, to provide for human household consumption. Cultivation with the explicit purpose of providing fodder for the animals is mainly found in families with a sedentary, "urban" base for their family economy. Nevertheless, even when the purpose is provision of food for people, durra stalks remaining in the fields after harvest do supply the animals with an important additional source of nutrition. Dukhn straw is in contrast valueless as fodder (Harrison 1955:39). The animals may by grazing off the fields in turn add some little benefit through their manuring and warding off pests, as indicated above. The relationship between pastoralism and farming is in this case supplementary rather than competitive.

The local grain trade versus the world market

There are extremely few studies of the structure of the internal grain trade in Sudan, whether in economic terms or in terms of its social organization. For example, the Agricultural Bibliography of Sudan, 1974-83 (A B Zahlan, ed) contains no spcecific reference to the marketing of sorghum. It appears to be a very sensitive issue. The trade is almost entirely in private hands (FAO 1982). In Port Sudan, the trade is dominated by a few international families of traditional traders, some of whom are also big landowners in the Gedaref area and who maintain large storehouses on the outskirts of the city.

Nevertheless, there are at least some Beja traders who specialize in supplying the Beja areas with grain. They sometimes buy from the big merchants, but they also have their own agents who buy grain for them in Gedaref and then transport it by lorry to Port Sudan. Some of them maintain stores in several of the small towns too, and may bring the grain there directly. But much of the grain actually passes through Port Sudan. In 1980 workers in Port Sudan sometimes got the durra ration for their Aulib families in Port Sudan itself. They paid for it there, and then transported it to Aulib by lorries which were frequently owned by the grain traders themselves. The lorries could take 50-80 sacks each time at a cost of SL 2 per sack. Such lorry transports were not very frequent, however. From Port Sudan to Khor Amur there was one roughly every third month, according to local estimates. If there was no motor transport, two sacks of 90 kg each could be loaded on to a camel, together with its rider, and brought back to Aulib in that way. During the drought, durra was available in Port Sudan all the time, albeit at a very high price, but there were few lorry movements from Port Sudan or from Gedaref into the mountain communities, and the camels of course were not enough to compensate for this.

If we disregard the delta Beja, it is only in exceptional years such as 1932 (quoted by Sandars) that some sections are able to provide all of what they need in terms of grain through their own cultivation. The World Food Programme (1985)[1] estimates that in good times the whole province — including the deltas — only meets one third of its cereal needs. It is reasonable to believe that an exchange of pastoral products for grain has been going on for centuries.

Before the introduction of cotton cultivation in the Gash delta, durra was the major crop there, grown for export to Jiddah and to Shendi on the Nile (Burckhardt quoted by Talhami 1975:70). This cultivation went back in time at least to the period of Ibn Hawqal, who noted that Nubians and "Beja" (probably Beja only in the widest sense of the term) were cultivating durra and dukhn there (Kheir 1982:108). We do not know whether the Beja proper also cultivated there, but the delta could certainly have served as a source of traded grain to them as well. To the north, the Beja could trade with the Nile Valley, according to the pattern which Fawzy (1978:60) describes for the present-day Ababda. She notes how they for example sell camels, charcoal, leather-work, drugs and herbs in the valley, obtaining flour,

---

[1] PM Ted Horton to OXFAM 15.12 1985

grain, tea, sugar and clothes from the riverine peoples, and she explains how they take on herding for the Nubians in order to get pastures or grain in exchange. Gleichen (1905) writes in the beginning of this century that in "years of good rainfall, there is considerable amounts of durra cultivated in the Wadis Alagi, Gabgaba and Diib etc, but the Arabs [i.e. the Beja] rely chiefly on Aswan and to a lesser extent on Halaib and Suakin for their grain supply". Jennings-Bramly (1910-11:11) also mentions Abu Hamad as a source of durra for the Aliab Bishariin. According to Sandars (1932) most of the Amar'ar imports of grain came via Port Sudan and Dungunab, "but I think the Gash is also now a buying market", and the Nazir had even arranged for durra to be imported from Umm Ruaba in Kordofan.

During recent decades, much of the durra consumed by the Atmaan and other Beja — as well as by the rest of Sudan's population — has come from the Gezira, and in particular from Gedaref. Gedaref for example exports Fetarita durra (shetariit), which is not very palatable but which stores well (Bacon, 1948:305). Other varieties of durra grown in Gedaref are Akar, also a <u>caudatum</u> type, Deber, Mogod (TuB: *adarharob*; Ar: *hayeri*) and Safra. By becoming dependent upon Gedaref, the Beja have grown economically integrated with the rest of the Sudan and of the world. Their access to durra is no longer just a question of local exchange with cultivating neighbours.

The harvest of Gedaref Fetarita starts in October, and the grain reaches the Port Sudan market in the end of November. "Red durra", which is much preferred to the white Fetarita, is cut in January or February and comes onto the Port Sudan market in March. Durra prices vary with the season. In March 1980 the price was SL 11 per sack, while in November it had reached SL 22. Normally the price remains high until the harvest of the "red durra".

Gedaref is situated south-east of Port Sudan (see Map 1), in an area which borders Ethiopia and which supplies 30 % of the total national production of sorghum (Kassala Province Profile, 1980:30). Sorghum has been grown there since the 1940's by means of intensive mechanized cultivation. This type of farming was introduced to Sudan by the British in order to supply British troops with grain (cf. Osman 1966:346). Gedaref and Gezira were early areas, but mechanized farming later expanded south and west into Darfur and Kordofan. This strong expansion of durra cultivation was first financed (in the period 1954-68) mainly by local private capital, and since 1968 has been

124

financed by IBRD, IDA and by international companies. While the area covered had expanded from the original 33,000 to over six million feddans in 1979 (Ministry of Finance and National Economy 1979-80:22, quoted by Kursani 1984:187), the result of this "resource mining" was in several cases severe exhaustion of the land and declining yields (*ibid*:192f). Mechanized cultivation has furthermore contributed to a loss of vegetation cover and forests, with possible secondary effects on the rainfall on which the Beja are dependant.

Certain features of mechanized cultivation, such as the necessary capital investment and the requirement for agricultural credit, promotes in Kursani's terms "the formation of a group of 'financiers' who monopolize most of the rainfed schemes and who manipulate both production and marketing of the produce" (ibid:189). These schemes belong to the class of "new men" — advocates, traders, civil servants, military officers, etc (*ibid*:191).

Export of durra is not a new phenomenon. Kursani (1984:194) quotes figures of 45,000 tonnes of sorghum export yearly in the 1930's and 10,205 tonnes in 1951. In the period 1970-74 Sudan had to import grain at an annual average of 107,000 tonnes, despite the expansion of mechanized cultivation. However, in 1975-78 99,000 tonnes were exported yearly, and in 1979-83 this average had risen to 299,000 tonnes, with no corresponding rise in the amount produced (Awad 1984:37). The FAO country report of 1982 concluded that "there is no general official policy governing such trade or the pricing structure other than the identification of surpluses or deficits of staple foods over domestic requirements ... Licenses from the Ministry of Commerce are fairly easy to obtain" (*ibid*:67).

Apart from the legal, licensed exports, a substantial amount of smuggling took place in the years preceeding the famine, both to Saudi Arabia and to Ethiopia (see FAO 1982). The consequences of this export were clearly perceived by the Beja. In 1980, many people in Musmar and Port Sudan complained that there were new difficulties in obtaining durra, and related these problems both to smuggling and to Government policy. In mid-November 1980 the price had gone up to SL 22 per bag. The relationship between local scarcity and smuggling is also suggested by the FAO report. The Beja were of the opinion that much of the durra that was exported ended up as animal fodder for Jiddahn stock-owners — with some resentment, for "here we want the durra and like to eat it; we only it give to the animals when there is no

125

grass; in Saudi it is just the opposite". Beja politicians raised the issue of rising sorghum prices in the parliament, complaining particularly over the outflow of durra from the country. The price was thereafter regulated to SL 10 per sack, a decision which however did not immediately penetrate into the trading centres of the Red Sea Hills. The durra price was to a great extent the yard-stick used when Beja outside the political elite were measuring the efficiency of Nimeiry's government. At the time of the FAO mission, the legal export of sorghum was restricted, but there was little the government could do about the smuggling. Prices remained high both in the neighbouring countries in and Sudan.[1]

One would perhaps have assumed that the extension of durra farming in Sudan generally would have made it easier for the Beja to get access to this good. However, this proved not to be the case in the early 1980's. During the years just prior to the famine, durra exports boomed, as we have just indicated. Thus we have a tragic example of how the attachment of a local group to an international trading system can be very detrimental. The Beja have had too little economic and political power to control the key decisions made about durra production and trade. The production apparatus, although geographically, and maybe even socially, close, has not been geared towards meeting any local basic needs. Durra has been available in towns but at high prices,[2] a fact which allows for stratified access, in reality no access to food for poor people.

---

[1] The smuggling "to Ethiopia" is perhaps to be seen as a continuation of an old tradition of grain sales from Kassala to Eritrea which caused concern to the British in the 1940s. See e.g. Kassala Province Monthly Diary January 1940 or Kassala Province Annual Report 1957.

[2] "Agricultural Prices in Sudan" has a table showing the durra price at Gedaref, deflated with the help of the consumer price index for the Three Towns (Khartoum, Khartoum North and Omdurman). This shows that in fact, at least relating to urban consumption, the durra price of 1980 was the worst since 1969, and that it then increased continuously during the drought period. For the years 1980-83 the relative figures are 136, 147, 226 and 285 % of the price of January 1970.

7

Family herds

The pastoralism of the northern Beja groups is mainly based on a combination of sheep and goat rearing with the rearing of camels. Cattle are only kept by certain Hadendowa groups. In this chapter, we will be concerned with the Atmaan practices of camel and small stock rearing, as they were described to us as having been before the big drought.

The Atmaan once used to be wealthy in camels. In the 1940's they were struck by a very serious drought which forced many Atmaan families to supplement their pastoral incomes with earnings from dock labour. Since then, the camel herds have never really recovered; yet in 1980, there were still many Atmaan who indeed supported themselves from camels, and the camels were very central to their notions of Beja identity. In the last drought, the camels also suffered severely, and it is an open question to what extent the herds can ever recover. The aid agencies operating during the drought appear generally to have assumed that camels were marginal to Beja subsistence (see for example Foster 1987).

The camel in local life

The Atmaan use their camels to produce subsistence food, and as a form of wealth which can be transported. Camel milk and durra form the basis of a household's diet. The camel has a distinct advantage, compared to cattle or fields, in that it provides food throughout the year. The quantity of milk depends on the breed, the quality of the pasture and the age and stage in the reproductive cycle. The yield is generally higher than that from cattle under comparable conditions. The Beja also utilize meat, skins and fat from the camels when these are made available through the slaughter of excess male calves or fairly old females. Any immediate need for meat is usually met by the slaughter of a sheep or a goat. Camel meat is not a preferred food, but when it becomes available it is readily eaten. Certain parts of the carcass may be stored in the form of fat and dried strips of meat. The camel hide is less important for household use, except as raw material for sandals and whips, but is usually sold. The wool is not used.

Many Beja claim that selling camels is improper. Nevertheless, there are many who do so in order to meet monetary expenses, which include the purchase of food items and consumer goods, payment of bridewealth and other transactions which may be made in cash as well as in livestock. In Musmar the price of a good riding camel is at least 500 LS. A top quality milking female will cost 400 LS; an immature female up to 200 LS and a female calf between 1.5 and two years of age at least 100 LS. Prices in the Port Sudan area are higher. These prices relate to the pre-drought situation in the early 1980's.

Many animals are taken away from the area to larger markets inside Sudan, in Egypt or in Saudi Arabia. The Sudanese markets are in Atbara, New Halfa and Ed Damer, from whence the camels are brought to Omdurman. Most of the demand in these markets is for good loading animals. Saudi Arabia buys riding animals and transporters, while the Egyptian market takes slaughter animals, female breeders and transporters. Beja traders drive herds of 50-150 animals in a 15 day day-and-night trek through the Nubian desert, preferably during the winter time, when the demand in Egypt is at its highest and the journey is least arduous. The camels are then sold at Daraw, Aswan, Esna or even in Cairo. Such traders should be formally licensed but a good deal of smuggling and black-marketing of currencies takes places at the boundary. The Rashaida Arabs are also heavily involved in camel exporting and handle much of the Saudi Arabian trade.

According to local opinion, the Beja trade in export camels has declined. There were small price differences between Egypt and Sudan in the early 1980's compared to fifteen years earlier. There is also severe competition from camel traders coming from the west of Sudan and using the traditional "forty day route" to Egypt.

The Atmaan differentiate between three categories of camels, *shallageea, aririit*, and *matiaat*. The shallageea are the sturdiest and are the best milk producers. The aririit are also fair milk producers but their main advantage is their endurance as transport animals; they can cover long distances at a steady pace without water. The matiaat are the most slender of the Atmaan camels and by far the fastest, although they tire quickly. They give comparatively little milk but are easier to manage than camels of the other categories.

The basis for the development of three different types of Atmaan camel lies more in differences in the feeding of the young camels than in any genetic differences. Different pastures used for feeding the young camels have different nutritional qualities. Selective breeding is not practised; in fact, inter-breeding occurs frequently. There may be a difference in physical appearance between matiaat and the other types. Both aririit and matiaat camel calves are said to develop into shallageea if they are brought to the coast and reared there from an early age. Three other local categories of camels, these perhaps being nearer to breed status, should be mentioned. Those of the Bishariin Beja (to the north) are better riding and transport animals than any of the Atmaan types. The Rashaida Arabs (to the south-east) have two different breeds, one being a better milk producer than any of the others, and one, the Anafi, being a renowned trotter. The economy of these two tribal groups is more clearly commercial than that of the Atmaan (cf. Dyson-Hudson, 1972).

The Atmaan camel, of whatever type, is a multi-purpose animal. An owner herding about a hundred female camels needs no more than one sire, which is selected on a basis of size, build, and his dam's milk record. A strong body and a slender "waist" are believed to indicate speed. The importance of hardiness, milk production and mobility accounts for the limited interest shown by the Atmaan in cross-breeding with for example the Rashaida camel, which is very productive but whose milk is said to be less palatable, and which above all is not a swift mover.

Occasionally, the owner of a female camel chooses a sire on the basis of the latter's running capacity. Thus he may contact the owner of a *kiliwau* camel, a breed originating from the Bishariin. Sometimes human assistance may be needed for copulation to be achieved, but generally the camels are left to manage mating by themselves. The male camel may be removed from the herd when the owner does not consider the season suitable from the point of view of the health of the animals, or when lactation, which is said to come to an end on the twelfth day after a successful mating, is required to continue.

The majority of male camels are either slaughtered as young calves for immediate consumption or are sold. Of the remainder, which are not castrated, some are maintained for pack and riding purposes and as sires. The loading capacity varies considerably between different breeds and types of camel. A standard load, however, is claimed to be two sacks of durra and a driver, making a total of about 250 kg for a walking baggage camel. A trotter carries less weight. The speed when trotting is approximately 12 km per hour. A five-hour trek is then possible for some five consecutive days (after which the animal should have a two-week complete rest).

Skill in camel riding is a highly valued masculine virtue in Beja culture, in contrast with that of the Cushitic herdsmen further south in the Horn of Africa, who do not ride their animals. The dexterity of the Beja rider and the high prestige value of the skill is demonstrated in camel racing. An Atmaan rider should be able to meet the proverbial test of riding standing upright with a bowl full of milk without spilling a drop while riding at a high speed. He should also be able to ride with a live camel fly held between his knee and the camel, without either killing the insect or allowing it to escape.

Although the Beja's role in long-distance trade has dwindled with the advance of transport technology, the camel still has an important part to play in shorter range travel. Pack camels are used to transport the purchases of grain. Camels are also important in carrying tents and household equipment when the household is on the move. Since the drought, they have become important assets for those who marketed firewood and charcoal.

Camel rearing is highly significant in the ethos of Atmaan society, and camel herding has a strong emotional appeal. *Mish'ariib*, those who tend the camels, are often young unmarried men who live a wild, independent, adventurous life. Their fathers, by their propriety control of the camel herds, tend to exercise a strict authority over their sons long after they have grown up.

To the Atmaan, camel life has a romantic glamour; the men are said to become strong, virile and attractive to women from their diet, which consists primarily of camel's milk. It is the right and duty of the oldest son to become a mish'ariib. When family labour is not available, a mish'ariib can be hired at the cost of one young male camel per annum (or the equivalent in sheep). Alternatively, the entire household may follow the family camel herd if other activities such as farming or small-stock rearing do not demand their attention. But camel tending is usually the responsibility of men. Women, by tradition, have a certain limited role to fulfil in the care of small stock whose needs they tend to in the morning before grazing begins, when they check the state of health of the animals. Occasionally, if no boys are available, the women may herd the small stock, but they do not milk sheep or goats and they take no part in the care of camels. Their domain is the home.

The nomadic home is the base of livestock herding. Only a few milch camels are kept in the vicinity of the settlement to cater for the daily needs of household members. If pasture is scarce the camels may be kept far away, distances being governed by the watering needs of the different species. Donkeys are used to carry household water, but one or two baggage camels are usually kept near to the camp to assist with transport requirements. All Atmaan recognize *i'damar*, the permanent home place where women, small children and old men dwell permanently when climatic conditions permit. It is the young and strong men who move with the camels.

Camel ownership is a male prerogative. As with many African pastoralists, an Atmaan man obtains stock from his parents by two processes. The first involves significant ante-mortem gifts, and the second inheritance according to Muslim law. The former benefits mainly or exclusively sons, and by the second (which probably is quantitatively less important) sons get a double share compared to their

131

sisters. Although women may nowadays get some formal title to stock, whenever Muslim law is followed rather than indigenous Beja traditions, they rarely get the practical control over the animals, but have to cede this to a male relative. This point relates primarily to large stock; small stock are more easily accessible for women. Young men are urged into early marriage by their fathers, who will contribute to the new conjugal herd in terms of small stock but who retain authority over the sons and over the camels that they have named for the sons. In this way the fathers maintain their authority until they die or retreat into senility. After the father's death all brothers ideally get a share in all kinds of stock, but if there are very few camels the older brother will act as a trustee for his younger brothers' animals.

The camel population

According to local opinion, the camel population was on the decline even before the last famine. The trend was rather towards small-stock keeping. It is difficult, however, to find a sound basis for accurate quantitative statements about such a trend or about the characteristics of the "area herd" of the Atmaan, that is all the camels to be found in the territory. There is a great scarcity of data on which to base research into all aspects of camel keeping among the Atmaan. A few rough censuses have been made in annual provincial reports, using simple extrapolating methods from "guesstimates" without compensating in the projections for climatic fluctuations and associated variations in mortality. For instance, a 1984 publication figure for the total number of camels in Red Sea Province is 70,000 (Kaspar and Moll 1984:107). In a 1985 publication, the figure given is 112,000 (General Statistics issued by the Regional Ministry of Finance and Economy, Eastern Region, Kassala, 1985, and quoted by Ahmed 1988:63). Bakhit (1988:148) claims that 95% of all livestock died in 1984.

Much of our discussion refers to the pre-1984 period. The least unreliable census of livestock in the Red Sea area seems to be an aerial count carried out in December 1975 (Sudan Veterinary Research Administration, 1977). This report identifies a few vegetation zones on which stock counts are based. However, the report neither provides any information on age structures in the area herd nor introduces data sufficiently detailed to make it worthwhile trying to separate the

132

Atmaan area from the entire Red Sea Province. The total number of camels in the Red Sea Province was around 100,000, according to the census. About half of this number was found on the coast or in the mountain area (*ibid*). Such a concentration is logical, given the fact that the winter rains were due on the coast at the time of the survey. This concentration is reflected in a high relative density of animals, 1.85 per square km. The vast inland area held about 20 per cent of the area camel herd, scattered at a density of about one-tenth of that of the coast. The animals kept in Aulib at the time of the survey were most likely being held in waiting for the summer rains as an alternative to trekking to the coast. High concentrations of camels were also observed in the Gash and Tokar (Baraka) deltas where another 20 per cent of the area herd was found.

If macro-data are difficult to get, micro-level herd "demography" puts us on no firmer ground. The above-mentioned report, referring to the clusters of camels that could be identified from the air, provides "mean group sizes". But while animals in a family herd certainly are kept together for herding purposes, one may wonder if the groups distinguished from the aeroplane really were complete family herds, or if they were animals from several families. With the sole exception of the Tokar delta, which held camel herds averaging 12.5 animals, the average herd size varied between 3 and 5.5 head. The value of this figure as an indication of size of houschold property is debatable. Firstly, camels do not keep together when browsing. And even if it is possible to identify a family herd, any herd may contain animals trusted to the herdsmen as well as property in the more narrow sense.

There were considerable obstacles to obtaining information on the sizes or age structures of family herds. Any interest from outsiders in numbers or ages of this sort raises suspicions. Every herd owner tries to keep secret his real wealth, having several good reasons for this. The Muslim charity to the pious and poor is regulated according to individual wealth; the exemption of the Atmaan from secular taxes is an insecure privilege that may be removed at any moment. Furthermore, the very right to individual animals is often an issue which could be debated. People who need to leave pastoralism temporarily for other ways of making a living may leave their remaining animals in the care of others. Time goes by, the migrant never returns but his camels and their offspring remain. The herdsman gradually starts to regard these animals as his own property, hoping that the former owner or his heirs have forgotten the whole issue. The more time that passes and the less talk there is about the background of these animals, the stronger will his claims to these animals be. Hence, there is a common understanding that the origins of individual camels should never be discussed, except on the occasion of negotiating an inheritance among heirs.

Three patterns of camel pastoralism

Aririit camel pastoralism in Aulib

The vast plateau area to the west of the Red Sea Hills is only sparsely covered with vegetation. Common trees on which camels browse are *sanganeeb* (Acacia tortilis) and *kitr* (Acacia mellifera). Among the shrubs attractive to camels one finds *singidd* (Indigofera spinosa) and *gefareeb* (Salsola baryosma). Grasses also provide the Aulib camels with fodder, notably the tall perennial *shuush* (Panicum turgidum), which can also be used for fodder when dried. Only if the rains fail completely for two consecutive years does it become grey and useless. Many annual grasses are excellent for camels but disappear comparatively quickly after the rains. Grasses like shuush are easy for the camels to graze, while they have difficulties with short grasses.

Aulib is suitable for camel and small stock rearing but not for cattle. Animals and people need to be dispersed over large areas. One seldom finds clusters of houses. Normally, each family lives by itself, but within walking distance (3 - 5 km) from a neighbour. This pattern was documented in the aerial survey (Sudan Veterinary Research Administration, 1977). It suggests an average of 0.18 nomadic houses per square km. The same report suggests a human population in Aulib of around 42,000, about equally divided between nomadic and sedentary settlements.[1]

In Aulib one can distinguish between two herding strategies. The first is to remain on the plateau, preferably fairly close to i'daamar, moving some 5-6 km daily or weekly in different directions. The second strategy is to carry out a few long-distance treks to new pastures. This is often done in groups where relatives help each other,

---

[1]For an evaluation of more recent population figures, and a discussion of the problems involved in comparing them with earlier figures, see Morton and Fre (1986:7-12). Allowing for the unreliability of the sources, Morton and Fre compare 1932, 1956 and 1983 figures for certain nomadic groups, and find that the figures suggest the possibility of a high rate of natural increase over the last fifty years.

with daily shorter movements for pasture at stopping points. Thus neighbours (kinsmen) cooperate and enjoy each others' company, agreeing daily on where to make the afternoon stop of the next day.

The hardy aririit camels are found in Aulib. After a successful rainy season (July to September), when the autumn pastures are fresh and good, the aririit can go 5-8 days without watering. Under very dry conditions they can be without water only for 2-3 days. On hot days one camel drinks 60-80 litres. A very large animal may take up to 100 litres. In the winter (November to January), when the weather is cool and dry, the aririit are usually watered every 5-8 days, but are in fact capable of going up to one month without watering if necessary. This is the best period of the year, when the animals give much milk. If proper pasture can be found, herdsmen claim that this period can be extended up to six months. Well-kept aririit give 2.5-5 kg milk at the midday and evening milking, and 3.5-5 kg in the morning. The volume of milk production depends heavily on the quality of pastures. Due to the seasonality of camel mating and the quality of pasture, access to milk may become difficult just before the rains, particularly when normal reproduction has been upset by a long drought, so that the competition between calves and people for milk becomes acute.

Availability of pasture rather than access to water decides the migration patterns for the Aulib camel herds. They move irregularly across Aulib in search of the little fodder available. If it rains in a locality for some three consecutive days, there will be a scramble for the anticipated grazing. Years with good rains see a gravitation of livestock toward the western slopes of the Red Sea Hills, where the potential for high quality grazing is best. During such years Aulib herds even penetrate down towards the Gunob strip without too much of an effort, and get a much-needed salt treat. The 'adlib bush (Suaeda fruticosa Forsk.), growing along the coast, offers salty pasture all the year around. Other plants, relying on rainfall, are not as salty and supplement the 'adlib browsing during the rainy season.

A slightly modified seasonal migration pattern exists north of the Red Sea Hills. Here, on the Atbai, camels are in a better position to browse their way to the coastal strip. Hence a pattern of transhumance emerges. The Atbai herdsmen are annually able to spend a couple of months browsing on 'adlib at the coast, as a salt treat for their camels. Some northern Atmaan people regularly inhabit the Atbai plains, which are otherwise dominated by the Bishariin.

135

Matiaat camel pastoralism in the khors

The khors and the mountain areas surrounding them present a special case of camel pastoralism. Here we find *matiaat* or *ti' hibqualda* camels which feed almost solely on the *hiib* tree (<u>Salvadora persica</u>; see for example Clark 1938:25). The Arab word for hiib, used frequently in conversation, is *araak*. These camels are so adapted to this rather unusual diet that they prefer this pasture for most of the year; only during the rainy months do they change diet. The matiaat dominate the khors because other camels do not eat hiib except in emergency. Both the aririit and shallageea (see below) can be fed hiib in critical times, but they react initially with diarrhea and refuse it until hunger forces them to eat it.

The matiaat live in the khors for most of the year. They do not migrate such vast distances as the aririit do. During the extremely hot and dry days they move up into the mountains to find water ponds, hiib trees and cool air. No herdsmen follow them during such days.

The major areas for matiaat are all in the Sinkat-Gebeit-Erba-Kamob Sanha area, as well as the remainder of Khor Amur, all of Khor Asot and the upper part of Khor Arba'at (Map 6). Hiib is also found in some small khors on the eastern side of the Red Sea Hills.

The matiaat become very thirsty from browsing on hiib and require daily watering for most of the year. One animal consumes typically 30 litres per watering during cold days and at least double that amount twice a day during the hot months. They give considerably less milk than aririit camels, typically only 1-2 kg at the midday milking.

If matiaat were to feed all year around on hiib they would develop chronic diarrhea and eventually die. During the rainy season most matiaat are therefore herded outside the hiib khors to feed on fresh grass pastures. Matiaat reproduction, like that of aririit, is geared to the rains, and mating as well as births occur in the July-September period. They are often taken to the Khor Arab area during these months.

Unlike other camels, matiaat are hardly ever sold on the market. It is difficult to move them the distances to any markets, and so there is little export demand for them. They are maintained in small numbers, usually between three and five animals per household. These households keep matiaat as a supplement to farming or small stock rearing. This shift in emphasis reflects a shift in priorities of risk-taking with employed herdsmen. During the rainy season a number of households cooperate in employing a man to take the animals to the pasture. Since this is a busy time for farming the matiaat owners are themselves too occupied with their farms to be able to move with the animals.

Many people in Khor Amor keep small stock flocks, mainly of goats, of 10-20 head per household. They are kept primarily to provide meat and milk for the household and are sold only occasionally. The goats feed on shuush and give 1-1.5 kg of good milk at morning and evening milking. Goats' hair also plays an important part in the household economy, providing material for the production of mats for bedding and the inner walls of the nomadic hut. The sheep are difficult to manage since they do not browse like goats and do not feed well on shuush Panicum turgidum). They give less than 1 kg of milk per day.

Shallageea camel pastoralism on the coast

The shallageea (coast) camels are adapted to the feed available on the coastal strip. They browse on the salty 'adlib (Suaeda fruticosa) (both the 'adlib variety and the similar but smaller *hadmal*), supplemented with the leaves and fruits of mangrove (*sha'warab*), which are also an emergency food for human beings. During the Mahdiia, when the region suffered from severe starvation, the survival of the coastal people was due to the fruits. The shallageea are very skilful at walking into the sea and nipping the lemon-like fruits from the mangrove stands. They learn where it is possible to walk on the sea bottom well enough to do it during the day and also at night. Frequently they wade so deeply that only the head and hump are visible above water. Mangrove trees are found along the entire Red Sea coast of Sudan.

The human population of the coast outside the towns reckoned from the December 1975 aerial survey was about 45,000, but the drought disaster of the early 1980s may have rendered this figure totally out of date. Statistics show an urban growth of 2.1% in the wake of that disaster (Bakhit 1988:150). We may, however, safely conclude that the density of the permanent and nomadic housing was much higher here than in Aulib, around one house per square km in the pre-drought situation.

The shallageea are larger than the aririit and the matiaat. They are herded on the coast at least six months of the year (December-May). If there is rain in Aulib, most shallageea will be taken to the western side of the hills for some months, and if it rains on Atbai to the north the

137

pasture there will be utilized as well. The shallageea herdsmen claim that their camels can feed well even on hiib and that the health status of their camels is so good that they never overeat on any fodder (in contrast to both matiaat and aririit). The reason given by mish'arib for the good health of the shallageea is their 'adlib diet. The urine of the shallageea is a traditional medicine and people come from as far away as Somalia to obtain it.

When on the coast the shallageea require watering daily or possibly every other day. This is due to the salty browsing, which causes them to urinate greatly. They drink 80 to 100 litres at each watering. In the Baraka delta, where the shallageea rely solely on 'adlib, the animals drink by night and browse during daytime. Their herdsmen build large mud containers next to the water holes for watering the animals. The containers are called *o'ser* in Tubedawiye and *girba* in Arabic. They are used by all Sudanese camel herders.

Apart from watering, the tasks of the mish'arib on the coast are limited to morning and evening chores and midday milking. During the day the camels are allowed to wander, a few leader camels having their forelegs tied together. This makes the entire herd less mobile and consequently easy to locate.

The shallageea herds are the only ones that the Atmaan systematically divide into dry and milking herds. Very few males are kept. One of our informants maintained only one bull to 150 females. By night, or when the herd is stationary for any particular reason, only the males are tied; this is enough to ensure that the females will not stray.

The shallageea are very good milkers, especially during the three one-month periods, roughly November, March and July, when the 'adlib is in fruit. At the early night milking one camel may give up to 6 kg. Three hours later it may give another 3.5 kg. The morning milk could then amount to between 6 and 7 kg. These figures, provided by the shallageea mish'ariib, represent an average good but not exceptional milk production for human consumption. The animals may be milked more frequently, and herdsmen claim that good camels give 3.5 kg each milking if milked at two-hour intervals during the day. With three milkings per day, which is a common practice, each animal gives a daily yield of 15-18 kg. During good rains and with excellent pasture on the Aulib side, each of the three milkings may provide some 6 or 7 kg. One wealthy camel trader was of the opinion that he had achieved the maximum milk production possible from shallageea. His few females were feeding on good quality cattle fodder purchased in Port Sudan and were yielding 22 kg per day with three milkings. He claimed that higher production could only be obtained from Rashaida camels.

Given such high yields and sustained production, two milking females can provide for a coastal family of man, wife and six children living near Port Sudan, the milk of one shallageea being kept for subsistence and that from the other being sold.

The shallageea have a different breeding season from the matiaat and aririit; they breed on the coast during the monsoon winter rains in November-December when the weather is cool and good pastures are available. If a mish'arib considers the condition of his animals too poor for breeding he simply keeps his males away from the family herd. However, this is only an extra preventive measure, since males are not normally interested in covering females when they are starving.

Those who specialize in providing the town market with milk products frequently themselves live in Port Sudan and employ salaried herdsmen, sometimes on a cooperative basis, as one herdsman can manage 60 to 70 head. When browsing becomes scarce the town shallageea are given about two kg of durra in the evening in order to maintain the supply. Town camels receive many kinds of waste materials, including *mushuk*, the date residue from wine production. There are mixed feelings about the appropriateness of keeping camels in town. To keep riding camels, however, can never be inappropriate, and many of the Atmaan tolerate the trouble and expense of having an animal tied outside the dwelling in order to satisfy leisure needs rather than to solve transportation problems.

Small stock herding

The *yategaab* shepherd, herding flocks of sheep (*t'anna*) and goats (*tonai*), earns his livelihood in an alternative to the mish'arib way. It is in theory an option open to those who will never be able to afford to build up a camel herd. Most yategaab families, however, have been herding small stock for many generations. Their livelihood is more vulnerable to drought than that of the mish'arib, a fact that could already be clearly seen in late 1980. At that time the summer rains had failed completely in most of the Aulib, and those of the preceeding

139

year had been insufficient. By November much grazing was practically finished in large areas. Camel herds were hard up but no really acute problems had developed, while small stock were generally in a very poor condition. As a result, market prices, both locally and in the big markets such as the *dekholia* outside Port Sudan, went down to such a low level that most yategaab felt it meaningless to make the effort of bringing animals to the local markets at all. And when the winter rains began in Gunob and Atbai, the Aulib flocks were generally too weak to make the journey. The only hope for many yategaab was that the animals would survive until the following rains, hoping that these would materialize. If not, it would mean total collapse for their small stock rearing, people said.

In the meantime, all yategaab who had the chance travelled to Port Sudan, Atbara or other smaller centres to seek temporary employment, in order to relieve the family household of the burden of supporting a consumer and in order to earn cash income until the rains returned. In the subsequent drought, the fears expressed were generally realised, even though it does not appear that the reproductive core was completely wiped out. Morton and Fre (1986:57) quote figures from Hazerjian (1986) showing that after the drought 80% of the rural population had at least one sheep or goat left, the average herd size being 4.3 sheep and/or goats. They also mention that (unspecified) interviews indicated that the average rural family in Red Sea Province had had 40 goats and 20 sheep before the drought.

The problems facing Babeker Ali illustrate the kinds of difficulties experienced by many herders. We met him in Ariaab in November 1980. He is a yategaab, and at that time was aged around 50. His family is very large; there were in 1980 about one dozen children, and one of his two married sons also lived with his household. Both married sons were yategaab just like their father, and they had been given enough small stock to establish independent households if they wished to do so. Babeker was extremely anxious that his children should marry as quickly as possible in order to make the family as large as could be. His arguments for this desire were twofold: primarily, that many people were needed for defence purposes in case he or a family member were to become involved in a conflict, and secondarily, that a large work force was a great asset for shepherding, granted that the flocks grew as they should. He had gone to great pains to provide his married sons with enough small stock at marriage. On the latest

140

occasion, the original family herd became unviable, and Babeker spent over one year involved in long distance trade in sheep to the dekholia outside Port Sudan in order to raise enough money to purchase additional small stock. When asked if it would not have been better for his son to wait that year until Babeker had achieved enough small stock, he refused such a suggestion with reference to the general importance of the fact that his children should reproduce as quickly as possible.

Most inhabitants of Ariaab are yategaab. They seldom see the Ariaab mish'arib at this time of the year, since their aririit camels are capable of moving long distances and go without watering for seven to ten days at this time of the year. The smallest Ariaab yategaab household needs a minimum of 20-30 good goats and sheep to have anywhere near a viable family flock.

Babeker was not the only one to help his son attain a viable family flock. In contrast to the practice among camel herders, it is common among yategaab families that close kinsmen such as brothers-in-law and a mother-in-law contribute, when capable, towards making a domestic flock big enough. Kinsmen of this distance or closer give *halagen* in the form of small stock on the occasion of marriage. This is done instead of giving cash, and possibly because each animal represents a smaller value than does one camel. When Babeker's oldest son Aden married he and his wife were given 15 goats and sheep by Babeker, five by Babeker's brother, three by Aden's mother, five by his future father-in-law and one each by his wife's-to-be's brother and one of her father's brothers. Almost all the animals were goats.

During less difficult years, Babeker Ali grew durra on a farm five by five qole in size. It provided the bulk of his household's grain consumption. The remainder was purchased from Musmar. Two or three times per year he made the three-day journey, bringing some two to five fat sheep each time to sell at the local market. The money earned was used for durra, but also for coffee and sugar.

In Ariaab there were very few examples of a mixed husbandry of small stock and camels in substantial numbers; most people were either mish'arib or yategaab. Babeker knew of very few cases where a yategaab had become a mish'arib, for how should he ever be able to accumulate the capital needed to buy some ten camels? Those who have tried have sooner or later been forced by dry years to sell off their few camels before they had built up a viable herd; the alternative would

141

have been to deplete the domestic flocks of goats and sheep so heavily that they lost their long-term viability. However, it is possible for a yategaab to combine their shepherding with farming during the summer months, according to Babeker. The harvests are good those years when the rain comes, and stores last for several years.

By the end of 1980 Babeker's household had consumed practically all the durra stored. The summer of 1980 gave absolutely no harvest, and the harvest of 1979 had been quite small. And since the 1980 rains failed, there was very little pasture remaining in the Ariaab area. All Babeker's animals were very thin and weak. He had decided earlier to remain, since water never posed a problem; the wells of the Nazir had never dried up. By 1980 he no longer had a choice, since his flocks were in no condition to do any long-distance trekking. When we discussed the prospects of the months to come, before the next rainy season, Babeker almost started crying; his animals, including now some 50 mature ones, were already then weak, and scores of them, if not all, would starve to death before the rains came. And all his wealth was in his goat and sheep flocks, which used to consist of 250-300 head. Had they only been in good health he would have sold them and purchased camels and employed a mish'arib to teach him camel rearing. This would not have been a viable solution for his household, but at least he would have kept some productive capacity intact. At the time of the interview he faced the prospect of losing everything. But God gave him the animals and God takes them away; what could he do? This was Babeker's way of closing the discussion about the future.

Shepherding: production and vulnerability

Throughout the Atmaan area one finds only one breed of sheep and one of goats. They are both local varieties. In the south, a smaller kind of goat is found as well, the Beni Amer goats. These originate from Eritrea. Milk production from goats and sheep is quantitatively of the same magnitude, but the composition is different. Only occasionally are goats reported to produce more milk than sheep. The less fat goats' milk is considered particularly suitable for small children, since its nutritional composition resembles that of human milk. As for meat, mutton is much preferred by the Atmaan to goat meat.

Small stock are usually bred according to how rainy seasons occur, so that the bulk of births takes place when there is fresh grass. The normal method to regulate births practiced by the yategaab is to tie a string from the male's penis to its pouch, loose enough to allow the animal to urinate and tight enough to prevent any sexual excitement. About five or four months before the anticipated rains the strings are removed from the rams and the bucks. If the owner expects the rains to fail or considers his animals too weak for breeding, he simply leaves the string in place. In the case of the Aulib this means that normally the string is tied only during *tubahala*, the bad period lasting from November to March. The Gunob practice is similar to that of Aulib but the tying is done during a period about three months later.

Milking animals are allowed one teat only for their young. The other teat is for human consumption and either it is simply tied with a string or, less painful for the female, a stick is tied along it so that a lamb or kid trying to suckle that teat only gets the stick into its mouth. Sometimes the mother has to be prevented from suckling her own milk intended for her offspring; this is done by use of a metal collar around her neck. Milk production for human consumption varies between 0.5 *rattel* (one rattel is approx. 0.45 kg) and 3 rattel, depending primarily on pasture quality. Medium quality goats and sheep under normal conditions give 1 to 2 rattel per day. Females which give below one rattel are seen as low-producers and are likely to be slaughtered later when their young have grown up. The milk production may begin in July for goats and August for sheep if they breed immediately after tubahala. August, September and October are the best months for milk in Aulib. Most sheep milk production is concentrated in these months. Goats give milk slightly earlier, in July. During good years they might breed again towards the end of the *tuhoobi* (rainy) period. Goats give milk for about four months, while sheep dry up after about three months. Variations are considerable in individual cases, due primarily to the quality of pasture. In November 1980, when grazing and browsing were of extremely poor quality in Ariaab, a large flock of some 150 head, which we might consider typical, had only five or six kids and lambs which, furthermore, would most likely die, since their mothers were unable to produce sufficient milk. The extremely low number of young was due to the fact that the yategaab had considered the health status of the flocks so poor that they had prevented most from breeding. Even this precaution thus proved to be insufficient.

The sheep and goats are normally kept until they have given birth

143

six times. After that the management differs between various yategaab; some practice selective breeding and keep good milkers only, others keep almost all females even after yields go down, since managing them causes very little extra labour input. Yet others make it a principle to get rid of all over-aged animals. Strategies vary not only with degree of specialization, however. An important issue is also whether the owners are the managers, or whether they have contracted herdsmen to look after their flocks. In the latter case husbandry strategies may tend to be less strictly adhered to by those who are in charge of the day-to-day care of the flocks. This inherent conflict is one reason for the owner to seek kinsmen for the job of yategaab.

With milk production as outlined above under favourable conditions, the Aulib yategaab who owns mixed goat and sheep flocks will get milk from July until January, with a peak in production during August-October. During the milk production months the yategaab get more milk than they need for household consumption. Those yategaab who look solely for milk require typically three milking sheep and six to ten milking goats for a family of husband, wife and six children. However, milk production is often only one aspect of food production from family flocks. The other is meat production. Slaughter for home consumption and sales of small stock occur throughout the year, of course, but reach a high towards the end of tubahala when many animals are weak and milk production is low. Market prices for small stock drop drastically at this time.

Marketing of small stock is one of the major regular sources of income. The final destination is for export, not least through smuggling to Saudi Arabia (a highly developed trade in the region). Yategaab do not, however, market their animals at urban centres such as Port Sudan or Atbara, except when travelling there to purchase consumer goods. Commercial trade in animals is either carried out with visiting middlemen or at local markets. The middlemen, as well as sometimes drawing from their own flocks, purchase a few head here and a few head there until they have collected some 50 head. These are then walked up to tarmac roads and transported by lorry from there to Atbara or Port Sudan. In the latter case, the flock is often split and part is sold legally at the official livestock market while the remainder is sold illegally for transport to Saudi Arabia. Prices depend on the condition of the animal and its age. Each animal is placed in an age category; this is calculated by counting the animal's teeth.

144

Flocks are managed differently, depending on production purpose. *Nagarii* flocks are kept close to the household for daily milk production. They are watered every other day. *Sermab* flocks are those kept far away "just like the camels". These flocks go two days without water. In Aulib they usually consist only of sheep, since goats require more frequent watering. Goats are accordingly more common in Gunob. The milk production from sermab is not immediately important to the household. The sermab can therefore be seen as a dry flock representing capital and a future milk and meat production capacity for the household. During the cool months of the year flocks of small stock manage to go longer without water; those which go three days without water are called *sumhaab* and those waiting four days are called *fadgab*.

The yategaab claim that milk production from lactating females in nagarii and sermab flocks does not differ significantly. Since the sermab stay longer without watering they can reach better pastures and hence compensate for the greater expenditure of energy necessary during their longer treks. The amount of water intake, of course, differs for animals belonging to the various flocks. A sheep in a sermab flock is the biggest consumer. It drinks one *safiia* at each watering. A nagarii goat is the smallest consumer (goats usually drink less than sheep); it takes 0.5 safiia (approx. 7 litres) at each watering.

More wealthy households, which spread their economic risk through diversifying into different activities, employ yategaab to herd their small stock. The normal salary is three sheep per annum for each 100 animals herded, plus food and clothing. It is also possible, but far less common, to pay the equivalent in cash. In families owning both camels and small stock, the oldest son has the right to work as mish'ariib and a younger son as yategaab.

In town and in the khors, sheep and goat keeping is of course combined with other activities. Small stock rearing combines well with keeping a few matiaat camels in the khor. Since araak is the dominating pasture available there, goats are preferred, even if one finds occasional sheep as well. Such goats give two to three rattel of milk per milking under very good conditions, while sheep in the khors rarely reach more than half of this quantity. In town the households are well integrated into the monetary economy.

One can thus distinguish between some basically different economic functions of small stock. For most yategaab they represent the sole or major source of cash and food. For camel herders and farmers, keeping small stock is a means of diversifying economic activities and achieving access to meat in suitable quantities and a seasonal milk supply. For townsmen it is important to keep a few milking animals for the milk consumption of the household.

Change and constraints

Between the three-year drought in the early 1940's and 1980, many Atmaan were forced out of their traditional niche. For them, camels ceased to be the main basis for their economy. The relative importance of small stock increased, and many Atmaan households were forced to take up paid employment in Port Sudan, or to rely on emergency relief. Such employment may be the major source of livelihood, or simply a supplementary venture in which a younger son can engage. In 1971 tribal wealth was considered to have dwindled so much that the Sudanese Government proclaimed a general exemption from taxation. Among those remaining in the pastoral sphere there were still herdowners who were quite wealthy if one counts the value of their capital, some having up to 150 camels. A balanced family herd, containing ten or more females of varying ages, can provide a relatively secure economic position, with enough milk being produced to cater for its herdsmen and other household members if these both live close to the herd and have good access to markets.

The minimum market value of a family herd was 2,500-4,000 LS in 1980. Even as things stood at that time, it would have been difficult for many ex-pastoralists to rebuild family herds solely by the purchase of new animals. The social organization of the Atmaan does not provide enough economic insurance or sufficiently efficient principles for redistribution to cater for those who loose a major part of their herd. To rebuild a herd solely through biological reproduction is a slow process which calls for skilful management as well as a substantial input of manpower, which may be difficult for people living from hand to mouth. With high mortality and low fecundity rates, the growth of the area herd is limited. Spencer (1973) has commented on the slow growth of camel herds of the Rendille in northern Kenya. Similar reflections can be made on the Atmaan situation. For a majority of Atmaan camel herders, the herd is at best a constant resource containing little promise of capital growth. A small herd, which if sold re-

146

presents a substantial amount of money, may if utilized for subsistence merely produce enough for making a living.

Old Atmaan men claim that before the 1940's each female used to give 10 to 11 calves during her lifetime. In the early 1980's, however, many females were not allowed to bear more than 7-8 calves, after which both strength and fertility seemed to decline. A restrictive strategy had its base in the small number of female camels available, which forbade the risk-taking that short inter-spacing would involve. In particular, camels should, according to the Beja, not be mated when droughts are anticipated. The age of first calving is five years or older. Old females were slaughtered at around the age of 21-23 years; formerly they were maintained until the age of 27-29 years.

The three different patterns of camel rearing among the Atmaan represent different ecological niches as well as differences in the importance ascribed to the camel. Shallageea and aririit were milk producers and trade goods for pastoralists who depended directly on their livestock for a substantial part of their diet while at the same time supplying the commercial camel markets. The role of matiaat was more adapted to farm production. The matiaat provided milk and meat for human consumption but without any substantial labour investment.

It must be repeated that there were already in 1980 considerable numbers of the Atmaan who had no camels and whose livelihood depended upon small stock shepherding, farming and urban occupations. When the great drought took place in the 1940's the British had long endeavoured, with little success, to recruit labour to, for example, the cotton schemes at Tokar and Gash, but found the Beja very unwilling to take up salaried work. After that crisis, however, the Atmaan never really recovered. Widespread poverty and the opportunities for wage income in Port Sudan and Atbara altered the logic of labour allocation for drought-stricken nomads. More recently, an increased demand for labour in Saudi Arabia in the late 1970's lured young men away from camel herding. At the same time, Saudi demand for camels was very great, and it is conceivable that this affected the availability of breeding stock among the Beja. When people were forced to sell camel heifers, contrary to cultural norms, these were likely to be bought by quite other categories of people than the poor brethren of the owner.

A majority of the Atmaan are now wage-earners in Port Sudan. They have varying degrees of commitment to the pastoral sphere.

147

Some are members of Aulib households who stay in town only for a limited period. Most common are those who work in port for a few weeks in order to earn enough to buy two sacks of durra and bring them home. Some, however, remain long enough to appear semi-permanently settled in town, even if they intend to return as soon as the family wealth allows them to do so. These may be men who have their family in Aulib and who send remittances regularly. Among those permanently living in town are some who have severed all links with pastoralism, and also those who have some security wealth in the form of camels, inherited or acquired by other means, or who invest their savings in animal wealth. Such livestock are kept in Aulib in the owners' absence by one of his relatives (normally a brother) or by an employee. If they are daring, such urban stock-owners may attempt some trade in small stock. One category of town people thus has as its main goal to regain viability of their household units in Aulib; for the other category the Aulib livestock is a subsidiary activity supporting a mainly urban-focussed economy.

The development of an urban market for meat and milk and the job opportunities offered in Port Sudan have become essential to Atmaan pastoralism and maybe even for the very existence of the Atmaan as a local group. Without the port, large parts of the community would have been scattered over various settlement schemes elsewhere in Sudan. As things stand, Port Sudan offers drought-stricken households a living, either by direct involvement in wage earning or trade, or indirectly through the exploitation of kinship links to those who have secure incomes. An opportunity is provided to live and work in the area for long enough to attempt to rebuild the family herds.

The factors which from one point of view seem to reinforce the viability of the pastoral undertaking, also threaten it. For people balanced on the margin of viability there is a clear risk that the temptations of good prices or emergency sales to meet short-term needs will cause excessive selling, particularly of female stock, beyond the point at which herds will be able to reproduce properly. Also, wage-earning opportunities divert manpower from camel rearing. Immediate needs may force too large a number of able-bodied persons to abandon herd management. The decrease of herding manpower tends to encourage the concentration of herds in the hands of the wealthy. In the end this may create a shift toward increased specialization both on the coast and in the interior, a more extensive form of pastoralism producing animals for the livestock market. Although there is a market for camel meat and riding camels, modern commercial livestock production puts a premium on small stock, which represent a more liquid capital, demand less specialized and well-trained herders and reproduce quickly.

Among the Atmaan there was already in 1980 a general belief that living conditions in the area had worsened within living memory. When both herds and land are considered, the entire Atmaan region has deteriorated in production capacity due to severe drought periods upsetting normal herd reproduction, which again has negative implications for a family's capacity to withstand drought. This goes both for camel and small stock rearing.

It is obvious that economic change is furthered by environmental stress. The change in land use implied by an altered consumption pattern divorced from the traditional pastoral land use not only puts pressure on land for cultivation but also leads to increased pressure on forestry resources. In the final chapter, we will discuss some of the issues involved.

The problem of competing land uses is particularly acute at the coast, and close to Port Sudan. This is also where those who are still active as pastoralists feel threatened by farmers. The cultivators are generally themselves former camel people of the same tribal unit, practicing dryland farming for lack of any alternative. Their only resource is a traditional claim on collective land, which they can transform into rights to carry out occasional farming, with the negative effect that the browsing that is a base for the communal exploitation of the land is destroyed. As in so many border areas between farming and pastoral areas, farming is primarily a symptom of poverty.

Aririit herders in the interior have not yet experienced competition from cultivation and perhaps are unlikely to do so. The matiaat in the khors graze close to cultivated fields but rely substantially on the Hiib, the supply of which does not appear threatened by khor cultivation. There are, however, other threats to a viable camel rearing system which stem rather from the labour demands associated with a mobile adaptation and the deleterious side effects of labour migration. The aririit rearing pattern is particularly vulnerable to manpower shortages, since it depends so much on a high degree of mobility. Experience in other pastoral communities (cf. Dahl 1979) shows that manpower shortages linked with labour migration tend to make the population of people and animals more stationary, which may create a situation of local overgrazing. Part of the adjustment may be a gradual transition to a commercially oriented, more stationary form of small-stock pastoralism.

When we asked about progressive desertification in 1980, the Beja were hesitant on the question of whether there was any general trend towards the country becoming more arid, although some people mentioned that there was more sand in the khors. In 1986, it was of course impossible to get an answer which was not dominated by the fact that the last few years had been devastatingly dry. Before the drought, when people were asked to explain the deteriorating living conditions that they had experienced during the 20th century, they usually emphasized the process of ever diminishing livestock resources, particularly the decline of camel holdings. They were also concerned about the availability of grain, which they felt had become much more difficult over the last decade. Desertification was not so much of an issue.

Many planners hope that keeping small stock might prove a more flexible strategy, still in line with cultural values. Investing in small stock is a traditional poor man's strategy in north-east Africa, and for various reasons all efforts from aid agencies in restocking the Beja or other impoverished nomads seem to have concentrated on small stock. However, using north Kenyan data, Mace (1988:10) has convincingly shown by statistical modelling that for people subsisting mainly from the produce of their flocks, the best strategy from the point of view of sustainability is to stop investing in small stock as soon as the flock is big enough to cover basic subsistence needs, and to invest the surplus small stock in camels. Mace starts from a subsistence point of view, which does not account for the use of, for example, salaries to cover risk periods. It is still thought-provoking that of her model population of 1000 pure small stock herders, only four survive after 50 years in the simulations. In planning for sustainability in the Red Sea Hills it would be advisable to take this perspective into account.

8

The dwindling resource base

In this final chapter, we want to depart from the idea that it is still pastoralism and the value systems, beliefs and ways of organizing social life connected to pastoralism that form the backbone of Beja culture (see for example Morton 1989:66). Therefore, in this conclusion, our primary aim is to show how the resource basis of Beja pastoralism has shrunk. We will do so by looking first at the Beja's experiences of pastoral crisis in the most concrete sense, by looking at the modern records of drought. Second, we will discuss the degree to which the processes of change in resources are available for observation and interpretation by the Beja, and what their discourse about these issues is like. This is a problematic task, since we operate neither with a bounded and distinct group nor with resources which have ever been fixed or completely bounded.

In talking about the Beja as a category, we are not thinking of a bounded and corporate group that exists as an entity in any way except as an aggregate of tribal confederations and households who speak the same language and share the same outlook on life. The Beja concept is not yet very significant as a "nation" or political entity, although it may come to be just that in the future. This would be a logical development of the Beja competing with people of other cultural backgrounds in the context of the Sudanese state. Politicians of Beja background and intellectual Beja in Port Sudan and Khartoum have tried to use an ethnic idiom since the 1950's, as other groups on the Sudanese scene also frequently do (Morton 1989:67f).[1]

Certain of the Beja are now getting access to new resources, which we will not deal with here, because they are not directly related to the pursuit of the traditional livelihood. What we are concerned with, mainly, are the changes that the Beja have suffered in relation to those land assets necessary for pastoralism that they could earlier gain access to just by proper reference to Beja values and by giving symbolic recognition of who is the host. We will consider their access to pastoral land in terms of quantity as well as quality.

The modern history of drought in Beja lands

A layman's view of drought is that it is concerned with lack of water, usually as the result of lack of rain. A drought is considered to be over when the rains return. For the victim of drought, however, the seriousness of a drought is not only related to the incidence of rain, but also depends to a great extent on the availability of other supplementary resources. And more important, among pastoral people the period of recuperation from drought may be much slower than the incidence of rains would lead us to assume (Dahl and Hjort 1976, 1979).

The temporal relationship between rainfall and food production is one of a certain delay in effects. In the case of the Beja, a good rain enables them to sow their durra, but the crop can only be harvested

---

[1] Morton (1989) provides a good summary of Beja regionalist politics.

after three to five months. The animals must get pregnant before they can give milk. How soon they can be milked after rains depends upon the type of animal, on how quickly they respond to an improvement in the pasture and on the length of their pregnancy. Sheep and goats give milk after half a year, but with camels and cattle the delay is longer, since they carry their calves for a more extended period. In the case of camels, the first calves are born in time for the rains of the following year. A good year can have effects for the Beja lasting for the whole of the following year, even if this should be bad. Those who have camels and cattle can still get milk. A durra cultivator who was lucky could store his surplus for the bad year and use his stores both for providing his family with porridge and his herd with fodder. But the system does not always work in this ideal way. A drought which lasts for several years can cause severe oscillations in the proportions of the herd which at any particular time are giving milk or are dry. A good year after a long drought makes all camels pregnant and the following year there will be plenty of milk but no animals who are free to be impregnated. The next year there will again be a shortage of milk, irrespective of the amount of rain falling. Besides such fluctuations in productivity, there are also the demographic effects of disaster, both on the animal and the human population. Disproportionate numbers of deaths of certain age categories of animals or people, or a hiatus in births, create very long-term waves of imbalance in the composition of the population. An even development of the herds and their production over time is thus a critical and difficult issue. Dependable pastures which can be used in dry years, and secure access to supplementary fodder in the form of bought grain, are the resources needed to meet such difficulties and thus preserve life.

The consequences of prolonged drought may have to be lived with for several years, even if the grass is green and the browse sprouting. It is the acute crisis of drought which tends to draw most attention, whether we talk of Western mass media, modern social and economic research, historical records or folk memories. The long-term effects are experienced as difficulties and poverty by the people directly hit by them, but there has so far been very little research done on them anywhere in the world. When the need for such research is realized, it is usually too late for the necessary baseline study to be done, and most development-oriented research operates with too short a time-span to be able to cover such processes.

153

Is the present crisis a new phenomenon? The following account offers a chronology of climatic events and acute periods of food crisis, and mainly deals with relatively recent phenomena. It starts with Sanasita, the disaster connected with the Mahdiya war. This does not mean that there were no disasters before that. It is unlikely that this was the first period of comprehensive starvation that had hit the Beja. Unfortunately, however, the historical sources tell us little about this, other than what can be gained from general knowledge of continental climatic trends. What appears clear is that the Mahdiya period brought armed conflicts into the Beja's own areas to a degree which appears to have had no precedent during the previous one thousand years. On the other hand, the historical continuity suggested by this statement and perhaps by our historical summary in Chapter 2 may be superficial. Historical discontinuities leave less trace than what remains; history is the history of survivors. The continuity of Beja life style is there as long as there are groups continuing to maintain it, but the groups who were absorbed by other ethnic categories, who migrated away, who starved to death after a drought or perhaps died in an epidemic, do not enter the record. There is no reason to use this spurious continuity as an argument either for or against an idea of the Beja as living "in a static equilibrium" with their environment. The present book should not be read as presenting such an argument (cf. Johnson and Anderson 1988:12). In Chapter 2 we concluded that the viability of temporal forms of adaptation for human survival cannot be taken for granted under changing macro-political regimes, and in fact that applies as well if their environmental advantages are taken into account instead. What works in one historical situation might be harmful in another. By saying this in order not to fall into the trap of idealizing the past, we can still maintain that the menace to continuity of Beja life has probably rarely been as serious as today, when access to grain is threatened at the same time as the herds and lands are dwindling.

The Sanasita period 1888-89

The concept of Sanasita goes back to the last years of the 1880's. The crisis began when, after a seriously dry 1888 with total crop (and probably pasture) failures, locusts attacked the crops in 1889. A new crop failure came in 1894. Pankhurst and Johnson (1988:57ff), in an overview article about the impact of the 1888-1889 disaster in Ethiopia and Sudan, emphasize the competition over grain between rural consumers, the newly swelling urban population of Omdurman and the Mahdist armies. The last-named had to feed themselves from the resources available in the areas where they were stationed. Food was also one of the main items used by the British and the Egyptians at Suakin in competing for the loyalty of people in the east. Grain prices, particularly in the urban and non-producing areas, rose ten and twentifold. In 1888 rinderpest had been introduced to Massawa by Italian imports of cattle,[1] probably from India, and within some few years large parts of Africa's pastoral areas were depopulated of people and livestock, the cattle-herds of the southern Beja not faring better than those elsewhere (*ibid.*:48). Smallpox had ravaged the Amar'ar and Hadendowa in 1886 (Jackson 1926:132). Many Beja were also killed in war. In 1888 Osman's troops killed 700 Amar'ar (*ibid.*:116-177).

Jackson (1926:140) writes about the following year: "That same year (1889) pestilence and famine swept through the Sudan. Many of the best cultivators had been ordered to Omdurman to serve with the Khalifa's armies: others were under arms elsewhere or had been killed in battle. The fighting and universal unsettlement of the past few years had depleted any little stores of grain that the people may have had and their supplies of seed corn had run low. Terrible though the losses by war had been during the past few years, they were dwarfed into insignificance by the appalling fate that overwhelmed the wretched inhabitants. Millions died in a few months and when the crops were ripe, locusts darkened the skies and devoured the only foodstuffs that people had. No part of the Sudan was spared: the natives dropped down in the streets and their friends were too weak to give them burial. Cannibalism became the horrible habit of many of the strictest of the true believers who in more normal times would not even eat a sheep unless its throat had first been cut in the name of God...In Kassala the hyaenas became so bold that...Osman Digna was compelled to marshal the whole of his army and lay siege to Jebel Kukram where most of the hyaenas had their lairs...".

All Beja talk about this time as abhorrent, but it should be said that the northern Beja, depending upon camels, were perhaps less hard hit than the ones living around the interior deltas of the Gash and Baraka.

---

[1] For this disaster, and its continental scope, see also Pankhurst (1966) and Pankhurst and Johnson (1988).

155

The latter were closer to the centres of disorder, more dependant on cattle-herds and thus also more vulnerable to rinderpest.

However, one source, Keimer (1954:118), states, on the basis of interviews with Bishariin elders in the 1940s, that Mahdist raids, drought and smallpox left the impoverished majority of Nubian Bishariin no other choice than to congregate around Luxor, Aswan, Kom Ombo, Daraw and other urban centres in Egypt. Sandars (1935:210) mentions that the famine drove many Amar'ar from various tribal sections down to Atbara in search of grain. Beja people are reluctant to talk about Sanasita, but there is a certain amount of folk lore about the conditions that prevailed. Some stories go further than the usually vague statements of how hunger made women forget their children and forced men to leave their wives and how people even killed each other to eat. It is impossible to know to what place or people such stories refer, as they are equally shocking and shameful to the Beja as they are to the reader. They mainly serve to emphasize the ultimately sinister character of those years. However, many families have stories following the general pattern of "my grandfather brought all his family and all his stock up into the mountains and hid them there against war and disease". But there are also stories which may not actually refer to things which happened just then, but which underline the character of Sanasita as the paramount disaster. There is for example the story of the young boy who was left with his sickly mother in their mountain glen when all others had migrated away or died. He found water at the foot of the mountain, and a green bush on its top which proved to be particularly attractive to the wild animals. To survive, he carried water uphill each day and poured it on the plant, so that he could trap the animals when they came to eat. This story is quoted as an example of human mental resourcefulness, a quality which the Beja praise highly and which is linked to their idea of stamina.

Environmental hazards during the post-Sanasita period

When we raise the issue of droughts after Sanasita, however, we enter the domain of experiences of living people, and we can also get information from British records. The latter tell us for example that in 1904 there was a serious drought "at Gebel Elba in the country of the Hamed Aurab Arabs" (Hunter, 1904). "As to exactly how long it is

156

since they had rain I cannot state accurately but feel pretty certain not for 5 or 6 years and probably longer, the whole country is parched, pasturage dead, nearly all the bushes dried up and only the sunt trees green: on these last camels and goats find a scanty livelihood". In 1910-11 there was no rain on the Atbai (Jennings-Bramly 1910-11).

World War I had favourable effects on the economy of the Beja. Newbold (1935:12) writes about the Hadendowa: "Animals were sale-able at fabulous prices and grain exportable ...to this tribe's favour. When the world wide reaction set in and prices declined, they suffered badly. 1919-26 perpetual taxation difficulty..." Later, 1925-27, 1941-2, 1948-9 and 1955-58 have been listed as drought years. In 1948-9 "a considerable number of Beja died in the rural areas" (Nur Deen 1982:102) and the number of Beja in Port Sudan increased by 2-4,000. The famine of 1925-7, particularly bad on the Atbai, is remembered as *O'kurbaji*, the whip. Old men can tell how hungry Beja came to ask for food at the administrative stations, and how in one case they were given a very small amount of sugar. Upset, they started to fight, and the police whipped them.

1929 is remembered as a year when the durra of the Amar'ar failed. The Amar'ar sheikhs reported a loss of 2/3 of all animals as compared with the situation five years earlier. Sandars (1932), who reports on this, thought "it quite certain that losses in camels did not exceed 1/3" but suggests for the following year that the hill tribes in the north had lost 3/4 of their sheep. 1931 exhibited an abundance of rain. Sandars estimated for the following year that the Bishariin and Amar'ar were in the exceptional situation of being able not only to cover all of their grain needs by their own production, but even to export some. 1936 was bad for Bishariin and Amar'ar in the north and the Beni Amer in the south.

1940 (*Tu'Tambili*) is remembered by the Amar'ar as the year when they first saw cars, but also as a year when very many animals died from the consequences of the drought, for example camel mange. The Amar'ar, along with Atbara and Halaib Bishariin, appear to have been the ones most hard hit by this disaster, but critical conditions were also reported from the Gash. The Atmur plains north of Wadi Amur and west of the hills had their third consecutive year without rain. This drought, although few of the Beja would know that, was part of a drought on the continental scale. One Amar'ar man told us how his father, who had had hundreds of sheep, goats and camels, had become

157

completely destitute. The sheep and goats of his particular clan group recovered after the war, but the camels never again became as many as they were before the drought of 1940. The provincial monthly diary for Kassala Aug 1941 reports that special arrangements had to be made at most railway stations and villages in order to take care of the dead animals. Famine relief was given for example to the Musmar population who had no chance of reaching Gash. Famine conditions in Musmar lasted well into the summer of 1942. The records also reflect a pattern of the livestock trade which is regular during drought periods. At the height of the famine, camels were sold cheaply, but as the drought continued they became scarce and Rashaida traders[1] travelled all over the province buying all available camels at high prices (KPMD Jan 1942).

The mid-1940's saw a change for the better, but then 1947-9 again brought a province-wide disaster. Drought conditions stretched towards Gedaref and Kassala, and some of the Hadendowa appear to have been especially hard hit. Compared to the 1940 drought, this crisis appears to have left a weaker impression on the Amar'ar. It was worst for those Beja who were living on the western plains. Harrison (1955:5 app 4) estimates that half of the camel population died and two thirds of the remaining stock. The animals of the Hadendowa had already begun to die by the end of 1947. A year later the Hadendowa asked to be given grazing concessions in Eritrea, free grain, reduced taxes and other support. But the British administration said firmly in the annual report "that conditions in the Gash as a result of the previous year's cotton crop and with another fine crop in view were as good as they had ever been, and should be able to carry people through to the coming season with little help from the Government". A year later even the Government had yielded to the pressure of the evidence and handed out grain as famine relief. In March, the author of the Kassala Province Monthly Diary noted "increasing mortality of camels, falling water levels and in some areas incipient famine..." and also that "the higher prices of grain [due to a bad harvest at Gedaref] has however

---

[1] The Rashaida are a group of Bedouins who arrived in Sudan from the Arabian peninsula in the 19th century, and who are still in cultural terms strikingly different both from the Beja and from Sudanese Arabs in general. They have during the last decades lived in Eritrea and in Sudan at Gash and Atbara and along the southern Beja coast. Once involved in the slave trade, they are now prominent in the camel trade to Egypt, and they rear camels and small stock. For obvious reasons, they do not have any "traditional" grazing grounds of their own, a fact which generates much conflict, particularly with the Hadendowa. See Hassan (1975), Salih (1976:97) and Young (1984).

upset the economy of those tribes which normally get through the dry weather under marginal conditions and has been the factor mainly responsible in the end for their present critical state...".

1950 was *Tu'Rasha*, the year of abundance, particularly in relation to subsistence cultivation. The good rains were immediately reflected in a crisis in the labour-dependent cotton production in the Gash and Tokar plantations. Some of the harvest was spoilt by locust attacks, a common feature when there is abundant rain after long drought.[1] In 1951, as a result of the good grazing and reproduction performance of the year before, the remaining herds gave plenty of milk; but the durra harvest was negligible in the Beja areas. There were then new reports of starvation and malnutrition in the areas north of Port Sudan. Presumably the herds, even if they had been in milk, were too small to cater for the population. Then followed some relatively good years, but in 1955 famine relief had to be handed out as a consequence of the local absence of rain and of bad river flushes. This was the case not only in the mountains but also in the rivers Gash and Baraka, which are watered from the Eritrean highlands. 1956 is remembered as a very bad drought, when grasses and trees are said to have died. Colonial records tell of an abundant supply of job-seekers in Sinkat and Kassala, and an influx of nomads into Gash. The population of Port Sudan swelled with immigrants from the northern Beja areas.

1967 (*I'Talawitmass-Sana*: "the year of the lightning") is noted as an exceptionally good year, when however some sheep and goats died from the abundance of rain: as people were taken unprepared, there were not enough sheds to house the animals in. Camels on the other hand fared well. They are sensitive to humidity, but do not suffer from rain in itself. Since most of the camel areas of the Beja have sandy soils with good drainage, there were no additional losses of camels.

In retrospect, people remember 1950-1972 as relatively good years, particularly in comparison with the late 1970s. Nevertheless, Abu Sin (1975:170) writes "The drought conditions prevailing in the region over the last decade imposed the first critical test to nomadism in the region. The loss of livestock forced a large number to desert nomadism. In the summer of 1972 there were over 18,000 families having no

---

[1]One explanation given is that farm residues are left in the fields instead of utilized by the (diminishing) livestock towards the end of a prolonged drought period. The residues offer good breeding facilities for insects, and the following season may therefore see a plague of locusts.

animals compared with 11,000 in 1964. During the same period over 20,000 persons moved from the hills to Port Sudan...".

Official documents on the latest starvation refer to 1983 as the beginning of drought. However, even the years preceding that had their problems. Cutler (1988), in a small survey of 31 Beja households, found that a majority of them identified the genesis of the drought as being between 1978 and 1979. In 1980, our Amar'ar informants in retrospect judged that the last five years had been bad. 1978 was serious enough to hamper camel reproduction for the Amar'ar, even if it did not kill off the herds. Another difficulty which was experienced even before 1981 was the sharp rise in durra prices. It is worth noting that in contrast to their judgment of climatic success, the Beja define grain price fluctuations as definitely being caused by political-economic factors, particularly by the Government's attitudes to illegal as well as licensed grain exports to Ethiopia and Saudia. Their analysis in this respect corresponds to that of the FAO Country mission (1982).

A survey undertaken by the UNICEF/WHO Joint Nutritional Support Programme indicates that in 1983 parts of the province were already on the way to starvation (El Tom and Bushra, 1984). In 1984, the rains failed completely, and according to Hale (1986) "the Beja and Beni Amer had lost 90% of their stock by the end of that year. The few remaining camels and donkeys were shared between families. Livestock prices slumped as people sold their dying animals. Most people with access to land did not plant that summer, and with poor harvests elsewhere in the Sudan the grain prices were treble that of a normal year..." Many men went to look for work in Gash, Gedaref and Port Sudan, and people who had not earlier sold charcoal, mats or water now turned to such activities. Many families who had lost everything they had or had sold the last remnants of their wealth congregated in camps particularly along the tarmac road from Port Sudan to Sinkat and near the urban centres, where conditions of famine were such that they shocked even experienced international aid workers.

Government agencies and voluntary organizations became alarmed in late 1984, but it was not until March 1985 that the first World Food Programme assistance reached its full scale. The drought continued and in 1985 few people were able to plant, particularly in the areas around Sinkat. Cultivation suffered not only from lack of rain, but also from lack of seeds and lack of saleable animals to buy them with, and from locust attacks (Hale 1986). The first assistance came from the Saudi Red Crescent, in the form of oil and sugar. The Saudi help met with some problems of distribution. To begin with, the assistance was mediated through one major clan group (diwab) who had traditional claims to leadership. As a result, complaints about selective nepotism were raised by other groups.

Later, as WFP started to cooperate with OXFAM, the distribution was instead organized through people appointed for each tribal group. The rations of food were trucked out to the "home villages" in order to encourage people to return to their homes and try to reoccupy themselves with subsistence activities. At the height of this distribution activity, aid reached 300,000 people in this way (Walker 1987). The "Responsible Men" were appointed on diwab-basis. One problem was for the aid organizations to resist the constant demands for the sub-division of the delivery units and the proliferation of such responsible men for smaller and smaller social units. The basis for fair distribution was left to the "Responsible Men", and varied between special rations for the needy, equal shares for all families and shares according to family size. There were also a number of cases where the "Responsible Men" sent the grain back to the towns and sold it there, or where the grain was sold by a joint decision within the clan group. The extent of such malpractices is impossible to ascertain. However, most of the distribution appears to have run well. Although the help was international with for example strong British and Norwegian inputs, most Beja, whether educated or illiterate, thought of it as coming as a result of the good disposition of President Reagan.

In 1986 there were very good rains, and prospects looked favourable for the durra harvest in, for example, Khor Amur. Other places were severely hit by locust attacks as a consequence of the lack of grazing animals. The durra stalks which are usually used as fodder were left on the fields for the pests to breed in. However, on the whole conditions turned better in the region and the aid organizations could gradually reduce their level of activity.

Most of the above description of the history of droughts during this century is based upon official documents. Talking with the Beja, it is clear that the experiences of Sanasita and the most recent drought overshadow the memories of all other arid periods. When we conducted our interviews in 1980, it was easier to get information on the intermediate droughts than it was in 1986, when apparently the last

161

disaster had made the previous ones seem rather bleak. Sanasita however stood out as the previous disaster, although there were no longer any people alive to tell us about it from first hand experience. Earlier disasters had been forgotten, perhaps since memories are only kept if revived in everyday discourse, and Sanasita would itself fulfil all needs for an historical archetypal catastrophe. Compared to Sanasita and the recent one, other droughts appear trivial. In an oral culture like that of the Beja, all anecdotes relating to starvation can easily be absorbed into the general idea of Sanasita. But also, Beja ideas about fortune make it inappropriate to talk too much of bad periods, lest doing so should invite them back, and complaints about the endowments of one's land are contrary to the code of honour. Memories of suffering are not cherished like the stories of brave heroes.

Some other considerations need to be emphasized. Wherever pastoral land resources are discussed, it is critical to distinguish between practical access and "property", and it is above all necessary to stress a regional perspective on land use. Losses of land must always be treated with an eye not only to the use of that piece of land as an isolated unit, but also to its place in a larger system of land use. Withdrawing 3% of the area from use may mean absolutely nothing to the rest of the system if the area concerned contains only lava boulders or sand, while it may mean the ruin of the land use system as a whole if it contains critical breeding grounds or drought resorts.

A summary of general trends in land control by the Beja

Our chronology of climatic crises in Beja lands goes back only to Sanasita, and we have chosen not to idealize the conditions under which Beja pastoralists lived before that, considering that "history is the history of the survivors" and that the data for either substantiating or corroborating such an idealization are far too scanty. However, it is not difficult to identify some serious new constraints, particularly relating to land.

The total area available for the livestock rearing of the Beja has diminished during the last fifty years or so.[1] The pressure on the cen-

---

[1] This summary of the general trends in Beja land control was in its original version published in SIDA Report (1984:24-7) but its general conclusions largely parallel Morton and Fre (1986:50-52). A classic discussion of the effects of pastoral land-loss can be found in Bondestam (1974) and Flood (1975).

tral regions owned and primarily populated by the Hadendowa and the Atmaan Beja has increased.

To the north, there has been pressure from other nomads dislocated by drought and the Aswan dam. When the latter was constructed, vast sums of money were invested in moving antique monuments in southern Egypt and in relocating the Nubian population from those parts of the Nile valley involved. Less known internationally was the fact that the grounds east of Aswan were important pastures. There the Bishariin Beja raised the best riding camels of the Arab world. The quality of pasture is critical when camels are to calve. They demand certain types of fodder and it is necessary for the welfare of the calves that the soil has good water drainage characteristics, and that it contains few ticks or harmful insects. The dam inundated areas of just this type used by the Bishariin. According to an Egyptian anthropologist, however, the Bishariin were not informed. Only three years after the official opening of the dam did they become aware that what they saw was not a temporary natural phenomenon. The result of the construction of the dam was for them a massive impoverishment of the pastoral families. Those who were not ruined were forced to turn southwards (Fawzy, 1978:121). Morton and Fre (1986 passim, esp. 51) emphasize that the period since 1967 has been one of more or less continuous drought in Bishariin (and Atmaan) areas and that this has contributed to a general southward migration by these pastoralists into Tibilol, Musmar and Atbara.

To the south, Rashaida livestock traders have not only moved in from Eritrea but have also expanded their herds. The Beni Amer, who used to graze over the border with Eritrea, have increasingly come to concentrate north of the boundary to escape war. The Gash and Tokar deltas were traditionally reserve pasture areas where the Beja also grew grain. Cotton and later castor have been focii for Sudanese agricultural development in these deltas, and this has meant a loss of important drought grazing. Although the Beja have not been completely estranged from these areas in terms of formal property rights, practical control has to a large extent passed into the hands of settled riverain and West African tenants or share croppers. The tensions thus created, particularly between the Hadendowa and the immigrant cultivators, have been described by Salih (1976, 1980). On a practical level, these tensions have resulted in cases of animal trespass and subsequent confiscation; on a conceptual and emotional level, they have

163

meant growing discontent, and complaints from the Hadendowa elders that the tribe's animal wealth was dwindling away due to the shortage of pastures. Salih (1980:131) notes that there were no records available to support this claim, and that it would be difficult to find out the impact on herding of the irrigation scheme without systematic sampling of opinion from a wide range of sections of the tribe. As indicated in the last chapter, the difficulties met by Salih in this respect are general, for there are no reliable figures which can allow us to quantify trends in the animal wealth of the Beja over a longer time period. In the context of both land losses and herd losses, it should be emphasized, though, that the most important aspect of pastoral impoverishment is one of quality. What we are talking of here are losses of critical drought resorts and of transport animals and reproductive stock of vital importance to the total productive system.

The scope of local observation

The diminishing of Beja pastures, which can be observed if we take an overall regional point of view, is not so easily visible from the ground. If there is population pressure, it will be felt as an increased number of strangers in the traditional pasture ground of the clan group, and as a serious social strain. This strain may lead to local skirmishes, but as we have seen these have to be explained by those involved in other symbolic forms than as mere resource competition. The relationship between drought and more violent conflicts over pasture and water is, however, complex; as water or grass become scarce people may quarrel over them, but only as long as they have living livestock to care for. People who have lost their herds, and who live in doubt of ever recovering, are not in a position to defend their rights to other natural resources.

The bird's eye view is totally inaccessible to the local people; they will see the local results of pressure and not the aggregate, and they will interpret them in terms of relations with neighbouring groups rather than attribute problems to "push factors" on the periphery of their area. Consequently, it is not very likely that references will be found in Beja discourse to the kind of idea that is presented by, for example, Kursani (1984b:23), who suggests that the large-scale mechanization of commercial sorghum cultivation on rain-fed arable land further to the south-west in Kassala province is responsible for the general decrease of humidity in the area. Deterioration in local conditions will not be seen as related to processes outside the local grazing ground.

The changes in the areal size of the pastures accessible to the Beja is only one aspect of the deterioration of their resources. The other is their productivity in terms of fodder. This is again an area where the individual Beja horizon is temporally and spatially limited. Here, the fact that the most important social group in the Beja community is based on a particular area of land becomes significant: the diwab is a unit which, even if only in a special sense, controls land. Members identify themselves with it, so that a Beja individual can be expected to be familiar mainly with the conditions in his or her own neighbourhood, and in alternative places where the family's livestock can be taken. As many Atmaan live in areas where they have "guest status", their knowledge of environmental conditions will not be limited purely to the territory of their own clan, but in many cases their own personal network is concentrated on the territories of one or two different clans only. Information on grazing and rain in areas of interest is freely circulated (Morton 1988) over such boundaries. Yet, it is within such limited areas that Beja herdsmen can be expected to observe the disappearance of certain plant species, the pressure of more sand in the river bed, increased exposure of tree roots and the like. This is important to remember when we consider local understanding of processes of drought, and the vague answers about progressive desertification that we were able to get in 1980 and to which we have already referred (see the end of the previous chapter).

Many of the demographic, historical and ecological processes with which we are dealing are of a numerical, geographical and temporal range which renders them inaccessible for observation. Thus what the researcher who has access to statistics on a regional or national scale and to long time-series of quantified documentation can see is not necessarily what can be seen from the grass-root perspective. The local nomad can only judge these trends from the actual experiences of subsistence difficulties and successes made by his immediate social network, and from the correlation of locally observable phenomena. Little (forthcoming), in the context of Njemps pastoralists, warns that "As local herders usually blame low rainfall rather than overstocking for lack of grazing, however, their citing climate as a variable may actually relate more to a decline in land and fodder availability than to precipitation". Processes outside the herder's own home range are generally only known to him in the form of stories about dramatic events that reach him by rumour, oral history or the selective eyes of the mass media.

Taking a perspective of some millenia, are there any signs that the ecological conditions under which the Beja live presently were at any time radically different? To be truthful, not many. Authors such as Harrison (1955) and Kennedy Cooke (1944) describe the pattern of climate, vegetation and rainfall as likely to have been more or less eternally static. However, Mawson and Williams (1984), on the basis of an examination of alluvial clays in the Red Sea river beds, suggest that 2,000 years ago the streams flowed permanently and the vegetation was more dense. This was due to the more generally favourable climatic conditions prevailing all over north-eastern Africa. In the shorter time perspective of the last 100 years, there is no firm evidence that any substantial wearing down of the local natural resources has taken place — probable as such a decline may seem. The area makes an extremely austere and dry impression on the Western observer (in spite of its rugged beauty and usefulness to the inhabitants). This may lead a casual observer to exaggerate the rate of environmental decline.[1] It is, however, known that the average amount of rain has steadily gone down from 150 mm in the early fifties to just above 50 in the late seventies (Norconsult 1986:13). This is part of a well-known general drying up of the Sahel belt, for which various explanations have been suggested, but which according to recent opinions among climatologists (Rapp 1988) can be directly related to changes in the circulation of water and air in the South Atlantic.

However, there were, even before the last drought, patterns in the prevalent land management of the Atmaan which ought to have caused concern and which may have worsened their situation during the last decades. The drought itself might also have had lasting effects which in the long run may prove irreparable. Swift (1986:9) reports on the fear among some experts that the stocks of grass seeds in the ground would have been depleted by the numerous but quantitatively insufficient light showers. Morton and Fre (1986:19) emphasize that the rate of environ-

---

[1] Haaland and al Hassan (n.d.:4) make a similar point about the reference frames of Beja and Western observers: "Although it is [starvation and tragedy] ... which is visible to us, we even tend to see their successes as misery. While we may agree with the Beja that starvation and diseases is bad life, we certainly have very different ideas about what constitutes good life".

mental decline appears to be much higher in other parts of the Sudan, such as Gedaref. Nevertheless, they say, in certain winter rain areas there is evidence of overgrazing, e.g. at Erkowit, where the wild olive has disappeared.

There was little systematic research on the state of vegetation and soils before the drought, so it is difficult to judge to what extent available evaluations simply rest on occasional and subjective observations. Some sources note the growth of sand dunes, for example Norconsult (1986:18, 55), who report from Sinkat, the Odrus and Huritri plains, and areas south of the Summit-Erkowit roads, and who mention cutting of trees and bushes as the direct cause of these signs of deterioration (*ibid*::55).

Swift (1986:9), who made a serious attempt to look for degradation during his mission, found little evidence for it while travelling through the areas of Derudeb west of the road, western Haya, the coastal plains and the mountains of rural Port Sudan and Halaib. "On the contrary there were good stands of Acacia Tortilis, especially in Halaib district, but also elsewhere...Considerable destruction of trees can be seen in a ring a few kilometres around the main villages, where no doubt villagers have cut firewood, but this does not seem to extend to the countryside at large". Furthermore, he could not see much evidence for large-scale natural death of trees as a result of the drought.

One pre-drought change in land management patterns which may have contributed to ecological problems was that of an increased dependence on sheep and goats. In addition, the shortage of camels may have made small stock rearing less mobile than before. A migratory form of husbandry is kind to the soil but requires great input of labour, which a poor family may not always be able to supply. Those who lack transport animals are forced to live with both animals and households close to places where there is permanent water. Wealthier families, on the other hand, may turn sedentary because of their involvement in trade, political offices or administrative jobs, and they can afford to pursue high-risk small stock rearing with less mobility and labour intensity, using commercial fodder to get through critical periods. These are double processes which are well documented from many parts of arid Africa. The ecological wear around fixed settlements is substantial and it becomes more difficult to supply animals with good grass and browse. Goats in particular are likely to be pastured freely without herdsman, and this may mean less monitoring of their browsing, for example on slopes in need of protection (Little, forthcoming). Sheep and goats also trample the soil, grazing and browsing in a more damaging way than camels when vegetation is scarce. It is important to see mobility not simply as a technical aspect of husbandry. Basically, land management forms are a question of what the individual household is able to carry out within the limits of its resources of human labour, food and transport animals. Presently, overgrazing is certainly no problem in Beja areas, as the number of animals is small, but in evaluating the future relationship between stock numbers and environmental wear it is essential to recognize that poverty limits the opportunities for a pattern of land management which does no environmental damage.

One might therefore argue that even if after the drought overgrazing did not seem to be a great problem, one would have to recognize that poverty limits the opportunities for a non-damaging pattern of land management when considering future relationships between stock numbers and environmental wear. This argument would seem to qualify the analysis made by Haaland and al Hassan (n.d.:23) who make a case for the classic "tragedy of the commons" interpretation of the Beja situation in relation to Hadendowa livestock keeping. They note that in terms of livestock management and investment strategies the households are independent units, and hence nobody is motivated to keep stock numbers down: "This is the fundamental dilemma for anybody dealing with human populations in arid regions. ... How can we relieve suffering without laying the grounds for ecological degradation and worse human disasters in the future?" (24). The concept of "tragedy of the commons" as a general tool for analysing pastoral systems has been criticized in several places. It is the aggregate of all resources, and not merely natural resources, which has to be analyzed before any discussion on sustainability can take place. This is also the perspective in which the Beja themselves evaluate such matters.

Trees and poverty

Another pattern of change in land management is that poverty has forced many pastoral families to cultivate areas formerly covered with soil-binding vegetation. As already mentioned, the Beja see land resources mainly in terms of plant cover, and it is clear that on the level of verbalized cultural rules there has existed an awareness of the fragility of this resource. One example quoted to us by Beja herds-people is that of the 'adlib bushes (Suaeda Fruticosa) on the coast. As we have mentioned, 'adlib is excellent fodder for camels. Camels never take so much that they threaten the root system. The 'adlib bush can however also be used as fuel, and, what is worse, its presence is a sign that finger millet cultivation is possible. This fact has caused great tension between those Amar'ar who primarily herd shallageea and those who have lost the bulk of their family herds and who try to use the coastal rains for rainfed farming during the months of November, December and January. The camel-herders complain that if the 'adlib is taken away in order to make room for cultivation, which happens more and more often, the result is frequently rapid local erosion and sand-dune migration.[1]

A well-known issue in environmentalist debates about land manage-ment patterns in arid regions is that of how fuel is procured and its relation to environmental destruction. Morton and Fre (1986:18) suggest that "at present intense charcoal-making could be the single most destructive factor and could be equally blamed [in upsetting the balance]".

Marketing of domestic fuel has a long tradition with the Beja, who make charcoal from trees such as *ti'sagane* (Acacia spirocarpa), *o'tawaj* (Acacia tortilis), *o'dala* (Acacia ehrenbergiana) and the *sunt* (Acacia arabica or nilotica). In 1936 Owen estimated that the Hadendowa sold 4,500 kantars of firewood and 280 kantars of charcoal yearly, and Sandars in 1932 estimated that Port Sudan needed 607,000 kantars of firewood yearly and 29,000 kantars of charcoal.[2] More recently Musa (1971) mentions charcoal and firewood as important cash sources for the Amar'ar. Similarly, for the Ababda and Bishariin on the Egyptian border, after livestock sales their most important source of cash is charcoal. Charcoal is exported northwards during all seasons and the quality of the product is renowned in all Egypt (Fawzy 1978:55,83,86, Keimer 1953 IV:173, Murray 1935:63, Winkler 1936:290).

Since early colonial times the Sudanese authorities have been con-cerned over the issue of whether the Beja are doing permanent harm to

---

[1]This is, however, a point on which alternative views are possible, as is obvious from Daballoub's study of ecological change at Tokar. Daballoub (1983) assumes that adlib is instead on the increase, and can be seen as a sign of erosion.

[2]One kantar is either 44.928 kg (small kantar) or 141.523 kg (big kantar). The latter seems to be used solely in connection with cotton production. We may therefore assume that Owen refers to small kantar.

their vegetation resources. For example, in 1910-11 Jennings-Bramly complained over fodder lopping in a military report from the Atbai, asserting that "this habit should be put a stop to as far as possible as it results in all the trees in the Atbai being continually lopped and prevented from growing to any size." In 1940, the colonial administrators found reason to make a particular check on this point. However, on inspection of the hills behind Suakin, where they expected that the demands of the town would have left its mark, they found no evidence of damage to live trees but an ample supply of dead trees and many new trees coming up. In dealing with external agents who talk to the Beja about Beja land management, whether representatives of the Sudanese administration or foreign organizations, the Beja know very well that whatever their practices, such people are likely to accuse them of destroying the forest cover.

In fact, Fawzy's observation (1978:55) that the Ababda have strict rules against lopping green trees holds also for the Atmaan and for the Hadendowa (Haaland and al Hassan n.d.:17). Despite the fact that commercial charcoal burning is an old practice, all the Beja have strict and explicit normative rules against such over-exploitation. They have a great love for trees and know that their own continued existence depends on the maintenance of the stock of trees. It is trees more than grass that are regarded as the basic source of fodder (see Alfred 1986:31). However, it is not known to us whether there is a general Beja belief in a relationship between tree cover and rain. We have indeed met Beja who suggested that extensive tree cutting would lead to drought, but they may only represent individual cases. Nevertheless, regardless of the reasons for Beja protectiveness vis-a-vis the trees, harsh economic circumstances force many Beja to break well-established principles, and charcoal burning is becoming one of the very few ways for a poor family to subsist.

In 1980, whenever we raised this issue, the Beja would say that it was acceptable to take dead trees, but that any Beja would regard it as immoral to cut from live trees for this purpose. "People are careful for this is their land. If you find other people burning live trees, you will ask them to stop, and you will always be respected for that," was a typical answer. In 1986 the response was strikingly different. The question would not be answered with a reference to moral norms but rather in an apologetic way, emphasizing that nobody can be blamed for mobilizing all resources to get cash in a situation of dire need.

Indeed, as OXFAM's figures from various parts of the region show, charcoal burning was the ultimate life-buoy for many nomads during the period of starvation. Before the drought charcoal production was generally restricted to particular families specializing in this trade. They burnt the charcoal in for example Aulib, the interior plain area, where the quality produced could be very high, and then brought it to the railway stations by camel. Drought turned this occupation into something that many families engaged in. For example, in December 1985 charcoal and firewood sales covered half of the sufficiency needs in Sinkat area, as estimated by OXFAM (Hale 1986). During their second surveillance cycle, half a year later (Hazerjian 1986), the overall figure for the province was 25%, and charcoal production involved one family in five. This opportunity for making a living was however mainly open to families living close to the main routes, with access to camels or donkeys and with ready access to markets. Trees in areas such as for example that along the Musmar-Haya route became very valuable in terms of cash. "One tree can keep a family alive for a month," one informant said "so people may even kill each other over the rights to it." Close to villages people collected firewood and sold it unburnt, in bundles stored along the roadsides. Apart from access to roads, local non-availability of suitable trees, particularly <u>Acacia tortilis</u>, was also a constraint in some places. Some distant areas with palm groves in the khors exported saaf, palm leaves, and mattings made out of them, or wooden poles from <u>Tamarix aphylla</u> (*amab*).

The negative attitudes of the authorities towards the lopping of trees, in combination with the old traditional norms of the Beja regarding how one should procure fuel, do not make it easy to get adequate information on actual practices, so little is known of whether the supply of goods for this growing export of fuel has been procured from trees that died naturally in the drought, or whether it also draws on green tree resources.[1]

It is not only the need the Beja have to find supplementary sources of cash which has grown, but also the urban demand for fuel. It is tempting for an external observer to wonder about the long term ecological effects of the increased demand for charcoal and firewood that will follow as a result of the urban growth of, for example, Kassala

---

[1] Haaland and al Hassan (n.d.:17): "... all firewood bundles inspected by this mission consisted of wood having signs of being eaten by white ants, thus indicating that it had been taken from dead trees".

and Port Sudan. This is the view offered by Schultz and Schultz (1983) and by Morton and Fre (1986:51). The degradation of land causes urban migration, and the demands of the new urbanites for charcoal (and milk) lead to further environmental destruction in a vicious circle.

According to the 1955-56 population census, Port Sudan had 47,600 inhabitants. The census of 1973 gave a figure of 132,632 and in 1981 the provincial authorities estimated that the town had 350,000 inhabitants. The expansion was largely accounted for by the influx of impoverished nomads from the surrounding hills and of large numbers of refugees. To these figures should now be added the large numbers of famished nomads that arrived there during the recent drought.

From the point of view of the Beja, the increased demand for charcoal has so far mainly been seen as a blessing to the impoverished rural household. It would be surprising enough if this demand was interpreted in a negative way by the Beja, who do not yet think of these things in terms of resource competition. What one can speculate about is however the long-term consequences of a parallel growth in the demand for fuel and the size of the population that is stockless and specialized in fuel production. Less careful attitudes to the sources of fodder can perhaps be expected if people on a large scale have lost hope of regaining their animals. In that case, we might find one sector of the Beja population re-established as pastoralists and maintaining the old rules, while others, who remain destitute, could not care less and reject the old norms. Such a situation would be rather tense, as trees are such a central cultural symbol, but so far this scenario remains in the future.

Talking about disaster

As we have seen above, Beja ideas of honour make it difficult for them to talk of the problems that they are presently facing. For a man to fail to be able to provide food for his family is regarded as utterly shameful and reflects negatively on his male status. In a situation of drought, individuals are of course not blamed and shamed in the same way as they would be if they failed to live up to expectations in times of abundance. Nevertheless, a general famine is not only a crisis for the stomach but also for the personal identity as well. How, then, do the Beja interpret the crisis?

172

It should be clear by now that there is no particular agent or practice within the sphere of traditional pastoral land management that it would appear "natural" or even decent for the Beja herds-people to blame for their misfortunes. The trend of degradation was not obvious enough to be an undisputed fact before the drought, except in terms of declining animal numbers. To the degree that a more long-term general degradation was observed, that as well as the disaster of the last years would be thought of as a phenomenon which existed on a level where direct human intervention was not a factor. Climate, and the fertility of livestock, is a matter of God's will. To the extent that humans influence these factors, it is rather through their relationship with Him than through the technical effects of their own activities. And if the Beja see that some of their land management practices might be harmful, they also see them as caused by poverty and not as the result of a free choice. However, as the Beja economy becomes differentiated, it is also likely that the discourse on these issues will be differentiated. Specialized cultivators may be more prone than the nomads to blame accelerating degradation on livestock, as is exemplified in Daballoub's study from Tokar (1983:78 f).

God and the Beja's new neighbours

Islam, as taught in Sudan, associates disasters such as droughts, floods, epidemics etc. with questions of the moral behaviour of humans. The traditions are not altogether coherent, for on the one hand the Prophet is recorded as having said "When God favours some people, he tests them with hardships" and on the other "God has never afflicted a people with drought except for disobeying him" (Awad, 1984). The second interpretation, however, appears to be the dominant one, and God's wrath was a recurrent theme in our interviews with the Beja. A good Muslim would of course not question God's goodness, so the moral blame is always with humanity. Who is regarded as the scapegoat varies, but the Beja are prone to associate moral decay closely with urbanism, and the Koran also says "Had the people of the cities believed and feared God, we would have unleashed upon them the benefits of Heaven and Earth" (Koran 7:96).

An old trader in Port Sudan complained: "The lack of rain is ordered by God. God's anger has been aroused when rich men do not help the poor. Before the Mahdiya war, people were few, but they lived very happily. Now Port Sudan has become the station for all kinds of refugees from Uganda and Eritrea. There are many thieves and bad people. The place is dirty. We are hospitable to these strangers, for they are refugees. We offer them houses, food, water. But we are very scared! I have houses and shops in the town, but my family have left them to live at our place down the coast in order to stay in peace in a clean place, where everybody knows each other. It would be much better if those people could return because they make everything expensive, including the water from Arbaat." In this quotation, the description of the dirt in the city should not be taken to mean just pollution in a western environmentalist sense. It is both moral and physical. Unschooled as well as highly educated Beja tend to think of epidemic disease as usually being transmitted from Ethiopia and Eritrea.

The Beja generally look upon towns as centres of filthiness, from which moral decay as well as disease is likely to spread. The city is thus contrasted with the arena of the mountains, where purity of the heart, health, honesty, clean water and cool winds prevail. Urban growth is thus equated with the growth of pollution: but this is pollution in a more ambiguous moral sense than the environmentalist would allow for. This is the general attitude to towns and town dwellers, but what about the specific categories of town dwellers the Beja come into contact with?

The blame for the Beja's troubles was only indirectly put on refugees, through their moral qualities and the displeasure that God might feel over those people. The spontaneous blame for a disasterous situation was equally frequently put "on the rulers of this country", particularly in retrospect. It was noted that the least drought-hit years during this century were associated with colonial rule, a period which tends to be idealized by the Beja as characterized by governmental fairness. The change of regime from Condominium to Independence took place in 1955-56, and so coincided with a period of difficulty for the Beja. Beja supporters of the Abboud regime, which was in power 1958-64, refer to that period as one of plenty and enough rain. "One loaf was enough for one man" (that is, bread was only supplementary food, and pastoralism could provide milk and meat in the necessary quantities). Serious droughts are said to have been associated with the corruption and avarice of Nimeiry's regime, particularly the latest climatic disaster. The late 1960's are remembered as good years, but "once Nimeiry was in power the rains stopped". After the overthrow of Nimeiry, the rains returned, it is said. Such statements are made with varying degrees of seriousness — and chosen according to political affiliation — but they regularly appear whenever Beja discuss the history of dry and wet years and the idea of a certain moral responsibility on the part of the ruler, reflecting upon the living conditions of his subjects through divine intervention, is certainly not alien to them.

Unification and division

The relocation of large sections of Beja society into an urban milieu as a result of the drought which has increased competition over urban resources has also made the Beja see themselves as a potential political unit. It has created the basis for forming a politicized Beja nation out of what was earlier only an aggregate of groups.

In the case of the Beja, the catastrophic drought has not led to any formulation of models of explanation that give weight to increased competition over grazing, fuel or water. The causes of the drought are not found by the Beja to lie in the observable, but they are relegated to more abstract phenomena, such as God's anger or the moral quality of the regime. Conflict in this situation does not relate to the already abandoned pastoral resources, but to other resources which could possibly offer a resort for the nomads when dislocated from their traditional niches. It manifests itself in competition over urban resources realised as class conflict between the poor and the wealthy layers of Port Sudan's population, with the latter seen as representatives of the power holders in Sudan. But the conflict is dressed up in the codes of ethnicity and honour. As Morton (1989:67) notes, the Beja see the city as built on their land and the Arabic speakers as transgressors. As one informant put it: "We will let these Balawict Sudanese whom we have always treated as guests know that they cannot come to Port Sudan which is Beja land and behave towards our central values with impunity."

Parallel to these processes, the drought may in the countryside create divisive processes that separate into competing groups with contrasting value systems those who earlier shared values and modes of subsistence.

The Osman Digna incident, mentioned in Chapter 5 in the context of symbolic collective insults, can be seen as an expression of such tensions. In the undercurrents of debate during the days following upon the riot, the theme was not only symbolic shame, but as much the airing of resentment over how strangers come and monopolize the wealth of the town, and over the general discrimination against the Beja. The position of the Beja was compared to that of the southerners, and there was speculation concerning the possible spread of resistance.

The traditional Beja economy was one of open or submerged conflict over resources, but at least all were herdsmen and devoted to the maintenance of the pastoral base. New social divisions may give rise not only to diverging ideas of the way to use the resource base in order not to spoil it, but also to intensified conflict over its components.

APPENDIX: Early Beja history

Beja country and Nubia in ancient times

Very roughly around 1000 BC a group of people, referred to in the archaeological texts as "the C-group", migrated from Lower Nubia (the area between present-day Aswan and Wadi Halfa) and settled in Upper Nubia (the Nile Valley north of Dongola in Sudan), where they developed the kingdom of Napata from about 750 BC. This kingdom for some time controlled even Egypt, supplying its 25th Dynasty. Contemporary with them are the archaeological remains of another cultural group, "the pan-grave people", about whom it has been held likely that they have a direct link to the Beja of later periods.

They have been identified with the Medjayu of written sources (Bietak 1986:17f). Sites related to them have been found at Khor Arba'at and Erkowit in the Beja heartland (Arkell 1955:78). The evidence suggests that only a minority of "the pan-grave people" lived in the Nile Valley, where they existed only in small enclave communities among the Egyptian and C-group populations, being periodically used as desert scouts, warriors or mine workers (Bietak, *ibid*). The majority of these people were probably desert nomads, breeding donkeys, sheep and goats.

After 600 BC the Napatan, C-group, dynasty lost control both over Egypt and over the desolate Lower Nubia. The latter area subsequently remained more or less without permanent settlements for four centuries. It was sparsely populated by desert nomads, but "politically a sort of no-man's land where caravans, unless they were provided with considerable escort, were delivered to brigands" (Török 1986:15).

The main explanation offered by science for the hiatus in the existence of a sedentary population from Lower Nubia has been a worsening of climatic conditions (*ibid*:18-19). The subsequent lowering of the Nile level could only be compensated for when, at the time of Christ, the *sagia* water-wheel was developed (Carlsson and Van Gerven 1979:55). There was then a gradual re-occupation of Lower Nubia mainly from 200 BC to 250 AD, the period when Napata's successor, the kingdom of Meroe, brought Lower Nubia under its influence (Adams 1977:379ff, Török 1986:26-7).

This renewed period of subordination of the area came to an end with the joint economic decline of Egypt (see Arkell 1955) and of

Meroe, leading to a new era of decentralization in upper and lower Nubia. Meroe's power had been based on the Egyptian trade with Sudan. It has for long been thought that a serious blow to Meroe came in 350 BC with an attack from King Ezanas of Axum, a kingdom centered on the region around present-day Massawa. In the context of this raid, there is a reference which used to be interpreted (Hartmann 1876:78; Macmichael 1922:I:3:VIII:38) as concerning the Beja. King Ezanas claims in an inscription among other merits to be king of the "Buiaites". Almkvist questioned this inscription's relevance to the Beja as early as 1881 (1881:10), and it has since been discussed by for example Behrens and Bechhaus-Gerst (1986). Disregarding the problem of the Buiaites, it is likely that the decline of Meroe was directly linked to the rise of Axum as an important commercial power exporting African goods.

There are few records of events in Upper Nubia during the centuries after Meroe's decline. It is clear, however, that there was a gradual development of three minor Christian kingdoms which were to remain as power centres of waxing and waning influence for many centuries to come: Nobatia (later Al-Maris), Makuria (Al-Muqurra) and Alodia (Alwa).

Makuria was orthodox, while Nobatia and Alodia practiced Coptic monophysism. Nobatia, having its capital at Bajrash (Faras) just north of the present Egyptian/Sudanese border, contained in its population "Nobadae" as well as "Blemmyes". The latter category, to which several Roman texts about this area refer, have been regarded as identical with the Beja. They had first been mentioned in an inscription describing a raid undertaken at the time of King Anlamani (623-593 BC).[1] In this raid, Blemmye women, children and cattle, but no men, had been captured.

Lower Nubia was during the period in question in the hands of Rome. To the Roman colonizers the Blemmyes were a problem. Repeated raiding is recorded between 250 and 297 AD. "They had developed from peaceful pastoralists into raiders and predators when they adopted the use of the camel" (Säve-Söderbergh 1979). The Roman garrison was forced to evacuate its positions several times, until they finally had to completely abandon the area south of Aswan to the Blemmyes and Nobadae (Hassan 1967:10). They were also a worry for

---

[1] Stela Copenhagen NCG (1709), quoted by Africa in Antiquity, p. 81.

the declining Meroitic power, and have even been suggested as the cause of its collapse. Török (1986:51), however, emphasizes that the real intensification of Blemmye raids in Lower Nubia came later than the Meroe decline. At the end of the 4th century, they carried out raids even as far away as Sinai (Desanges 1978), and they controlled part of the Nile Valley south of the Elephantine route as well as the emerald mines in the desert (*loc.cit*).

Olympiodoros, who came to Syene (Aswan) in 420 AD, was taken to its emerald mines with the explicit permission of the Nobatian king. These mines were situated in the present Beja areas and he was brought there by "the spiritual and worldly leaders of the Blemmyes".[2] At this time, the desert dwellers and the Nobadae were allied (Pa I:396ff, Kirwan 1937:53). In a text dating from the early 6th century, however, the king of Nobatia prides himself on having driven Blemmyes out from his country northwards from Ibrim to Shellal on the frontier with Roman Egypt (Kirwan *op.cit:*54).

The sources consistently differentiate the Nobadae and the Blemmyes from each other. The identity of the latter has not been discussed as much as that of the Nobadae, which is somewhat uncertain but generally taken to be "Nubian". Nevertheless, it is possible that "Blemmyes" in itself was no simple category. If Reinisch (1895:47) is right in deriving the word from *balami* — desert dweller — the category might have included an ethnic mixture and not only Bedawic proper.

During Roman times, the harbours of the Beja coast were of some significance. The fragrant goods of the wealthy kingdoms of Southern Arabia and also luxury items from Africa, India and the Far East had long attracted European traders (Doe 1971:13). However, the opportunities for the competing Phoenician, Egyptian and Greek powers to expand trade beyond the Red Sea were limited both by their navigational skills and by their naval technology. The small flat-bottomed vessels had to creep along the western (Beja) shore to avoid storms, dangerous currents and pirates. When the Roman interests in Far Eastern trade revived Red Sea traffic, they do not seem to have been concerned with the local resources available on the present Sudanese coast (Crowfoot 1911:526). The author of the Periplus, for example, mentions one of these hunting stations, Ptolemais, as the only harbour between Berenice (at the latitude of Aswan) and Adulis (close

---

[2]Kraus (1930:21-2) quoting Olympiodor, ed. Niebuhr, Bonn (1829:465-66).

to present-day Asmara). However, as Roman interests expanded south-wards, Ptolemais was used as a stopover.

Despite technological improvements, it was not possible to use the same kind of boat in the Red Sea as was used in the Indian Ocean. Hence the cargo had to be reloaded in Aden. Pauses were necessary on the route to the destinal port at the northern end of the Red Sea, where the goods were reloaded on camels and brought to the Mediterranean. For the latter purpose Tor, a port on the southern tip of Sinai, was one alternative. The loads could also be taken to Berenice and transferred by desert routes up to the Nile, a manoeuvre made advantageous by the difficulties of Red Sea navigation (East 1935:26), and these goods must clearly have passed through Beja areas.

The treaty of 831 (which repeats several of the points made in an earlier treaty) also gives the chief of the Aswan Beja, Kannun bin Abd-Al-Aziz, the nominal status of the caliph's tributary king for all the area between Aswan and the Dahlak islands off the Eritrean coast (Hassan 1967:39 ff). This is an enormous, and probably unrealistic, area, as is apparent if it is compared even to the size of the territories of present-day Beja tribal federations such as Hadendowa or Bishariin. In 846 the gold and emerald mines in Wadi Allaqi were rediscovered by the Arabs. The Beja made some initial resistance against the exploitation of these mines (Hassan 1967:50 quoting Maqrizi 1922 III:270 along with Tabari 1879-90 III 1429-31, and Ibn Hawqal 1938:53). A military expedition was sent against them, in which an apparently not yet converted chief "Ali Baba" was captured (Baladhuri 1932:234; Taghribirdi in Vantini 1975:728-31 and Hawqal 1938:53). Sandars (1933:124) suggests that this might be a corruption of the Beja name Olbab. "Ali Baba" was brought to the caliph in Baghdad, where he was treated as a tributary king. The sources give different versions as to whether or not he was actually a king (Holt and Daly, 1979:17, Hassan 1967:51, Vantini 1981:94).

The Beja in Early Arab times

Of the territorial and inter-ethnic organization of the medieval Beja, the little we know has been distilled from a number of Arab writers who wrote in the 9th and 10th centuries, notably Yacubi, Aswami and Ibn Hawqal. Zaborski, who provides a good critical summary of Arab medieval writers, notes (1965:291): "For nearly 200 following years,

180

the contacts between the Arabs and the Beja were limited to the frontier disputes caused by Beja raids against the settled population of Egypt but the usual exchange of produce between the Beja nomads and Egyptian agriculturalists was peacefully conducted as well". It was suggested in a first treaty with the Arabs — dating from the early 700s — that the Beja should supply 300 young camels yearly (Hassan *loc cit*). By the same treaty they agreed to fines to be paid when individual Beja stole sheep or cattle, and promised not to harbour slaves who had run away from Muslim owners and not to enter Upper Egypt except as merchants. A similar treaty of 831 (Vantini 1975:625-7, 1981:92, after Maqrizi, 1922) followed upon two decades of very intense raiding against Nubian towns. It rendered the Beja liable to payment of *zakat*, Muslim charity taxes, and guaranteed the protection of mosques built at H.j.r and S.n.ja. The former has not been identified with any certainty (but see Crawford 1951:104-6 and Zaborski 1965:291-2 for suggestions and discussion). The latter is probably Wadi Ceija at long. 34 o 10', lat. 22o 31' (Kheir 1982:296), a place described by Linant (1884) as a great mining centre. Vantini (1981:92), Hassan (1973:40) and Zaborski (1965) have all read this information to mean that at this time at least some Beja had come under the influence of Islam. Some of the medieval Arab writers offer descriptions of more southerly "Beja areas" than those referred to in for example the Roman descriptions of disturbances and Blemmye raids. Trying to disentangle the facts that actually relate to Bedawiet-speakers offers a problem, since it is apparent from the records that the notion "Beja" was used by the Arabs as a term also covering Tigre-speakers (the Khasa) and para-Nilotic groups such as the Baria and the Kunama[3] in Northern Ethiopia and Eritrea (Crawford 1951:106, see also Marquart 1913:315 and Zaborski 1965). Still, certain facts can be deduced from the material.

Yacubi, who relied for his description on hearsay, wrote sometime between 872 and 891 (Newbold 1935:149, Vantini 1981:96). He gives a short description of five Beja "kingdoms", which may not have been kingdoms at all, and which judging from their names and the descriptions refer only partly to Bedawiet areas. Scepticism concerning these "kingdoms" was shown by Crawford as early as 1951, but other, and later, authors, such as Darar (1965:57) and Shaaban (1970), have taken them more seriously. One name which appears to refer unambiguously

---

[3]The Baria live north of Gash, and the Kunama in the Barentu area between Setit and Gash.

both to ethnic Beja and to the present Beja land is that of N.q.y.s. This kingdom extended from the limit of Muslim rule at Aswan to Khor Baraka, and had its capital at H.j.r. (Hajar) 25 "marhalas" from Wadi Allaqi. It comprised the district of the gold and emerald mines, and its population lived in peace with the Muslim mine-workers. They were divided into several branches, *butun* (Ar.).[4]

Yacubi's texts are not altogether coherent. His Kitab al-Buldan and his Universal History give contradictory information, and in the available versions the names lack diacritical marks and are generally difficult to read.

Hawqal visited the area between 945 and 950 (Vantini 1981:96). He, too, mentions some groups who appear to us to be Bedawiet-speakers. The most obvious cases are H.n.d.y.ba, and, among sub-categories of the Hadarab, names such as Arteiga, al S.w.t.badowa, al-H.w.t.ma, Hadendowa/hadandiwa, and al-n.rendowa. Another unit is comprised by al-J.n.y.tika, al-Wah.tika, and Gerib. The reason why we can safely assume these groups to be Beja proper is that they have obvious similarities to the names of Beja groups of today (such as Arteiga, Hadarab, Hadendowa or Gerib) or that their names end with "end-dowa", meaning tribe, or "tika", meaning men in TuBedawiye (Zaborski 1965:299, 300; Reinisch 1895:224). Crawford (1951:107-108) identifies his "Sitrab" with the inhabitants of the mountains and canyons of Sitrab, 20 to 30 miles west of Tokar, and links the H.nd.yba with Khor Handuba west of Suakin. More debatable is the claim that the Rigbat, presently part of Beni Amer, were a Beja group. They might not have spoken TuBedawiye either then or later, and certainly they do not do so now. Hawqal also mentions the Khasa, who are bi- or trilingual nowadays, with Tigre[5] as the dominant language. According to Zaborski it is still a puzzle whether this group were originally Tigre or Beja (1965:301). The Khasa at that time were living in the hills and coastal plains around the mouth of Khor Baraka, and the Rigbat stayed

---

[4]Their names are given here according to Zaborski's compilation and spelling, but alternative transcriptions offered by Crawford or Trimingham are: Hedareb, Hadarat; Hijab, Higab, Hajat; 'Ama'ir; Kadbin, Kawbar; Manasa, Rasifsa; Arbaba'ah, Arbab'a or Gharirigha; and Zanafig, Zanafaj. Vantini (1981) renders the names given by Yacubi as Aritika, Sutabaru, Hawtama, Junitika. Newbold (1935:149) takes 'Ama'ir to be the Amar'ar.

[5]Tigre (Khasa) is a separate language of Semitic origin related to Tigrinya and Amharinja. It is spoken by the Dahlak islanders and the population of the eastern lowlands and northern hills of Eritrea, for example by the Mensa, Marya, Ad Temariam, Ad Tekles, Habab and a majority of the Beni Amer. See Ullendorff (1973:122).

close to Suakin. Ibn Hawqal further names some four other as yet unidentified groups.

Another of the present major tribal groups, the Bishariya, or Bishariin, are not included in any of the lists of Beja kingdoms, unless N.q.y.s. refers to "Umm Nagi", one of their important sub-groups. They are however mentioned by Abu Nasr al-Maqdisi (d. 996) (Vantini 1975:148). He claims them to be Christians, and living in tents. There is also mention of another tribe, the Balliyin, who according to Idrisi and Al-Harrani (Vantini 1975:276, 449 respectively; see also 1981:91) were Jacobite Christians. According to Khaldoun they originated from Sinai and Yahtreb in Arabia. Idrisi says that they were to be found at Aswan and roaming the desert as far as the land of the Habash, also coming into the country of the Nuba. The reason why the Balliyin are of interest is that several authors, including Paul (1954:64 f) and Hassan (1973:14-15), have identified them with the Balaw, a group which ruled the southern Beja coast in the 16th to 18th centuries AD. These authors have seen them as the source of the Beja expression "Balawiet", now meaning non-Beja, primarily Arabic/Nubian. Whether this is correct, is hard to say.

Tribal names like these, even when they coincide with present-day names, cannot do more than hint at a continuity in the identity of the groups as such. The fact of a continuity in naming practices can on the other hand not be contested. Pastoral communities are usually assemblages of rather independent units, and their demographic fate may vary substantially. Kinship groups have a duration above individual people's life, but they also grow and dwindle, merge and scatter and are rearranged in new ways. Though the Hadendowa/Hadandiwa and the Gerib were at one time separate groups, still the Gerib could be found at a later stage as a subgroup of the Hadendowa (as in fact they are today in that particular case). In theory, a subordinate splinter group may even grow and absorb its former superordinate as a subgroup. Nevertheless, even if the chances of reconstructing the true historical relations between tribal sections are limited, it is extremely rare in African ethnography that one can establish such time-depth in the current tribal names among pastoralists.[6]

---

[6]In the case of Hadendowa and Arteiga, the dating of the name as stemming from at least the 10th century contradicts much later myths of origin current in the tribes.

Bibliography

Abir, M. 1980: *Ethiopia and the Red Sea: The rise and decline of the Solomonic dynasty and Muslim-European Rivalry in the Region.* London: Frank Cass

Abou Zeid, A. M. 1965: Honour and Shame among the Bedouins of Egypt pp. 245-9 in: J. G. Peristiany (ed.) *Honour and Shame. The Values of Mediterranean Society.* Weidenfeld and Nicholson

Abu Sin, M. E. 1975: *A Survey and Analysis of Population Mobility within Northern and Central Sudan.* University of London, Bedford College. Ph D Thesis

Acland, P. B. E. 1932: Notes on the Camel in Eastern Sudan. *Sudan Notes and Records* 15:119-149

Adams, W. Y. 1977: *Nubia, Corridor to Africa.* London: Princeton University Press

Ahmad, 'al-R. N. 1969: *Ta'rikh al-Abdallab, min kha'il ru ruwayatihim al-sima`iya.* Khartoum

Ahmed, A. 1976: *Millenium and Charisma among Pathans.* London: Routledge and Kegan Paul

Ahmed, El-A. El-A. H. 1988: *The migration of the Hadandawa to Port Sudan with special reference to its impact on their identification.* Bayreuth: Universität Bayreuth (Dissertation)

Ahmed, H. A. 1974: Aspects of Sudan's foreign trade during the 19th Century. *Sudan Notes and Records* 55

al Deen, M. M. A. N. 1985: *Ethnicity and Politics in Northern Sudan with Special Reference to the Beja and the Nuba.* University of Khartoum: Institute for African and Asian Studies. MA Thesis

Alfred, C. 1986: *Famine and Food Aid among the Beja: Report of Resarch into some Aspects of Relief Food Aid in the Red Sea Province of the Sudan.* OXFAM, Port Sudan, mimeo

Amin, M. A. 1968: *Historical Geography of Trade Routes and Trade Centers in Northern Sudan 1500-1939.* University of California. Ph. D. Thesis

Anderson, D. M. and D. H. Johnson 1988: Introduction: Ecology and Society in Northeast African History in D. H. Johnson and D. M. Anderson (eds.) *The Ecology of Survival: Case Studies from Northeast African History.* London: Lester Crook Academic Publishing. Boulder, Colorado: Westview Press

Arkell, A. J. 1955: *A History of the Sudan.* London: University of London and Athlone Press

Asad, T. 1970: *The Kababish Arabs: Power, Authority and Consent in a Nomadic Tribe.* London: C. Hurst & Co. New York: Praeger

Aswami, I. S. al- in Maqrizi: Khitat edn ΛH 1324, pp. 313-19

Awad, M. H. 1984: Economic Islamization in the Sudan; a Review. *DRSC Seminar* no 50 Oct 1984

Bacon, G. H. 1948: Crops of the Sudan, chapter 16, pp. 302-400 in: John D Tothill (ed.) *Agriculture in the Sudan.* London

Bakhit, A. 1988: The Highland Hadendowa and their Recent Migration in: Fouad N. Ibrahim and H. Ruppert (eds) *Rural Urban Migration and Identity Change: Case Studies from the Sudan.* Bruckhaus Bayreuth Verlagsgesellschaft

Balamoan, G. A. 1976: *Peoples and Economics in the Sudan 1884-1956: A Study in Migration Policies and Economics.* Harvard University Centre for Population Studies

Bank and Kahn 1982: *The Sibling Bond.* New York: Basic Books

Barradas 1633: *Tres tractatus historico-geographici* in: Beccari (ed) 1905-1917

Barth, F. l965: *Political Leadership among Swat Pathans.* London: Athalone Press

Battuta, M. b. I. Ibn- /d.1368/ 1958: *The Travels of Ibn Battuta AD 1325-1354* (transl. HAR Gibb, Cambridge: Hakluyt Society

Beccari, C. 1903-17: *Rerum Aethiopicarum Scriptores Occidentales Inediti a Saeculo XVI ad XIX Rom.*, 15 vols.

Behrens, P. and M. Beckhaus-Gerst, 1986: The "Nubian" of Nubia and the "Noba" of the Ezana- inscription: A matter of confusion. *Sixth International Conference for Nubian Studies*, Abstracts of Communications, ed. Rita Dehlin and Tomas Hägg

Beshir, M. O. 1984: *Ethnicity, Regionalism and National Cohesion in the Sudan in The Sudan, Ethnicity and National Cohesion.* Bayreuth African Studies Series

Bietak, M. 1986: The C-group and the Pan-Grave Culture in Nubia pp. 1-30 in: *Proceedings of Sixth International Conference for Nubian Studies.* Prepublication of Main Papers, vol 1 Bergen:Klassisk Institutt, and Society for Nubian Studies

Black-Michaud, J. 1975: *Feuding Societies.* Oxford: Basil Blackwell

Bloss, J. F. E. 1936: The Story of Suakin. *Sudan Notes and Records* 19:2:271-300

Bloss, J. F. E. 1938: The Story of Suakin (concluded). *Sudan Notes and Records* 21:2:247-280

Bondestam, L. 1974: People and Capitalism in the North East Lowlands of Ethiopia, *Journal of Modern African Studies* 12

Born, M. 1964: Bevölkerung und Wirtschaft in der Näheren Umgebung von Kassala *Geographische Zeitschrift* 52

Brandström, P., J. Hultin and J. Lindström 1979: *Aspects of Agro-pastoralism in East Africa.* Research Report no 51: Scandinavian Institute of African Studies

Browne, G. W. 1799: *Travels in Egypt, Syria and Africa.* London

Bruce 1790 (1804): *Travels to Discover the Source of the Nile in the years 1768-73.* First edition of five volumes J. Ruthven for G.G.J. and J. Robinson, Paternoster Row, London, second edition of 1804 seven vols. Edinburgh (esp. vol IV s.529 ff)

Bulliet, R. N. 1975: *The Camel and the Wheel.* Cambridge, Massachusetts: Harvard University Press

Burckhardt, J. L. 1819: *Travels in Nubia.* London: Published by the authority of the Association for Promoting the Discovery of the Interior of Africa. pp. ix,439 esp. s. 148-151, 170 ff

Carlsson. D. and D. P. van Gerven 1979: Diffusion. Biological Determinism and Biocultural adaptation in the Nubian Corridor. *American Anthropologist* 81:562-80

Christensen, A. 1944: *L'Iran sous les Sassanides*

Christiansson, C. 1981: *Soil Erosion and Sedimentation in Semi-arid Tanzania. Studies of Environmental Change and Ecological Imbalance.* Uppsala: Scandinavian Institute of African Studies

Clark, W. T. 1938: Manners, Customs and Beliefs of the Northern Bega *Sudan Notes and Records* 21:1-29

Cockrill R. (ed.) 1984: *The Camelid. An All-purpose animal.* Volume 1. Proceedings of the Khartoum Workshop on camels. December 1979. Uppsala: Scandinavian Institute of African Studies

Coser, L. A. 1956 (reprinted 1965): *The Functions of Social Conflict.* London: Routledge and Kegan Paul

Crawford, O. G. S. 1951: *The Fung Kingdom of Sennar.* Gloucester: John Bellows Ltd

Crossland, C. 1913: *Desert and Water Gardens of the Red Sea: Being an Account of the Natives and the Shore Formations of the Coast.* Cambridge University Press.

Crowfoot, J. W. 1911: Some Red Sea Ports of the Anglo-Egyptian Sudan. *Geographical Journal* 38: 523-550

Cutler, P. 1986: The Response to Drought of Beja Famine Refugees in Sudan, *Disasters* 10, 3, 181-188

Cutler, P. 1988: The Political Economy of Famine in Ethiopia and Sudan. Paper presented to the *Conference on Environmental Stress and Security,* Stockholm 13-15 December 1988. The Royal Swedish Academy of Sciences and the Swedish Ministry for Foreign Affairs and the Ministry of Environment and Energy

Daballoub, M. A. 1983: *The Ecological Factor in Environmental Change in Tokar Area,* University of Khartoum, M Sc Thesis

Dahl, G. and A. Hjort 1976: *Having Herds: Pastoral Herd Growth and Household Economy,* Stockholm: Stockholm Studies in Social Anthropology, University of Stockholm

Dahl, G. and A. Hjort 1979: *Pastoral Change and the Role of Drought.* SAREC Report R2:1979

Dahl, G. 1979: *Suffering Grass. Subsistence and Society of the Waso Borana.* Stockholm: Stockholm Studies in Social Anthropology, University of Stockholm

Dahl, G. 1985: Bejafolket i Sudan. När livsrytmen blir störd — då kommer torka och svält. *SIDA Rapport* 2:24-7

Darar, M. S. 1965: *Tarikh el Sudan, al bahr el Ahmar.* Iqlim el-Bescha Beirut

Dareer, A. El- 1982: *Woman, Why do you weep? Circumcision and its consequences.* London, Zed Press

de Munck, V., 1990: A Study of Cross-Sibling relations and the dowry in Sri Lanka, *Ethnos*:1-2

Doe, B. 1971: *Southern Arabia.* New York, St Louis and San Francisco: Mc Graw-Hill

Dyson-Hudson, N. 1972: Introduction. In: W. Irons and N. Dyson-Hudson (eds) *Perspectives on Nomadism.* Leiden: E. J. Brill 2-29

Ehret, C. 1976: Cushitic Prehistory p.85-96 in M. L. Bender (ed.) *The Non-Semitic Languages of Ethiopia.* Publ. by the African Studies Center, Michigan State University, East Lansing, Michigan and Southern Illinois University, Carbondale, Illinois

Eisa, M. el H. 1978: *Smuggling in East Sudanese Borders.* University of Khartoum: Institute for African and Asian Studies. MA Thesis

Eltom, A. R. and H. E. Bushra 1984: *Results of Base-line Survey. Joint Nutrition Support Project, Red Sea Province.* UNICEF 1984

Euro Action Accord 1984: *Programming in Northern Sudan. Report of Preliminary Investigations.* Khartoum. (mimeo)

FAO 1982 Country Report ESC/FSAS/SUDAN Jan 1982: *A Policy and Action Plan for Strengthening National Food Security in the Sudan*

Fawzy, S. 1978: *No Margins: Lake Nasser and the Ecological and Socio-economic Dislocations among the Nomads of the South-Eastern Desert. A Policy-Oriented Study.* American University in Cairo. MA Thesis

Flood, G. 1975: *Nomadism and its Future; the Afar.* Royal Anthropological Institute News (RAIN) 6

Foster, T. 1987: *Recommendations for the future role of OXFAM in the Red Sea Province of Sudan.* Oxfam, Port Sudan

Friedl, E. 1975: *Women and Men: an anthropologist's view.* New York: Holt, Rinehart & Winston

Garcia, J. C. 1972: Jean-Léon l'Africain et `Aydhab. *Annales Islamologiques* 11:189-209

Ghirshman, R. 1962: *Iran, Parthians and Sassanians.* London

Girard, P. S. 1818: Memoire sur l'agriculture, l'industrie et le commerce de l'Égypte. *Description de l'Égypte, État Moderne, II,* 419-714 2nd ed.: XVII, Paris 1-436

Gleichen, 1905: *The Anglo-Egyptian Sudan: A Compendium prepared by Officers of the Sudan Government.* London: Harrison and Sons, for Her Majesty's Stationary Office. 2 vol.

Goffman, E. 1959: *The Presentation of Self in Everyday Life.* New York: Doubleday

Gutbi, O. S. A. 1989: *Dockers of Port Sudan: From Pastoralists to Urban Workers in The Red Sea Area Programme (RESAP).* Proceedings from a Workshop in Khartoum, Jan 1989, University of Khartoum and University of Bergen

Haaland, G. and H. M. al Hassan (n.d.): *Report on Mission to Derudeb* (mimeo)

Hakam, Ibn 'Abd al- 1920: *Kitab, Futuh al-Misr wa Akhbariha.* Leiden

Hakem, A. A. al-, et al. 1979: Preliminary Report of the Multidisciplinary Mission of the Joint Sudanese-French Expedition to the Red Sea Region 1981 (sic). *Sudan Notes and Records* 60:87-108

Hale, S. 1986: *OXFAM Nutritional Surveillance Team. The OXFAM Food Targeting and Monitoring Programme in the Red Sea Province, Sudan.* Port Sudan: Oxfam 55 pp. mimeo

Harrison, M. N. 1955: *The Beja Tribes.* Appendix 4, Report on a Grazing Survey of the Sudan. Ministry of Animal Resources, Khartoum

Hartmann R. 1876: *Die Nigritier* B I Berlin

Hartmann, R. 1865: *Naturgeschichtliche Medizinische Skizze der Nilländer*. Berlin

Hassan, Y. F. 1975: Hijrat al-Rashayda ila al-Sudan (The migration of the Rashayda to the Sudan) in Y. F. Hassan (ed.) *Studies in the History of Sudan* vol 1 Khartoum, Khartoum University Press, 227 pp. 173-223

Hassan, Y. F. 1967: *The Arabs and the Sudan from the seventh to the early sixteenth century*. Edinburgh: Edinburgh University Press, reprinted 1973 by Khartoum University Press

Hawqal, A. 'l K. Ibn- 1938: Kitab surat al-ard in J.H. Kramers (ed.) *Opus Geographicum auctore Ibn Hawqal spec. tome I*, pp. 50-56 Lugduni Batavorum

Hazerjian, J. 1985-86: *OXFAM Nutritional Surveillance Team*, Red Sea Province, Sudan: First Province-wide Cycle of Tours. Report on the Nutritional Status of 2226 Children and Economic Life of 557 families in Red Sea Province, Nov. 85-Feb. 86, mimeo and: Second Province-wide Cycle of Tours March 1986-July 1986, Food aid research and Development Office, OXFAM, Port Sudan

Hejazi, N. B. 1975: *Port Sudan: A Social and Economic Study*. Khartoum. MA Thesis

Hekekyan, Y., *Papers*, 7 vol., British Museum Add 37448-37454

Herrman, G. 1977: *The Iranian Revival*. Oxford

Hill, R. 1959: *Egypt in the Sudan 1820-1881*. London

Hjort, A. 1981: Herds, trade and grain: Pastoralism in a regional perspective. In: J. G. Galaty, D. Aronson and P.C. Salzman (eds): *The Future of Pastoral Peoples*. Ottawa, IDRC, pp. 135-143

Hjort af Ornäs, A. 1989: Environment and the security of dryland herders. In: A. Hjort af Ornäs and M. A. Mohamed Salih (eds): *Ecology and Politics. Environmental Stress and Security in Africa*. Uppsala: Scandinavian Institute of African Studies pp. 67-88

Holt, P. M. and M. W. Daly 1979: *The History of the Sudan from the Coming of Islam to the Present Day*. Third edition. London: Weidenfeld and Nicolson

Holy, L. 1976: Knowledge and behaviour. In: L. Holy (ed): *Knowledge and Behaviour*. Belfast: Queens University

Holy, L. 1988: Cultivation as a long-term strategy of survival in Johnsson and Andersson (eds): *The Ecology of Survival. Case Studies from North East African History*. London: Lester Crook Academic Publishing

Hunter, G. 1904: *Letter G Hunter to Ministry of Finance 10 Feb 1904*, DAKHLIA 112-11-75)

Idrisi, M. b. 'A. al-A. al- 1864: *Sifat al-mahgrib wa al Sudan wa Misr wa'l-Andalus*. Leiden

Ingold, T. 1987: *The Appropriation of Nature: Essays on Human Ecology and Social Relations*. Iowa City: University of Iowa Press

Jackson, H. C. 1926: *Osman Digna*. London: Methuen Co

Jackson, M. 1991: Free Will and Determinism, in: Jan Ovesen (ed.) *Texts and Contexts: Models, Metaphors and Meanings in African Symbolism* Uppsala Studies in Cultural Anthropology

Jacobsson, A. 1990: The Shadow as an Expression of Individuality in Congolese Conceptions of Personhood in: Michael Jackson and Ivan Karp (ed.): *Personhood and Agency: The Experience of Self and Other in African Cultures*. Uppsala Studies in Cultural Anthropology

James, W. 1969: Port Sudan's Overspill, *Sudan Society*

James, W. 1980: *The Shanty Towns of Port Sudan*

Jennings-Bramly A. 1910-11: *Appendix: Report on the Atbai Patrol 1910-11 Military Intelligence Reports*. Sudan Government Archives DAKHLIA 112/11/75

Johnson, D. H. and D. M. Anderson (eds.) 1988: *The Ecology of Survival. Case Studies from North East African History*. London: Lester Crook Academic Publishing

Jubayr, M. bin A. ibn- 1907: *Rihlat Ibn Jubayr*. Leiden

Junker 1876: Geogr. Bericht uber das Chor Baraka und das angrenzende Beni-Amer und Hadendou-Gebiet *Petermanns Mitteilungen*. 1876:383-88

Kamal, Y. (1928-51) *Monumenta Cartographica Africae et Aegypti*. Cairo and Leiden

Kaspar, Ph. and W. Moll 1984: IV The case of Sudan, in K. Klennert (ed.): *Rural Development and Careful Utilization of Resources: The Cases of Pakistan, Peru and Sudan*. Baden-Baden: Nomos Verlagsgesellschaft, pp. 93-115

Kennedy-Cooke 1944: The Red Sea Hills. Appendix 1 to *Sudan Government Soil Conservation Committee Report*. Mc Corquadale and Co.

Khaldoun, 'Abd al-R. b. M. ibn- (1956-61) *al-Ibar wa-diwan al-mubtada' wa'l-khabar*. Beirut 7 vols.

Kheir, H. M. 1982: *Medieval Eastern Sudan and the Arabs: A study in the Evolution of Economic Relations, 640-1400 AD*. University of Khartoum. MAThesis

Kheir, H. M. 1977: *Matrilineal Elements in the Political Organization of Medieval Eastern Sudan*. University of Khartoum. MA Thesis

Khogali, M. 1963: *The Significance of Railways in the Development of Sudan with special references to Western Provinces*. Swansea. MA Thesis

Khogali, M. 1980: *Sedentarization of Nomadic Tribes in the North and Central Sudan*. University of Khartoum. Ph D Thesis

Khusraw, N.-i, 1945: *Safar Nama*, transl. from Persian into Arabic by Yahya al-Khashshab, Cairo

Kirwan, L. P. 1937: A Survey of Nubian Origins. *Sudan Notes and Records* 20:1:47-62

KPMD ... *Kassala Province Monthly Diary* Sudan National Archives

Kraus P. J. 1930: *Die Anfänge des Christentums in Nubien*. Inaugural-Dissertation zur Erlangung der theologischen Doktorwurde der hochwurdigen katholisch-theologischen Fakultät der Universität Munster Wien, Missionsdruckerei Sankt Gabriel

Kursani, I. 1984: *Eritrean Refugees in Kassala Province of Eastern Sudan: An Economic Assessment* 20 aug 1984, manuscript

Kursani, I. 1984b: The Dynamics and Limits of Private Capitalist Development in Sudanese Agriculture. *Development and Peace*, vol 5, Spring

Lane, E. W. 1860: *An Account of the Manners and Customs of the Modern Egyptians*. London: John Murray. (Written in 1833-35 based on notes taken 1825-28) Reprinted by Everyman's Library, 315, Dent and Dutton

Lewis, B. A. 1962 Deim el Arab and the Beja Stevedores of Port Sudan. *Sudan Notes and Records* 43:1:16-49

Linant de Bellefonds, L.-M.-A. 1884: *L'Etbaye ou pays habité par les arabes Bichariehs* Paris: Arthur Bernard [built on experiences in 1833]

Lindholm, C. 1982: *Generosity and Jealousy. The Swat Pukhtun of Northern Pakistan*. New York: Columbia University Press

Little, P.(forthcoming): *The Elusive Granary: Herder, Farmer and State in Northern Kenya*. Cambridge University Press

Lobban, R. 1980: A Genealogical and Historical Study of the Mahas of the Three Towns. *Sudan Notes and Records* vol LXI p 89-109

Mace, R. 1988: A Model of Herd composition that maximizes household viability and its potential application in the support of pastoralists under stress. *ODI Pastoral Development Network* Paper 26 b September 1988

Manger, L. O. (n.d.): *Development in Sinkat, The Red Sea Hills*. A report based on a feasibility study of Norwegian Red Cross proposals for development projects in Sinkat District, in the Red Sea Province of the Sudan. The Social Anthropological Report. 41 p. (mimeo)

Maqrizi, A, bin 'A, al- 1922: *Kitab al-mawa' iz wa' l-i`tibar bi-dhikr al-khitat wa' l - athar* G. Wiet (ed.), 4 vol, Paris and Cairo. [Beja particularly in vol I]

Mariam, A. G. 1986: *Economic Adaptation and Competition for Scarce Resources: The Afar in North East Ethiopia*. Bergen. Department of Social Anthropology, University of Bergen. MA Thesis

Marsh, J. 1985: *Comments* In: The Sibling Relationship in Lowland South America, Bennington (vt): Bennington college, Working Papers on South American Indians v. 7

Masudi, al- 1861: *Les prairies d'òr*. Transl. by C. Barbier de Meynard and Pavet de Courteille. Paris

Mawson, R. and M. A. J. Williams 1984: A wetter climate in eastern Sudan 2000 years ago? *Nature* 308:49-51

Mc Evedy, C. 1980: *The Penguin Atlas of African History*. Penguin

Mc Loughlin, P. F. M. 1966: Labour Market Conditions and Wages in the Gash and Tokar Deltas 1900-1955. *Sudan Notes and Records* 47:111-126

Milne, J. C. M. 1976: *The Changing Pattern of Mobility and Migration of the Amarar Tribe of Eastern Sudan*. London, SOAS, unpubl. thesis

Milne, J. C. M. 1974: The Impact on Labour Migration on the Amarar in Port Sudan. *Sudan Notes and Records* 55: 70-87

Mohamed, A. A. 1980: *The White Nile Arabs*. London School of Economics Monographs on Social Anthropology 53. New Jersey: Athlone Press

Mohamed, A. H. 1965: *Pastoralism and the Southern Beja Problems*. University of Khartoum, Department of Geography. Diss.

Morton, J. 1988: Sakanab: Greetings and Information among the Northern Beja *Africa* 58(4) 423-436

Morton, J. 1989: Ethnicity and Politics in Red Sea Province, Sudan *African Affairs* vol 88 no:350: 63-76

Morton, J. and Z. Fre 1986: Red Sea Province and the Beja. A Preliminary Report to OXFAM. Food Aid Research and Development Office, OXFAM, Port Sudan

Morton, J. 1984: (forthcoming) *Ethnicity and Politics in Red Sea Province*

Muir, A. 1986: *Red Sea Province Tour Report*. Mimeo

Murdock, G. P. 1959: *Africa — its Peoples and their Culture*. New York

Murray, G. W. 1923: Note on the Ababda. *Journal of Royal Anthropological Institute* 53:417-22

Murray, G. W. 1926: Graves of Oxen in the Eastern Desert of Egypt. *Journal of the Egyptian Archaeology* 12

Murray, G. W. 1927: The Northern Beja. *Journal of Royal Anthropological Institute* 57:39-55

Murray, G. W. 1935: *Sons of Ishmael, A Study of the Egyptian Bedouin*. London: George Routledge and Sons Ltd

Musa, A. A. 1971: *Nomadism in the Southern Etbai*. University of Khartoum. Unpubl. Geogr. Thesis

Myers, F. 1982: Always ask: resource use and land ownership amongst Pintupi Aborigines of the Australian Western Desert. In N. M. Williams and E.S. (eds): *Resource Managers: North American and Australian hunter-gatherers* eds. Hunn, AAA's selected Symposium 67, Boulder Colorado: Westview Press

Nadel, S. F. 1954: Notes on the Beni Amer Society. *Sudan Notes and Records* 26:51-94

Newbold, O. B. E. 1935: The Beja Tribes of the Red Sea Hinterland in J. A. de C. Hamilton (ed.) *The Anglo-Egyptian Sudan from Within*, p.140-160 London: Faber and Faber

Norconsult and the Red Cross 1986: *Integrated Development Project, Sinkat District, Sudan: Assessment of Water Potential*, 25800/3703 May 1986

Nordenstam, T. 1968: *Sudanese Ethics*. Uppsala: Scandinavian Institute of African Studies

Nuwayri, A. 'bin 'A. al-W. al- (ms): *Nihayat al-Arab fi funun al-adab Dar al-kutub al-Misriyya*, Ma'arif 'ama, Cairo

O'Fahey, R. S. and J. L. Spaulding 1974: *Kingdoms of the Sudan*. London: Methuen & Co.

Oliver, J. 1966: Port Sudan, the Study of its Growth and Functions. *Tijdschrift voor Econ. en Soc. Geografie* 57:54-61

Olympiodor, (1829) ed. Niebuhr, Bonn

Osman, M. S. 1966: The Possibilities and Problems of the Mechanization of Agricultural Production in the Sudan in: D. J. Shaw (ed.) *Agricultural Development in the Sudan* vol 2. Khartoum: Philosophical Society of the Sudan 1966: 336

Owen, T. R. H. 1934: *Notes on the Methods of Beja Courts and Meglisses*. Received 28/11/34 Sudan Government Archives, Dakhlia 112/11/75

Owen, T. R. H. 1936: *Economic Survey of Hadendowa Resources*

Owen, T. R. H. 1937: The Red Sea Ibex. *Sudan Notes and Records* 20:150-165

Pankhurst, R. and D. H. Johnsson 1988: The great drought and famine of 1888-92 in northeast Africa, p. 47-70 In Andersson & Johnsson (ed.) *The Ecology of Survival. Case Studies from North East African History*. London: Lester Crook Academic Publishing

Parker 1901: *Letter of Inspector of Kassala to Mudir*, SGA 112/11/77

Paul, A. M. 1950: Notes on the Beni Amer. *Sudan Notes and Records* 31:2:223-246

Paul, A. M. 1954a (repr.1971 with corrections by the authour): *History of the Beja Tribes of the Sudan* Cambridge and London: Frank Cass

Paul, A. M. 1936: Aidhab: a Medieval Red Sea Port. *Sudan Notes and Records* 36:1:64-70

Paul, A. M. 1959: The Hadareb. *Sudan Notes and Records* 40:75-78

Penn, A. E. D. 1934: Traditional Stories of the Abdullab tribe. *Sudan Notes and Records* 17:1, 59-82

Peristiany, J. G. 1965: Introduction, p. 1-16 in J. G. Peristiany (ed.) *Honour and Shame: The Values of Mediterranean Society*. Weidenfeldt and Nicholson

Pitt-Rivers, J. 1968: The Stranger, the Guest and the Hostile Host: Introduction to the Study of the Laws of Hospitality, pp. 13-29 in Peristiany (ed.) *Contributions to Mediterranean Sociology* (Acts of the Mediterranean Sociology Conference Athens July 1963). Paris and Hague: Mouton and Co

Pitt-Rivers, J. 1973: The Kith and the Kin in Goody, J. (ed.) *The Character of Kinship*, Cambridge University Press, pp. 89-105

Rapp, A. and J. O. Mattson 1988: The Recent Sahelo-Ethiopian Droughts in a Climatic Context. Paper presented at the *International Conference on Environmental Stress and Security*. 13-15 December, 1988 Royal Swedish Academy of Sciences, Stockholm, Sweden

Rapp, A. and J. O. Mattson 1987: Afrikas torkkatastrofer och nordisk kyla styrs av svag golfström *Svensk Geografisk Årsbok* 1987, Lund

Reinisch, L. 1895: *Wörterbuch der Bedauyesprache*. Wien

Riches, D. 1979: Ecological Variation on the North West Coast: Models for the Generation of Cognatic and Matrilineal Descent pp. 145-166 in: Burnham, Philip and Roy Ellen (eds.) *Social and Ecological Systems* ASA Monographs 18 Academic Press

Riesman, P. 1977: *Freedom in Fulani Social Life. An Introspective Ethnography*. University of Chicago Press

Rossini, C. Conti- 1928: *Storia d'Etiopia*. Bergamo

Sacks, K. 1974: Engels revisited. In: M.Z.Rosaldo and L. Lamphere (eds.) *Women, Culture and Society* Stanford: Stanford University Press

Sahlins, M. D. 1972: *Stone Age Economics*. London: Tavistock

Salih, H. M. 1976: *The Hadendowa: Pastoralism and Problems of Sedentarization*. University of Hull. PhD Thesis

Salih, H. M. 1980: Hadendowa Traditional Territorial Rights and Interpopulation Relations within the Context of Native Administration System 1927-1970. *Sudan Notes and Records* LXI: 118-133

Sandars, C. E. R. 1932: *Note on the Amar'ar*, Dakhlia 112/11/76, Sudan National Archives

Sandars, C. E. R. 1933: The Bisharin. *Sudan Notes and Records* 16:119-149

Sandars, C. E. R. 1935: The Amarar. *Sudan Notes and Records* 18:195-219

Schultz, M. and J. Schultz 1983: *Port Sudan Small Enterprise Programme Final Report on the Programme Design Phase*, Report for Euro Action Accord

Schultze, J. H. 1963: *Der Ost-Sudan, Entwicklungsland zwischen Wüsten und Regenwald* Abhandlungen des Geographischen Instituts der Freien Universität Berlin, 7. Berlin

Schultze, J. H. 1963: *The Eastern Sudan: Development between Desert and Rain Forest*. Berlin: Dietrich Reimer Verlag

Schulz, J. and M. 1983: *Port Sudan Small Enterprises Programme: Final Report of the programme design phase*, Euro-Action Accord, London

Seligman, C. G. 1913: Some Aspects of the Hamitic Problem in the Anglo-Egyptian Sudan. *Journal of the Royal Anthropological Society* 43:593-705

Seligman, C. G. and Z. Brenda 1930: Note on the history and present condition of the Beni Amer (South-Beja). *Sudan Notes and Records* 13:83-97

Shaaban, S. 1970: *Die Hadendowa-Bedscha*. Reinischen Friedrich Wilhelms-Universität zu Bonn. Ph D Thesis

Shami, S. 1961: *Sudanese Ports*, (in arabic) Cairo: Misr Library

Shaw, S. J. 1962: *Ottoman Egypt in the Eighteenth Century*. Harvard Middle Eastern Monographs VII, Cambridge Massachussets: Harvard University Press

Shepherd, A. 1985: *The Food System and Food Policy Issues*. Paper for workshop for Eastern Region Govmt Kassala dec 4th and 5th 1985, mimeo

Spencer, P. 1973: *Nomads in alliance: Symbiosis and Growth of the Rendille and Samburu of Kenya*. London, New York, Toronto, Nairobi: Oxford University Press

Stern, P. H. 1985: *Proposals for developing low cost small scale irrigation in the Red Sea Province, Sudan*. Report No GP 3378.01 to UNICEF by Gifford and Partners, Southampton, UK

Strathern, A. 1973: Kinship, descent and locality: Some New Guinea Examples in Goody (ed.): *The Character of Kinship* Cambridge, Cambridge University Press 21-35

Stuchlik, M. ed., 1977: *Goals and Behaviour*, Belfast, Queens University

Stuhlmann, F. 1909: Die Getreide-Gräser und Futter-Gräser. *Beiträge zur Kulturgeschichte von Ost-Afrika. Deutsch Ost-Afrika* 10:165-76, 344-7, 410-4

Sudan Survey Department 1974: *Vegetation of Sudan*

Swift, J. 1986: *Rehabilitation and Long-Term Development for Pastoralists in Red Sea Province, Sudan*. UNICEF, Khartoum

Säve-Söderbergh, T. 1979: *Scandinavian Joint Expedition to Nubia*. vol 8:4 Copenhagen

Tabari, al- 1901 (ed. M.J. de Goeje): *Annales III*, Lugduni Batavorum

Tahir, M. I. el- 1972: *Stevedores in Port Sudan*. unpubl. paper

Talhami, G. H. 1975: *Egypt's Civilizing Mission. Khedive Ismail's Red Sea Province 1865-1885*. Univ of Ill. Ph D 1975

Talhami, G. H. 1979: *Suakin and Massawa under Egyptian Rule 1865-1885*: Washington, University Press of America

Trigger, B. 1965: *History and Settlement in Lower Nubia*. Yale University Publications in Anthropology 69, New Haven

Trimingham, J. S. 1952: *Islam in Ethiopia*. Oxford

Tubiana, M. J. and J. Tubiana 1977: *The Zaghawa from an Ecological Perspective. Food gathering, the pastoral system, tradition and developments of the Zaghawa of the Sudan and the Chad*. Rotterdam: A.A. Balkema

Török, L. 1986: Meroe, North and South. *Proceedings of the Sixth International Conference for Nubian Studies*, Prepublications of Main Papers, Uppsala 11-16 aug. 1986, Bergen: Klassisk Institutt and Society for Nubian Studies

Ullendorff, E. 1973: *The Ethiopians: An Introduction to Country and People*. London: Oxford University Press

Unpubl. report in CRO file DAKHLIA 112/11/75-6

Vantini, G. 1981: *Christianity in the Sudan*. Bologna: EMI

Vantini, G. (ed.and transl.) 1975: *Oriental Sources Concerning Nubia*. Heidelberg and Warszaw: Polish Academy of Science and the Society for Nubian Studies

Voll, J. O. 1969: *A History of the Khatmiyya Tariqa in the Sudan*. Cambridge: Harvard University. Thesis

Walker, P. 1987: Famine Relief amongst Pastoralists in Sudan: A Report of Oxfam's experience. *Disasters* 12:3

Walz, T. 1978: *Trade between Egypt and Bilad as-Sudan 1700-1820* Cairo: Institut Francais d'Archéologie Orientale du Caire

Wilson, F. 1984: *Women and the Commercialization of Agriculture: A Review of Recent Literature on Latin America*: Copenhagen CDR Research Report no 4:57 ff

Winkler, H. A. 1936: *Ägyptischen Volkskunde*. Stuttgart

Yacubi (Yaccoubi), al- [d.893] 1892 (ed.M.J de Goeje): *Kitab al-Buldan* in Bibliotheca Geographorum Arabicorum 7

Young, W. C. 1984: Heterodoxy and Reform among the Rashayda Bedouin, *Nomadic Peoples* 15:35-39

Zaborski, A. 1965: *Notes on the Mediaeval History of the Beja Tribes*. Folia Orientalia 7:289-307

Zahlan, A. B. *Agricultural Bibliography of the Sudan* 1974-83

Zarins, J. 1978: The Camel in Ancient Arabia: a Further Note. *Antiquity* 52:204:44-46

Zeuner 1963: *A History of Domesticated Animals*. New York

Stockholm Studies in Social Anthropology

1. *Caymanian Politics: Structure and Style in a Changing Island Society* by Ulf Hannerz. 1974.
2. *Having Herds: Pastoral Herd Growth and Household Economy* by Gudrun Dahl and Anders Hjort. 1976.
3. *The Patron and the Panca: Village Values and Pancayat Democracy in Nepal* by Bengt-Erik Borgström. 1976.
4. *Ethnicity and Mobilization in Sami Politics* by Tom Svensson. 1976.
5. *Market, Mosque and Mafraj: Social Inequality in a Yemeni Town* by Tomas Gerholm. 1977.
6. *The Community Apart: A Case Study of a Canadian Indian Reserve Community* by Yngve G. Lithman. 1978 (Available from the University of Manitoba Press.)
7 *Savanna Town: Rural Ties and Urban Opportunities in Northern Kenya* by Anders Hjort. 1979.
8. *Suffering Grass: Subsistence and Society of Waso Borana* by Gudrun Dahl. 1979.
9. *North to Another Country: The Formation of a Suryoyo Community in Sweden* by Ulf Björklund. 1981.
10. *Catching the Tourist: Women Handicraft Traders in Gambia* by Ulla Wagner. 1982.
11. *The Practice of Underdevelopment: Economic Development Projects in a Canadian Indian Reserve Community* by Yngve G. Lithman. 1983.
12. *Evil Eye or Bacteria: Turkish Migrant Women and Swedish Health Care* by Lisbeth Sachs. 1983
13. *Women of the Barrio: Class and Gender in a Colombian City* by Kristina Bohman. 1984.
14. *Conflict and Compliance: Class Consciousness among Swedish Workers* by Mona Rosendahl. 1985.
15. *Change on the Euphrates: Villagers, Townsmen and Employees in Northeast Syria* by Annika Rabo. 1986.
16. *Morally United and Politically Divided: The Chinese Community of Penang* by Claes Hallgren. 1987.
17. *In the Stockholm Art World* by Deborah Ericsson. 1988.
18. *Shepherds, Workers, Intellectuals: Culture and Centre-Periphery Relationships in a Sardinian Village* by Peter Schweitzer
19. *Women at a Loss: Changes in Maasai Pastoralism and their Effects on Gender Relations* by Aud Talle. 1988.
20. *First We are People...The Koris of Kanpur between Caste and Class* by Stefan Molund. 1988.
21. *Twenty Girls: Growing Up: Ethnicity and Excitement in a South London Microculture* by Helena Wulff. 1988.
22. *Left Hand Left Behind: The Changing Gender System of a Barrio in Valencia, Spain* by Britt-Marie Thurén. 1988.
23. *Central Planning and Local Reality: The Case of a Producers' Cooperative in Ethiopia* by Eva Poluha. 1989.
24. *A Sound Family makes a Sound State: Ideology and Upbringing in a German Village* by Karin Norman. 1991.
25. *Community, Carnival and Campaign: Expressions of Belonging in a Swedish Region* by Ann-Kristin Ekman. 1991.
26. *Women in a Borderland: Managing Muslim Identity where Morocco meets Spain* by Eva Evers Rosander. 1991.
27. *Responsible Man: The Atmaan Beja of Northeastern Sudan.* Anders Hjort af Ornäs and Gudrun Dahl. 1991.
28. *Peasant Differentiation and Development: The Case of a Mexican Ejido* by Lasse Krantz.(to be published during 1991)

Available from Almqvist & Wiksell International